EL SABELOTODO
The Bilingual Teacher's Best Friend

Contributing Writers

Shirley Costigan

Carmen Muñoz

Mark Porter

Juan Quintana

HAMPTON-BROWN BOOKS

FOR BILINGUAL EDUCATION

Quien sabe dos lenguas vale por dos.

Reviewers

We are very grateful to the following people who helped in the development of this book:

María Guerrero
Principal
The Sunnyslope School
Hollister, California

Carrol Moran
Resource Teacher
Mintie White
 Elementary School
Pajaro, California

Carmen Muñoz
Educational Consultant
Pharr, Texas

Every effort has been made to secure permission, but if any omissions have been made, please let us know. We gratefully acknowledge the following permissions:

"Los siete días" by Oscar Jara Azócar is from ANTOLOGÍA DE LA POESÍA INFANTIL, compiled by Blanca de la Vega. All rights reserved. ©1954 Editorial Kapelusz, S. A. "La tijera de mamá" by Germán Berdiales is from ALBORADA, published by Editorial Kapelusz, S. A. Both are reprinted by permission of the publisher.

"A catalog of imaginative ideas to promote reading, writing, listening, and speaking" is adapted from "Instead of 'Write a story,' try . . ." in IF YOU'RE TRYING TO TEACH KIDS HOW TO WRITE, YOU'VE GOTTA HAVE THIS BOOK! by Marjorie Frank. Copyright ©1979 by Incentive Publications, Inc. All rights reserved. Adapted by permission of Incentive Publications, Box 120189, Nashville, TN 37212.

"La voz de los animalitos" is from PETALITOS by A. L. Jáuregui. All rights reserved. © Editorial Avante, S. de R. L. Reprinted by permission of the publisher.

"El burro flautista" is from FÁBULAS by Tomás de Iriarte. © Editores Mexicanos Unidos, S. A. Reprinted by permission of the publisher.

"La rueda de San Miguel" is from JUEGOS INFANTILES CANTADOS EN NUEVO MÉXICO, compiled by Richard B. Stark. Published by Museum of New Mexico Press, Santa Fe. Reprinted by permission of the publisher.

"Que llueva" appears in LET'S PLAY GAMES IN SPANISH, compiled by Loretta Burke Hubp. This song was originally published by Cooperative Recreation Service, Inc. of Delaware, Ohio. Extensive research failed to locate the copyright holder of this work.

A number of the palindromes used come from EL PALÍN DE LOS DROMOS by Mauricio Charpenel. © 1980 and published by Mauricio Charpenel. Used by the kind permission of the author and publisher.

The proverb "Quien sabe dos lenguas vale por dos" has been taken from SPANISH PROVERBS OF THE SOUTHWEST, collected and translated by Rubén Cobos. Published by San Marcos Press, P. O. Box 53, Cerrillos, NM 87010 and used with their permission.

Some of the riddles are from ADIVINANCERO POPULAR ESPAÑOL I and II edited by Jose Luis Gárfer and Concha Fernández. ©1984 Taurus Ediciones, S.A., Madrid. Used by permission of the publisher.

Some of the riddles and tongue twisters are from ANTOLOGÍA DE LA LITERATURA INFANTIL ESPAÑOLA 1 and 2 compiled by Carmen Bravo-Villasante. © Carmen Bravo-Villasante and Editorial Doncel. Used by permission of the publisher.

Some of the riddles are from UNA, DOLA, TELA, CATOLA by Carmen Bravo-Villasante. © 1976 Carmen Bravo-Villasante © Edición española, Miñón, S. A. Excerpt also from CHINA, CHINA, CAPUCHINA by Carmen Bravo-Villasante. ©1981 Carmen Bravo-Villasante and Miñón, S. A. All are used by permission of Miñón, S. A.

Some riddles and tongue twisters are from POESÍA INFANTIL by Elsa Isabel Bornemann. First edition published in 1976. All rights reserved. Used by permission of Editorial Latina, a division of Ediciones Preescolar, S. A., Buenos Aires.

Some riddles and "Los meses del año" are from PINCELADAS FOLKLÓRICAS DOMINICANAS, compiled by Mercedes R. de González. © Mercedes R. de González. Published by Ediciones Abra. Extensive research failed to locate the publisher and/or copyright holder of this work

Hampton-Brown Books
P.O. Box 223220
Carmel, California 93922

Printed in the United States of America
ISBN 0-917837-01-0

   6 7 8 9 0 96 95 94 93 92

CONTENTS/CONTENIDO

PART 1 PALABRERÍA
A collection of words for every occasion

PART 2   LA CULTURA
Things and people Hispanic, and a brief anthology of traditional Spanish children's folklore and literature

PART 3   VOCABULÁLOGO
Instructional words for reading, writing, and the content areas

PART 4 TEMAS HASTA POR GUSTO
Ideas for implementing a theme-oriented approach to teaching, and ten sample themes to get you started

PART 5 MANOS A LA OBRA
Imaginative ideas to promote reading, writing, listening, and speaking

PART 1

PALABRERÍA

A collection of words for every occasion

¡SALUDOS!

Greetings! *Welcome to* EL SABELOTODO, *the book that's a real know-it-all when it comes to helping you teach reading to your bilingual students. What would a book that calls itself a sabelotodo have in it? Just about everything! It's got list after list of Spanish word wisdom, creative teaching ideas, and other indispensable information just waiting at your fingertips whenever you need it. To get you started, here's a warm welcome and a wealth of other ways to say hello.*

¡Bienvenidos!
¡Buen día!
¡Buenas!
¡Buenas noches!
¡Buenas tardes!
¡Buenos días!
¿Cómo andas?
¿Cómo amaneciste?
¿Cómo estás?
¿Cómo has estado?
¿Cómo te ha ido?
¿Cómo te han tratado?

¿Cómo te va?
¿Cómo va la cosa?
¡Hola!
¿Qué haces?
¿Qué has hecho?
¿Qué hay?
¿Qué hay de nuevo?
¿Qué hubo?
¿Qué pasa?
¿Qué tal?
¿Qué te pasa, calabaza?
¿Quihúbole?

WORDWISE

*HOLA*balloo   The Spanish *hola* is just one variation of an exclamation that is truly multilingual. Spanish records *hala* and *ala* as well as *hola*. The French variant is *holà*. The German variant is *hallo*. Within English, the forms *hallo*, *hello*, *halloo*, *hollo*, *holla*, and *holloa* are known.

Ola que viene.   Ola que va.   ¡Hola!   ¿Qué tal está?

PINTEMOS CON PALABRAS

*These **color words** will add to your vocabulary spectrum.*

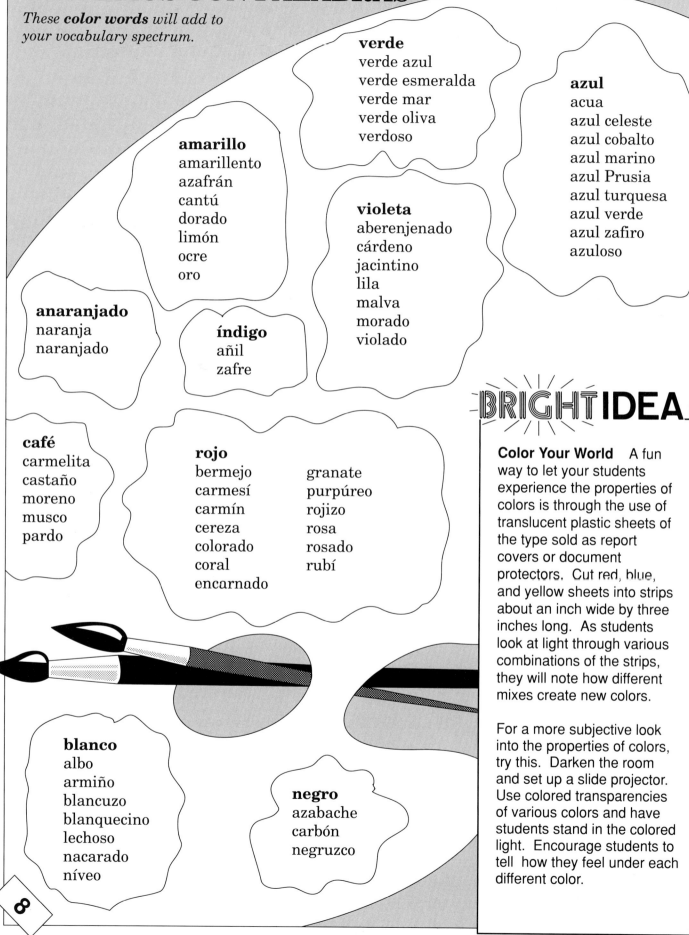

verde
verde azul
verde esmeralda
verde mar
verde oliva
verdoso

azul
acua
azul celeste
azul cobalto
azul marino
azul Prusia
azul turquesa
azul verde
azul zafiro
azuloso

amarillo
amarillento
azafrán
cantú
dorado
limón
ocre
oro

violeta
aberenjenado
cárdeno
jacintino
lila
malva
morado
violado

anaranjado
naranja
naranjado

índigo
añil
zafre

café
carmelita
castaño
moreno
musco
pardo

rojo
bermejo
carmesí
carmín
cereza
colorado
coral
encarnado
granate
purpúreo
rojizo
rosa
rosado
rubí

blanco
albo
armiño
blancuzo
blanquecino
lechoso
nacarado
níveo

negro
azabache
carbón
negruzco

BRIGHT IDEA

Color Your World A fun way to let your students experience the properties of colors is through the use of translucent plastic sheets of the type sold as report covers or document protectors. Cut red, blue, and yellow sheets into strips about an inch wide by three inches long. As students look at light through various combinations of the strips, they will note how different mixes create new colors.

For a more subjective look into the properties of colors, try this. Darken the room and set up a slide projector. Use colored transparencies of various colors and have students stand in the colored light. Encourage students to tell how they feel under each different color.

FORMAS Y TAMAÑOS

Shape words and size words come in all shapes and sizes.
Here's a sampling of some of the most common ones.

GRANDE

ciclópeo, colosal,
descomunal,
desmesurado,
enorme, exagerado,
excesivo, fenomenal,
gigantesco,
monstruoso,
monumental,
tamaño, titánico,
tremendo

MEDIANO

moderado, normal, regular

PEQUEÑO

chico, chiquitín, chiquitito, chiquito,
diminutivo, diminuto, enanito, invisible,
liliputiense, menor, microscópico,
miniatura, mínimo, minúsculo, parvo,
pequeño, pigmeo, tamañito

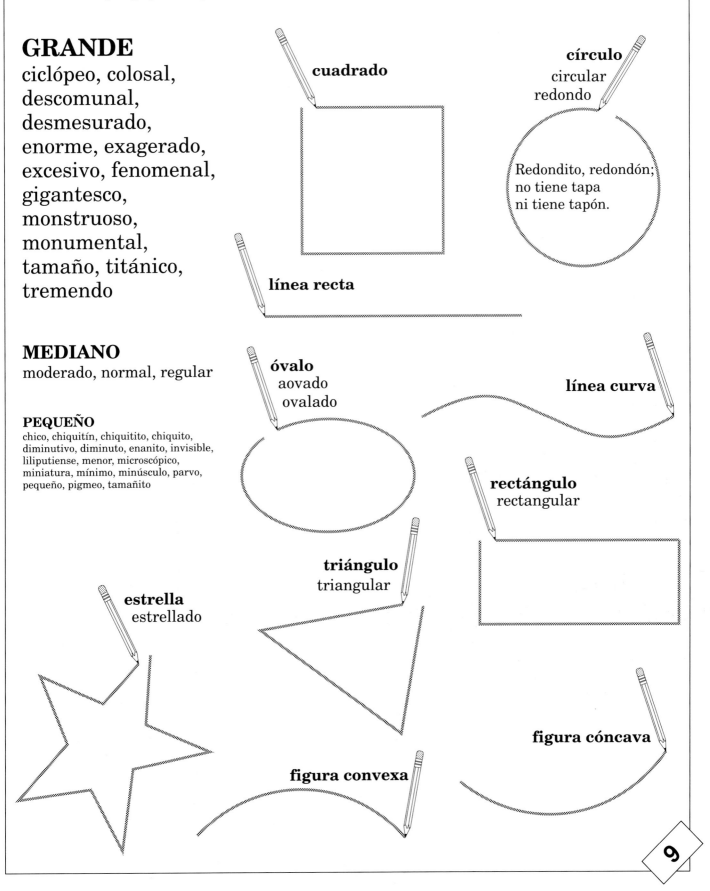

cuadrado

círculo
circular
redondo

Redondito, redondón;
no tiene tapa
ni tiene tapón.

línea recta

óvalo
aovado
ovalado

línea curva

rectángulo
rectangular

triángulo
triangular

estrella
estrellado

figura convexa

figura cóncava

9

UN SINNÚMERO DE NÚMEROS

*The spelling of **number words** in Spanish can be confusing.*
Here is a list that spells it all out. Each Arabic numeral is
followed by the corresponding cardinal and ordinal number.

0	cero	
1	uno, un	primero, primer
2	dos	segundo
3	tres	tercero, tercer
4	cuatro	cuarto
5	cinco	quinto
6	seis	sexto
7	siete	séptimo
8	ocho	octavo
9	nueve	noveno
10	diez	décimo
11	once	undécimo
12	doce	duodécimo
13	trece	decimotercero, decimotercer, decimotercio
14	catorce	decimocuarto
15	quince	decimoquinto
16	dieciséis	decimosexto
17	diecisiete	decimoséptimo
18	dieciocho	decimoctavo
19	diecinueve	decimonoveno, decimonono
20	veinte	vigésimo
21	veintiuno, ventiún	vigésimo primero, vigésimo primer
22	veintidós	vigésimo segundo
23	veintitrés	vigésimo tercero, vigésimo tercer
etc.		
30	treinta	trigésimo
31	treinta y uno, treinta y un	trigésimo primero, trigésimo primer
32	treinta y dos	trigésimo segundo
33	treinta y tres	trigésimo tercero, trigésimo tercer
etc.		

40	cuarenta	cuadragésimo
50	cincuenta	quincuagésimo
60	sesenta	sexagésimo
70	setenta	septuagésimo
80	ochenta	octogésimo
90	noventa	nonagésimo
100	ciento, cien	centésimo
101	ciento uno, ciento un	centésimo primero, centésimo primer
102	ciento dos	centésimo segundo
etc.		
200	doscientos	ducentésimo
300	trescientos	tricentésimo
400	cuatrocientos	cuadringentésimo
500	quinientos	quingentésimo
600	seiscientos	sexcentésimo
700	setecientos	septingentésimo
800	ochocientos	octingentésimo
900	novecientos	noningentésimo
1,000	mil	milésimo
1,001	mil uno, mil un	milésimo primero, milésimo primer
etc.		
2,000	dos mil	dosmilésimo
3,000	tres mil	tresmilésimo
etc.		
10,000	diez mil	diezmilésimo
100,000	cien mil	cienmilésimo
500,000	quinientos mil	quinientosmilésimo
1,000,000	un millón	millonésimo

*The following are the most common **Greek and Latin roots** that indicate number.*

Raíz	Número	Ejemplo
mono, uni	1	*monólogo, unilateral*
bi, duo	2	*bicicleta, dual*
ter, tri	3	*ternario, triciclo*
tetra, cuadro	4	*tetraedro, cuadrúpedo*
penta, quin	5	*pentágono, quíntuple*
hexa, sexa	6	*hexagonal, sexteto*
hepta, septa	7	*heptágono, septiembre*
oct	8	*octagonal*
enea	9	*eneágono*
deca	10	*decálogo*
endeca	11	*endecasílabo*
dodeca	12	*dodecaedro*
icos	20	*icosaedro*
hect	100	*hectárea*
kilo	1,000	*kilómetro*
poli, multi	muchos	*políglota, multitud*

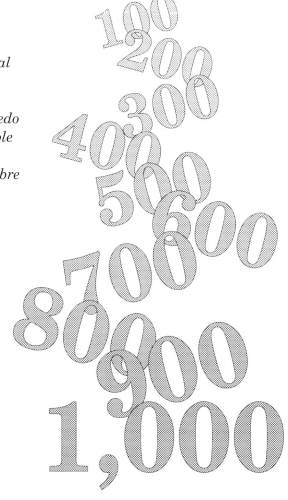

SIEMPRELISTOS

Number Sense Here are some basic rules that you can really count on about the use of number words.

• The noun following a number word ending in *un* or *una* always goes in the plural: *veintiún hombres, treinta y una mujeres.*

• A number word expressing 200 to 999 agrees in gender with the noun it modifies: *doscientas tres niñas.* The singular, masculine *ciento,* however, is used regardless of the gender of the noun it modifies: *ciento tres niñas.* This rule also applies when numbers contain values in the thousands place and beyond: *mil doscientas tres niñas,* but *mil ciento tres niñas.*

• In Spain, as in many other European countries, it is customary to use a period to set off thousands, millions, etc., and to use a comma to set off decimal place. Thus the quantity one thousand, seventy-two and five one-hundredths would be written 1.072,05. Most countries of Latin America follow the style used in the U.S.: commas to set off thousands, millions, etc., and periods to set off decimal place: 1,072.05.

• In the U.S. the word *billion* is used to denote a thousand millions—10^9, or a 1 followed by nine zeroes. Throughout the Spanish-speaking world, the seemingly equivalent word, *billón,* is used to denote a million millions—10^{12}, or a 1 followed by twelve zeros. Thus, the proper Spanish translation of *one billion* is not *un billón,* but *mil millones.*

NO ES LO MISMO NI SE ESCRIBE IGUAL

Homophones are words that sound exactly alike, but which have different spellings and different meanings. Homophones arise in Spanish because of the similar pronunciation of b and v; soft c, s, and z; soft g and j; ll and y; and because of the silent h. Here is a list of some of the most common ones.

Me voy a cazar con mi novia.

B - V

baso *Yo me baso . . .*
vaso

basta *¡Basta ya!*
vasta amplia, grande

bello lindo, bonito
vello pelo del cuerpo

beses *¡No me beses!*
veces *Muchas veces . . .*

bienes posesiones
vienes *¿Vienes con nosotros?*

bote
vote *Vote por mí.*

hierba zacate, vegetación
hierva *No dejes que la leche hierva.*

rebelar *rebelarse contra algo*
revelar *revelar un secreto o una foto*

sabia instruida, sensata
savia líquido de las plantas

varón del sexo masculino
barón título de nobleza

vota del verbo *votar*
bota

votar *votar en elecciones*
botar *botar a la basura*

C - S - Z

abrasar quemar
abrazar dar un abrazo

azada
asada *carne asada*

azar suerte, casualidad
asar *asar carne*

casa
caza acción de cazar

casar unir en matrimonio
cazar matar animales salvajes

CEDA EL PASO

ceda
seda *una blusa de seda*

cien 100
sien

cierra *Cierra la puerta.*
sierra serrucho; cordillera

cocer cocinar
coser *coser con aguja e hilo*

hacia *hacia el sur*
Asia el continente

hacía del verbo *hacer*
asía agarraba

meses *los meses del año*
meces del verbo *mecer*

peces *los peces del mar*
peses *No peses la mercancía en esa balanza.*

risa acción de reírse
riza *María se riza el pelo.*

rosa la flor
roza *El zapato me roza el tobillo.*

senado *el senado de los Estados Unidos*
cenado *Hemos cenado ya.*

12

sumo del verbo *sumar*; supremo
zumo jugo de las frutas

ves *¿No ves lo que hay ahí?*
vez *la primera vez*

G - J
agito del verbo *agitar*
ajito ajo pequeñito

ingerir comer
injerir insertar, injertar

H
arte *una obra de arte*
harte *Déjalo que se harte de comida.*

hablando *hablando con una persona*
ablando *ablando los frijoles en la olla*

habría *Si lloviera más, habría más flores.*
abría *Abría la puerta.*

hasta *¡Hasta mañana!*
asta

hay *Hay mucho que hacer.*
ay *¡Ay, qué dolor!*

haya *Cuando haya tiempo, iré.*
halla del verbo *hallar*
aya niñera

hecho *Es un hecho.*
echo *Lo echo a la basura.*

hola *¡Hola, qué tal!*
ola

LL - Y
aboyar flotar
abollar producir una depresión con un golpe

cayo isla pequeña
callo *Tengo un callo en la mano de tanto trabajar.*

cayó *Se cayó de la escalera.*
calló *Se calló y no dijo más nada.*

malla *unas medias de malla*
maya de los indios mayas

rayar hacer líneas o rayas
rallar *rallar queso con un rallador*

rayo descarga eléctrica; del verbo *rayar*
rallo del verbo *rallar*

vaya *Vaya a mi casa cuando guste.*
valla cerca hecha de madera para defensa

BRIGHT IDEA

Homophone Pop-Ups   A good way to help students to distinguish between homophones is through homophone pop-up cards. Using Blackline Master 1 on page 152, the children can make a pop-up page for each member of a homophone pair (see Part 5, page 139 for directions on how to use the Blackline Master). The front of each page contains the homophone itself. A picture that the child has drawn, which illustrates the word, pops up when the page is unfolded. The picture should be accompanied by a sentence that uses the homophone correctly. By taping the two pages together next to each other, the pop-up book demonstrates at a glance the difference between the homophones.

cayo   callo

El bote pasó cerca de un cayo.

callo

13

NO ES LO MISMO, PERO SE ESCRIBE IGUAL

*Here is a list of common **multiple-meaning words** in Spanish.*

araña	1. animal	2. forma del verbo *arañar: El gato me araña.*	3. candelabro
botón	1. capullo	2. pieza que se empuja para hacer funcionar algo: *Si quieres tocar el timbre, aprieta el botón.*	3. pieza que se usa para sujetar la ropa
cara	1. rostro	2. que cuesta mucho dinero: *Esa blusa de seda es muy cara.*	
cola	1. goma, pegamento: *Le pegamos la pata a la silla con cola.*	2. rabo de un animal	3. fila de personas: *Tuvimos que hacer cola para entrar al cine.*
corriente	1. común, ordinario: *Es un aparato común y corriente.*	2. movimiento del agua de un río: *El río no es muy hondo, pero la corriente es muy fuerte.*	3. electricidad: *Las baterías proporcionan corriente para operar el auto.*
cubiertos	1. utensilios que se usan para comer	2. participio del verbo cubrir: *Los pollitos estaban cubiertos de finísimas plumas amarillas.*	
dura	1. no blanda o suave: *El ébano es una madera muy dura.*	2. difícil: *La maestra nos dio una prueba muy dura.*	3. forma del verbo *durar: La película dura dos horas.*
enseñar	1. Instruir: *La maestra va a enseñar al niño a leer.*	2. mostrar una cosa para que otros la vean: *La maestra les va a enseñar a los niños unas láminas muy bonitas.*	
hoja	1. Página de un libro	2. parte de un planta	3. parte de una espada

lengua	1. órgano muscular de la boca	2. idioma: *El español es una bella lengua.*	3. parte de una campana
lima	1. fruta	2. herramienta	3. (con mayúscula) capital del Perú
lista	1. franja: *Tenía puesto un vestido blanco con una lista azul.*	2. enumeración escrita: *He hecho una lista de las cosas que quiero comprar.*	3. inteligente: *Es una chica muy lista.* 4. preparada: *Estoy lista para salir.*
llama	1. animal	2. fuego	3. forma del verbo *llamar: Llama a tu hermano para que venga a almorzar.*
planta	1. parte inferior del pie: *Tiene un callo en la planta del pie.*	2. ser del reino vegetal	3. fábrica o instalación industrial: *Trabajamos en la planta petrolera.*
vela	1. cilindro de cera con mecha para alumbrarse	2. lona usada en barcos para navegar	3. forma del verbo *velar: La madre vela por el bienestar de sus hijos.*

BRIGHT IDEA

Multiple-Meaning "Pictionary" Pictures and context phrases or sentences are two of the most effective ways to help students grasp the various definitions of multiple-meaning words. Putting together a "pictionary" gives students experience in both.

To use cooperative/collaborative learning techniques, create small groups and assign each group one or more multiple-meaning words. Each group then creates pictures and/or context sentences to clarify the various meanings. You can show them these pages to give them the idea. In addition to the words listed on these pages, other good words to use are: *campo* (country, playing field); *clases* (kinds, lessons, classes); *estación* (season, station); *mañana* (morning, tomorrow); *pelo* (hair, I peel); *peso* (weight, unit of money); *pata* (leg, female duck); *pluma* (pen, feather).

Put together the final products of all the groups to come up with a class "pictionary" of multiple-meaning words.

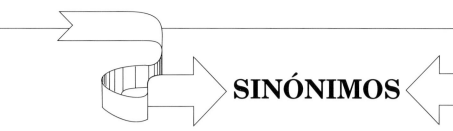

SINÓNIMOS

Synonyms *are words that have the same or almost the same meaning.* **Antonyms** *are opposites. The following lists offer appropriate examples of both for a variety of difficulty levels.*

Adjetivos

adversario — contrario, enemigo
afligido — triste, acongojado
alegre — contento, feliz
amable — agradable, atento, sociable
bello — lindo, bonito, hermoso
cómico — divertido, gracioso
desconcertado — turbado, confundido
entero — completo, total
excelente — magnífico, maravilloso
famoso — conocido, distinguido, ilustre, célebre
flaco — delgado, fino
grueso — gordo, corpulento
habituado — acostumbrado
hondo — profundo
ocupado — atareado
pequeño — chiquito, chico, diminutivo
perezoso — flojo, haragán, vago
preciso — justo, exacto
rápido — veloz, pronto
sencillo — simple, fácil
suficiente — bastante
terco — testarudo, cabeciduro, cabezudo
tranquilo — quieto, callado, calmado
vanidoso — presuntuoso, presumido
verdadero — cierto, real, auténtico

Sustantivos

aeroplano — avión
alumno — discípulo, estudiante
amor — afecto, cariño, ternura
asombro — sorpresa, admiración
barro — lodo, fango
bestia — animal
calamidad — desastre, catástrofe, desgracia
cara — rostro, faz, semblante
cárcel — prisión
cima — punta, cumbre
defecto — falta, imperfección
engaño — mentira, burla
ganas — deseos
grito — alarido, chillido
motivo — razón, causa
principio — comienzo, origen
rabia — ira, furia, cólera

riesgo — peligro, amenaza
temor — miedo, timidez, espanto

Verbos

acabar — terminar, finalizar, concluir
acumular — amontonar, almacenar, juntar, aglomerar
botar — echar, tirar
cambiar — variar, mudar
colocar — poner, situar
chocar — tropezar
derramar — echar, esparcir
elevar — alzar, levantar
escuchar — oír, atender
hacer — crear, producir, fabricar
ocultar — esconder, tapar
opinar — creer, pensar
persuadir — convencer
quebrar — romper, partir
recordar — acordarse
socorrer — ayudar, auxiliar
soportar — aguantar, tolerar, resistir
tomar — beber; asir, agarrar

BRIGHT IDEA

Synonym-Antonym Centipede   A centipede (*ciempiés*) like the critter below can stretch students' vocabulary and build understanding of shades of meaning. Three-by-five index cards, each with an oval shape and feet, form the sections of the centipede. To start, pin up cards with two appropriate antonyms written in different colors. Students extend the centipede in both directions by writing synonyms for each word on other index cards and attaching them to the appropriate end. Encourage students to arrange their synonyms denoting greater and greater degrees of intensity the farther they are from the center of the centipede.

This activity also works well as a timed game for two teams. Each team focuses on synonyms for one of the antonyms. The team that comes up

magnífico · extraordinario · tremendo · excelente · bueno

ANTÓNIMOS

Adjetivos

abierto — cerrado
acompañado — solo
alto — bajo, chico
barato — caro
blando — duro
bonito — feo
bueno — malo
calmado — intranquilo,
    inquieto, nervioso
cobarde — valiente
cómodo — incómodo
cuidadoso — descuidado,
    abandonado
defectuoso — perfecto
derecho — izquierdo;
    curvado
dulce — salado, amargo
enfermo — sano, saludable
entero — incompleto, parcial
estrecho — ancho
fácil — difícil
femenino — masculino
frío — caliente
fuerte — débil
generoso — egoísta
gordo — flaco, delgado
grande — chico, pequeño

igual — distinto, diferente
legal — ilegal, prohibido
liso — áspero, desigual
loco — cuerdo, prudente
mejor — peor
menor — mayor
nuevo — viejo, gastado,
    usado
pesado — ligero, leve,
    liviano; simpático
pobre — rico; afortunado
positivo — negativo
rápido — lento, despacio
sencillo — complicado, difícil
simpático — antipático
tímido — sociable
tranquilo — excitado,
    entusiasmado, animado
triste — alegre, contento
último — primero
vacío — lleno

Adverbios

arriba — abajo
cerca — lejos
delante — detrás
dentro — fuera
mejor — peor
rápido — lento, despacio

Sustantivos

abundancia — escasez
alegría — tristeza
amigo — enemigo
calor — frío
campo — ciudad
claridad — oscuridad
confianza — duda,
    desconfianza
día — noche
paciencia — impaciencia,
    desespero
presencia — ausencia
silencio — sonido, ruido,
    bulla
verdad — mentira, falsedad

Verbos

abrir — cerrar
agarrar — soltar
amar — odiar
aumentar — disminuir
comprar — vender
congelar — derretir
construir — destruir
dar — quitar
dormirse — despertarse
empezar — acabar, terminar
encender — apagar,
    extinguir
ir — venir, regresar
limpiar — ensuciar
meter — sacar
mojar — secar
perjudicar — beneficiar
recordar — olvidar
retroceder — avanzar
separar — juntar, unir
tapar — destapar
vencer — perder, rendirse

with the most synonyms gets to add a head on its end of the centipede.

Good antonym pairs for lower grades are: *grande/chico, bonito/feo, bueno/malo, triste/alegre.* For higher grades, try: *tranquilo/animado, aumentar/disminuir, empezar/acabar, tímido/sociable.*

Word Wheels are another good way to practice with and collect synonyms and antonyms. Reproduce Blackline Master 4 (page 155) on heavy paper and cut out the word wheels. Students write a word in the center and think of synonyms or antonyms, as appropriate, to write on the spokes. Finished synonym or antonym word wheels can be kept in the writing center as a resource.

malo   terrible   horrible   funesto   pésimo

CULTIVANDO PALABRAS

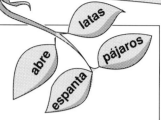

PALABRAS COMPUESTAS

When two or more small words join together, they blossom into a **compound word** *with a new meaning. Spanish compounds may be formed by the union of a verb and a noun, of a noun and an adjective, of a verb and an adverb, of two nouns, or of two adjectives. Other compounds are merely strings of words that usage has fused into one. Here are some examples of each type, along with their English meanings.*

Verbo + Sustantivo

guardabosque/*forest ranger*
guardaespaldas/*bodyguard*
guardarropa/*clothes closet*
hincapié/*emphasis*
lavamanos/*sink*
lavaplatos/*dishwasher*
limpiabotas/*shoe shiner*
limpiaparabrisas/
 windshield wiper
matamoscas/*flyswatter*
parabrisas/*windshield*
paracaídas/*parachute*
paraguas/*umbrella*
parasol/*parasol*
pasamano/*railing*
pasatiempo/*pastime*
picaflor/*hummingbird*
portarretratos/*picture frame*
rompecabezas/*puzzle*
sacacorchos/*corkscrew*
sacapuntas/*pencil sharpener*
salvavidas/*lifeguard; life
 preserver*
tocadiscos/*record player*

Sustantivo + Adjetivo

alicaído/*crestfallen*
bajorrelieve/*bas relief*
boquiabierto/*amazed*
camposanto/*cemetery*
carirredondo/*round-faced*
ciempiés/*centipede*
 hispanoparlante/*Spanish
 speaker*

lanzallamas/*flame thrower*
marisabidilla/*Miss Know-
 it-all*
mediodía/*noon*
Nochebuena/*Christmas Eve*
pelirrojo/*red-haired*
puntiagudo/*sharp-pointed*
supermercado/*supermarket*
tiovivo/*carrousel*
zanquilargo/*long-legged*

Adverbio + Verbo

altoparlante/*loudspeaker*
malcriar/*spoil*
malograr/*waste, ruin; fail*
maltratar/*mistreat*
menospreciar/*despise;
 depreciate*

Sustantivo + Sustantivo

balompié/*soccer*
bocacalle/*entrance to a
 street*
bocamanga/*sleeve opening*
carricoche/*jalopy*
coche-cama/*sleepingcar (in
 a train)*
coliflor/*cauliflower*
compraventa/*buying and
 selling*
hojalata/*sheet metal*
hombre-rana/*frogman
 (diver)*
hora-punta/*peak hour*

maniobra/*maneuver*
marimacho/*tomboy*
puntapié/*kick*

Adjetivo + Adjetivo

agridulce/*sweet-and-sour*
altiplano/*mesa*
mexicano-americano/*Mexican
 American*
sordomudo/*deaf-mute*
tontiloco/*crazy*

Otros compuestos

anteojos/*binoculars;
 eyeglasses*
correveidile/*tattletale, gossip*
cualquiera/*any one*
deprisa/*in a hurry*
dieciséis/*sixteen (See other
 compound numbers on
 p. 10.)*
enhorabuena/*congratulations*
hazmerreír/*laughingstock*
metomentodo/*nosy person*
nomeolvides/*forget-me-not
 (flower)*
quehacer/*chore*
sabelotodo/*know-it-all*
sinfín/*a very high number*
sinnúmero/*a very high
 number*
subibaja/*seesaw*
tampoco/*neither*
tentenpié/*snack*
vaivén/*coming and going*

18

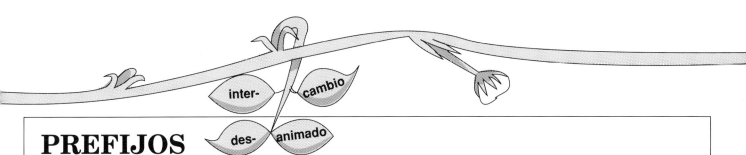

PREFIJOS

*A list of numerical prefixes appears on page 11. Here are some other common **prefixes**, along with their meanings and examples of words in which they appear. All are of Latin origin, except the ones with an asterisk, which are Greek.*

Prefijo	Significado	Ejemplos
*a-	no	*anormal, apolítico*
*anti-	contra	*antivenenoso, antitanque*
*archi-	muy, el más	*archienemigo, archivillano*
*auto-	de o por sí mismo	*autobiografía, autorretrato*
co-	junto con	*cooperar, colaborar*
des-	lo contrario de	*desanimado, descuidar, deshacer*
dis-	no	*discontinuo, disconforme, disculpar*
ex-	fue en un tiempo pero ya no	*ex-gobernador*
extra-	fuera de	*extraordinario, extraterrestre*
extra-	muy, más que	*extraplano, extrasabroso*
im-, in-	no	*imposible, invisible, inútil*

Prefijo	Significado	Ejemplos
inter-	entre	*intercambio, intercontinental, interponer*
post-	después	*postguerra, postmoderno*
pre-	antes	*predecir, previsión, presuponer*
re-	de nuevo, otra vez	*recomenzar, reajustar, reanimar*
re-, requete-	muy	*reguapo, requetelindo*
semi-	medio, a medias	*semiabierto, semicircular*
sub-	debajo	*submarino, subrayar, subterráneo*
super-	encima	*superponer, superestructura*
super-	muy, grande,	*superfino, supermercado*
trans-, tras-	de un lado a otro	*transatlántico, transportar, traspasar, trasplantar*

19

SUFIJOS

*For finishing touches, here is a list of **suffixes**.*

Sufijo	Significado	Ejemplos
-able, -ible	digno de, que se puede	*demostrable, probable, temible*
-áceo	aproximación	*grisáceo, rosáceo*
-ada, -azo	golpe dado con algo	*pedrada, puñalada, pelotazo*
-ador, -edor, -idor	agente, oficio	*comprador, corredor, seguidor*
-ano	gentilicio	*cubano*
-bilidad	capacidad, propensión	*responsabilidad, irritabilidad*
-ción, -sión, -xión	acción o efecto	*invención, confusión, conexión*
-dero	lugar donde se hace algo	*comedero, lavadero, embarcadero*
-ero	ocupación, utensilio	*zapatero, fregadero, mosquitero*
-ería	lugar donde se vende o se repara algo	*zapatería, joyería, relojería*

Sufijo	Significado	Ejemplos
-esco	propio de, semejante a	*gigantesco, carnavalesco*
-ico, -ín, -ito, -illo, -cito, -cillo	diminutivo	*Juanico, pequeñín, perrito, pajarillo, trencito, hombrecillo*
-ísimo	superlativo	*lindísimo, buenísimo*
-ista	ocupación	*ciclista, taxista, artista*
-izo	tendencia, aproximación	*enfermizo, rojizo*
-mente	de cierto modo	*locamente, absolutamente, finalmente*
-miento	acción o efecto	*crecimiento, cumplimiento, nacimiento*
-ón, -ote	aumentativo	*apretón, empujón, grandote*
-oso	lleno de	*luminoso, sudoroso*
-oso	tendencia, aproximación	*verdoso, lechoso*
-ucho	despectivo	*medicucho, delgaducho*

RAÍCES

*Here is a list of some of the most common **classical roots** used in Spanish word formation.* All are of Greek origin, except for *cid*, which is of Latin origin.

Easier Roots

Raíz	Significado	Ejemplos
bio	vida	*anfibio, biología, simbiosis*
fobia	miedo	*fotofobia, claustrofobia*
fono	sonido	*fonética, sinfonía, fonógrafo*
foto	luz	*fotografía, fotofobia, fotoeléctrico*
geo	la Tierra	*geografía, geología, apogeo*
graf	escribir	*biografía, autógrafo, grafología*
homo	igual	*homófono, homogéneo*
logo	estudio, descripción	*biología, arqueología*
macro, mega	grande	*macroclima, megalomanía*
metro	medir	*cronómetro, metrónomo*
micro	pequeño	*microscopio, microbio*

More Difficult Roots

Raíz	Significado	Ejemplos
antropo	ser humano	*antropología, antropomorfo, filantropía*
arqui	mando, gobierno	*anarquía, monarquía, arquitecto*
cid	matar	*insecticida, bactericida, homicidio*
cracia	gobierno	*democracia, autocracia, teocracia*
crono	tiempo	*cronómetro, cronología, sincronizar*
demo	pueblo	*democracia, demagogo, epidemia*
filo	amor, tendencia	*filosofía, cervantófilo, hemofilia*
hidro	agua, líquido	*hidráulico, deshidratado, hidrosfera*
psico	mente, alma	*psiquiatra, psicología*

¿ME PRESTAS UNA PALABRA?

Spanish is richer for the words it has taken from other languages.
*Here are just a few examples of those **borrowed words.***

Del árabe

ajedrez
ajonjolí
alacena
albañil
albaricoque
alcohol
almanaque
almohada
arroba
azafata
azúcar
berenjena
bujía
garra
jabalí
jaque
jarabe
jinete
quintal

De otras lenguas del Viejo Mundo

Del francés

bayoneta (de *baionnette*)
bicicleta (de *bicyclette*)
bisturí (de *bistouri*)
blusa (de *blouse*)
crema (de *crème*)
cretino (de *crétin*)
croqueta (de *croquette*)
cupón (de *coupon*)
chaqueta (de *jaquette*)
ducha (de *douche*)
flan (de *flan*)
fricasé (de *fricassé*)
fusil (de *fusil*)
gabinete (de *gabinet*)
gripe (de *grippe*)
guillotina (de *guillotine*)
oboe (de *hautbois*)

pantalón (de *pantalon*)
parque (de *parc*)
peluca (de *perruque*)
petardo (de *pétard*)
pompón (de *pompon*)
quepis (de *képi*)
quincalla (de *quincaille*)
raqueta (de *raquette*)
taller (de *atelier*)
zigzag (de *zigzag*)

Del inglés

béisbol (de *baseball*)
bistek/biftek (de *beefsteak*)
caqui (de *khaki*)
comité (de *committee*)
cheque (de *check*)
fútbol (de *football*)
galón (de *gallon*)
gol (de *goal*)
radar (de *radar*)
vagón (de *wagon*)

Del italiano

acuarela (de *acquarella*)
cascada (de *cascata*)
corbata (de *corvatta* o *crovatta*)
cuneta (de *cunetta*)
escopeta (de *schioppetto*)
macarrón (de *maccherone*)
remolacha (de *ramolaccio*)

Otros ejemplos

aspirina (del alemán *aspirin*)
bambú (de una lengua de la India)
banana (voz del África occidental)
cacatúa (del malayo)
café (del turco)
cobalto (del alemán *kobalt*)
chacal (del turco)
chimpancé (de una lengua del África occidental)

esquí (del noruego)
orangután (del malayo *orangutan*, "hombre de la selva")
pistola (del alemán *pistole*)

De lenguas indígenas del Nuevo Mundo

Del taíno u otras lenguas arauacas

ají
bejuco
cacique
canoa
comején
guanajo
guayaba
güira
hamaca
huracán
iguana
maíz
mamey

WORDWISE

A Word About Words   If you enjoy learning about the histories of words, curl up some evening with an etymological dictionary—the *Breve diccionario etimológico de la lengua castellana* (by Joan Corominas; Madrid: Editorial Gredos, 1973) is the standard work in the field. You'll be in for hours of word-sleuthing fun!

Del náhuatl u otras lenguas aztecas

aguacate (de *auácatl*)
atole (de *atúlli*)
cacahuete (de *tlalcacáuatl*)
cacao (de *cacáuatl*)
coyote (de *cóyotl*)
chicle (de *tzíctli*)
chile (de *chílli*)
chocolate (de formación
   incierta)
elote (de *élotl*)
guacamole (de *auacamúlli*)
guajolote (de *uexólotl*)
mecate (de *mécatl*)

mole (de *múlli*)
nopal (de *nopálli*)
ocelote (de *océlotl*)
sinsonte (de *zenzóntli*)
tamal (de *tamálli*)
tomate (de *tómatl*)
zacate (de *çácatl*)

Del quechua

cóndor (de *cúntur*)
llama
papa (de *pápa*)
poroto (de *purutú*)
puma (de *púma*)
vicuña

Otros ejemplos

caimán (del caribe
   acayuman)
jaguar (del tupí-guaraní
   jaguará)
ñandú (del guaraní)
ombú (del guaraní *umbú*)
papaya (probablemente del
   caribe)

SIEMPRE LISTOS

Pre-Columbian Cultures   The following is a brief outline of the various cultures indigenous to the New World from whose languages some of the above words were borrowed.

The **Aztec** civilization flourished during the 1400s and early 1500s in Mexico. There were several regional variants or dialects of the Aztec language, the main one of which was **Nahuatl**. Today some Mexicans still speak a modern form of Nahuatl.

The **Carib** Indians lived in South America before migrating to the Caribbean Islands in 1300. Only a few survive.

Quechua was the mother tongue of the ancient Incas of the central Andean highlands of Peru. As the Inca conquest expanded in the 15th and early 16th centuries, Quechua became the administrative and commercial language of the empire. Quechua is still spoken today by some of the Indians in the highlands of Peru and neighboring countries.

The **Guarani** Indians were the first people to live in what is now Paraguay. They migrated inland from Brazil and Argentina to the Río de la Plata in the 14th and 15th centuries. Today in rural Paraguay, Guarani is more widely spoken than Spanish.

The **Tupi-Guarani**—different tribes that spoke related languages—lived in eastern South America. Tupi-Guarani is one of the major language families of South America and has become widely dispersed and differentiated since the 15th century. It served as the basis for the Indian language spoken throughout Brazil before the European colonization.

Some tribes of the **Arawak** Indians came from South America in about A.D. 1000 to settle the Greater Antilles (Cuba, Puerto Rico, Haiti and Santo Domingo, Jamaica); others lived in the Amazon River Valley. The Arawaks were the first American Indians Columbus met when he landed in the West Indies in 1492. The **Taínos** were a subgroup of the Arawaks.

REGALITOS

Spanish has given as well as received. Here is a list of some of the many
English words that have come into the language from Spanish.

adobe
aficionado
alfalfa
alligator (from *el lagarto*)
armada
armadillo
avocado
banana
barbecue (from *barbacoa*)
bolero
bonanza
bongo (from *bongó*)
bronco
cabana (from *cabaña*)
calabash (from *calabaza*)
canyon (from *cañón*)
cargo
castanet (from *castañeta*)
cayman (from *caimán*)
chaparral
chaps (from *chaparreras*)

chili (from *chile*)
chocolate
cocoa (from *cacao*)
condor (from *cóndor*)
cork (from *corcho*)
corral
coyote
desperado (from *desesperado*)
fiesta
flamenco
guava (from *guayaba*)
guerrilla
hacienda
hurricane (from *huracán*)
iguana
jai alai
junta
lariat (from *la reata*)
lasso (from *lazo*)
machete
mesa
mesquite
mosquito
mustang (from *mestengo*)

palomino
papaya
parakeet (from *periquito*)
patio
peccadillo (from *pecadillo*)
plantain (from *plátano*)
plaza
poncho
potato (from *patata*)
pronunciamento (from *pronunciamiento*)
ranch (from *rancho*)
rodeo
rumba
salsa
sierra
siesta
stampede (from *estampida*)
tango
tobacco (from *tabaco*)
tomato (from *tomate*)
tornado
vanilla (from *vainilla*)
vigilante

BRIGHT IDEA

What's in a Name?   From **Florida** to **California**, there are a myriad of place names that are Spanish or derived from Spanish. Having your students research the origin of such names is a good way to introduce them to word histories. The names to research don't have to be geographical features. Often there are fascinating histories behind the names of streets, neighborhoods, and government or historic buildings. This activity will also foster pride in, and awareness of, cultural heritage.

PAREJAS FAMOSAS . . .

*Here are some Spanish celebrity couples—**pairs of words** that go together hand in glove.*

abrir y cerrar
aceite y vinagre
agua y jabón
ahora o nunca
aquí y allí
arroz con frijoles
arroz con leche
arroz con pollo
bate y pelota
besos y abrazos
bistek con papas
blanco y negro
brincar y saltar
café con leche
cara o cruz
casa y comida
comal y metate
compra y venta
común y corriente
crimen y castigo
cuello y corbata
de una vez y por todas
día y noche
entra y sale
felices pascuas y
    próspero año nuevo
gato y ratón
ida y vuelta
increíble pero cierto
ir y venir
leer y escribir
mal nacido y peor aconsejado
mamá y papá
más o menos
mesa y sillas
pan con mantequilla
pan y agua
papel y lápiz
pares y nones
paz y tranquilidad
por sí o por no
puertas y ventanas
punto y aparte
sal y pimienta
sangre y fuego

sano y salvo
siempre y cuando
soltero y sin compromiso
sube y baja
tarde o temprano
uña y carne
vida o muerte
viento y marea

. . . Y TRÍOS

*And some **threesomes** too.*

agudas, llanas y esdrújulas
a la una, a las dos y a las tres
bueno, malo y regular
garganta, nariz y oídos
Jesús, María y José
hombres, mujeres y niños
lunes, miércoles y viernes
Melchor, Gaspar y Baltasar
músico, poeta y loco
papá, mamá y nené
tierra, mar y aire

BRIGHT IDEA

Word Collections One good word always leads to another, and pretty soon students will have entire collections that keep their love of language alive!

Take a good look at language—you'll find a treasure trove of words to collect: sound words (see p. 26), multiple-meaning words (see pp. 14–15), rhyming words (see pp. 28–29), people words, scary words, palindromes (see p. 27), bird words, word pairs and trios.

Some collections become important resources for writing and should be a permanent part of a big classroom scrapbook in the writing corner, or smaller card files for individual use. Blackline Master 2 on page 153 of this book may be reproduced on card stock to provide collection cards for a 5" x 7" file, or students can create their own format. As the Blackline Master suggests, however, you will want to encourage students to do more than merely write the word and its definition. There is a space to attach a symbol which serves to classify the word (as a sound word, a place word, a word that describes people, etc.). Children will also need space to illustrate the word; to write synonyms, antonyms, and other related words for it; or to use it in a sentence.

Other collection activities, like the pairs and trios on this page, should be just for fun. Time the collection to coincide with a seasonal event (scary words for Halloween), with a content-area topic (desert words when studying the American Southwest), or with the theme of a story you've just read. For such collections, plan a temporary display of the words on mobiles or bulletin boards, for example.

The collection of word pairs and trios works well for a bulletin board display depicting a springtime scene. Once the background has been drawn, children can add butterflies and clover, using the patterns on Blackline Master 3 on page 154. The butterfly pattern is for collecting word pairs: each word in the pair is written on a wing of the butterfly, with the conjunction on the butterfly's body. The three-leaf-clover pattern is for collecting trios. Select a few examples from this list to spark the brainstorming. Then let students show off their ideas.

¡QUÉ RUIDO!

*An **onomatopoeia** is a noisy word whose sound imitates what it describes. Every language has its share. Here are some Spanish ones.*

tilín talán

run rún

zas

cataplum

pum

ja ja ja

mu

pim **pam pom**

rataplán

jau jau

chiqui**chaque**

purrr

p a f

crac

tuturu**tú**

quiquiri**quí**

miau

tic toc

gua-a-a-**á**

pío pío

Here are some sound words that have been incorporated into the language as regular parts of speech.

bofetón/*slap*
cacarear/*to cluck*
cuchichear/*to whisper*
chacharear/*to gossip*
chancleta/*flip-flop*
chaparrón/*downpour*
chapotear/*to splash*

chasquear/*to chew noisily*
chasquido/*smack*
chicharra/*cicada; noisemaker*
chirriar/*to make a grating sound*
fofo/*overly soft*
gárgaras/*gargling*
maullar/*to meow*

piar/*to peep*
refunfuñar/*to complain under one's breath*
ronronear/*to rumble, to purr*
susurrar/*to whisper*
tartamudear/*to stammer*
zumbar/*to hum*

LOS PALÍNDROMOS ME DAN LO MISMO

Palindromes are words and phrases that read the same from right to left as from left to right. Single-word palindromes are relatively easy to find. If you haven't had a good headache in a while, try making up some whole-sentence palindromes. Here's some inspiration.

ANA	AMA	SOMOS	AMOR A ROMA	ALLÍ VES A SEVILLA
OJO	ADA	RADAR	ANITA LAVA LA TINA	SE VAN SUS NAVES
ALA	ORO	RAPAR	¿SOMOS O NO SOMOS?	SOPAS Y SAPOS
OSO	SALAS	SOLOS	OIRÁS ORAR A ROSARIO	ANILINA
			DÁBALE ARROZ A LA ZORRA EL ABAD	

CORTOS DE VISTA

Here are some common Spanish **abbreviations** *and* **acronyms**.

Abreviatura o sigla	Significado
a.C.	antes de Cristo
A.D.	*anno Domini*, año del Señor
cap.	capítulo
c.c.	centímetro(s) cúbico(s)
Cía.	compañía
D.	Don, domingo
Da.	Doña
doc.	docena
dom.	domingo
Dr.	doctor
ed.	edición, editor, editorial
EE.UU., E.U.A.	Estados Unidos

Abreviatura o sigla	Significado
F. de T.	fulano de tal
fig.	figura
Fr.	fray
g	gramo(s)
gral.	general
H.	hermano (en órdenes religiosas)
hect.	hectárea(s)
hnos.	hermanos
km/h	kilómetros por hora
l	litro(s)
lic.	licenciado
m	metro(s)
núm.	número
O.E.A.	Organización de Estados Americanos
O.N.U.	Organización de las Naciones Unidas
O.T.A.N.	Organización del Tratado del Atlántico Norte
P.	padre
pág., págs.	página(s)
P.D.	posdata
p. ej.	por ejemplo
S.	san, santo, sábado
S.A.	sociedad anónima
Sr.	señor
Sra.	señora
Sres., Srs.	señores
Srta.	señorita
Sto., Sta.	santo, santa
U., Ud., V.	usted
Uds., Vds.	ustedes

SIEMPRE LISTOS

Metric-System Abbreviations In Spanish-speaking countries, the following metric-system prefix abbreviations are used.

m = *mili*	= 1/1,000	*da* = *deca*	= 10	
c = *centi*	= 1/100	*h* = *hecto*	= 100	
d = *deci*	= 1/10	*k* = *kilo*	= 1,000	

These prefix abbreviations are combined with the abbreviations for the basic units—m, l, and g—to designate the derived units. For example, *hectometers* is abbreviated *hm*; *centiliters* is abbreviated *cl*.

CON SON Y TON

*Spanish, like the other Romance languages, is rhyme-rich. Here is just a sampling of some **rhyming words**.*

-abo, avo acabo, centavo, lavo, nabo, octavo, pavo, rabo, trabo

-ad bondad, edad, maldad, oportunidad, piedad, responsabilidad, seguridad, suavidad, variedad, verdad

-aco bellaco, chamaco, checoslovaco, empaco, flaco, guanaco, opaco, polaco, saco, tabaco, taco, verraco

-ado cuidado, delgado, demasiado, dorado, lado, mercado, plateado, recado, tratado, *todos los participios terminados en* -ado

-ajo abajo, ajo, bajo, contrajo, debajo, distrajo, escarabajo, estropajo, trabajo, trajo

-al al, animal, cabal, cal, corral, cual, especial, fatal, final, igual, mal, musical, sal, tal, total

-alo dalo, halo, igualo, malo, palo, regalo, señalo

-allo, ayo caballo, callo, cayo, fallo, gallo, rayo

-ama ama, brama, cama, clama, drama, exclama, fama, llama, mama, payama, proclama, programa, rama, reclama, trama

-ante adelante, aguante, bastante, brillante, constante, durante, elefante, estante, estudiante, importante, interesante, guante, restaurante, semejante, vigilante

-ar azar, azahar, hogar, lugar, paladar, yaguar, *todos los infinitivos terminados en* -ar

-ario armario, calendario, contrario, escenario, extraordinario, horario, ordinario, vestuario

-ás, -az además, aguarrás, atrás, capataz, capaz, detrás, estás, jamás, más, quizás

-ato contrato, chato, gato, grato, inmediato, maltrato, mato, pato, rato, relato, retrato, sensato, trato

-echo cosecho, derecho, estrecho, hecho, lecho, satisfecho, techo, trecho

-elo caramelo, celo, lelo, paralelo, pelo, terciopelo

-ella aquella, bella, botella, ella, estrella, paella

-ema anatema, crema, emblema, flema, gema, lema, problema, quema, rema, sistema, tema, teorema, yema

-eno ajeno, freno, heno, lleno, moreno, pleno, sereno, terreno

-ente agente, caliente, continente, corriente, diferente, gente, gerente, inteligente, mente, repente, serpiente, siente, siguiente, suficiente, valiente, *todos los adverbios terminados en* -mente

-ero acero, agujero, alero, bolero, caballero, carnero, cero, dinero, febrero, granjero, pero, primero, quiero, sendero, verdadero, zapatero

-esto apuesto, arresto, cesto, detesto, esto, funesto, gesto, molesto, presto, puesto, resto

-eta aleta, careta, carreta, caseta, cometa, gaveta, maleta, meseta, meta, nieta, paleta, trompeta

-ico acuático, científico, eléctrico, folklórico, lógico, mágico, México, músico, simpático, técnico, único

-ida bienvenida, comida, despedida, enseguida, guarida, medida, mordida, salida, vida, *todos los adjetivos participios terminados en* -ida

-illa arcilla, ardilla, barbilla, bombilla, brilla, camilla, comilla, costilla, maravilla, orilla, parrilla, rodilla, semilla, Sevilla, silla, vajilla, varilla

-illo bolsillo, castillo, grillo, rastrillo, sencillo

-ina camina, cocina, colina, fina, gallina, golondrina, harina, Josefina, letrina, madrina, margarina, mina

-ino bovino, camino, cochino, comino, destino, fino, imagino, lino, molino, remolino, termino, vino

-ío frío, mío, río, tío, vacío

-ista arista, artista, ciclista, dentista, lista, pista, realista, vista

-oma asoma, coma, doma, goma, loma, Mahoma, maroma, paloma, Roma, toma

-ojo acongojo, enojo, flojo, mojo, ojo, reojo, rojo

-oso, -ozo arenoso, famoso, hermoso, jugoso, nervioso, orgulloso, oso, pozo, ruidoso, trozo

-ubo, uvo cubo, detuvo, entretuvo, estuvo, hubo, sostuvo, subo, tubo, tuvo

-uelo abuelo, consuelo, pañuelo, señuelo, suelo, vuelo

-uro apuro, aseguro, canguro, duro, figuro, impuro, juro, maduro, muro, oscuro, puro, seguro

-usto arbusto, busto, gusto, justo, susto

Hink Pink = Poco Loco   Are you familiar with the rhyming game known as "Hink Pink"? You might adapt this game to Spanish, calling it "Poco Loco." Here's how it works.

At least two players are needed to play the game. One of the players must think of a two-word phrase in which the words rhyme and have the same number of syllables, for example: *otro potro*. Then this player gives a clever clue that will elicit the rhyming phrase.

To illustrate with the *otro potro* example, the player would start off by saying something like: "*Estoy pensando en algo que es un poco loco. Es un caballo joven distinto.*" The words *poco loco* in this example are a signal to the syllabic structure of the phrase to be guessed by the other players. (For clues to two one-syllable words, use *poc loc*; for two three-syllable words, use *poquito loquito*; etc.) The players take turns guessing the rhyming phrase until someone guesses correctly. Then it is that player's turn to think of a rhyming phrase.

Here are some more clues to get you started:

- *calzado que no es caro = zapato barato* (poquito loquito)
- *una hacienda no estrecha = rancho ancho* (poco loco)
- *una obra de cine de muy mal gusto = película ridícula* (poquitito loquitito)
- *un plátano muy pequeño = banana enana* (poquito loquito)
- *que no tiene terminación = sin fin* (poc loc)

The game can be varied by allowing the rhyming pairs to have a different number of syllables. For example, a *poquito loco* for "*cartas que no son bonitas*" would be *correo feo* and a *poquito loquitititito* for "*un doctor que sabe mucho*" would be *médico enciclopédico*.

MODISMOS DE MODA

*In any language, a good way to say what you mean is to use **idioms**, which don't really mean what they say! Here is a group of commonly used Spanish idioms.*

A duras penas Con gran dificultad. *A duras penas consiguió la viejita subir las escaleras.*

A toda vela Muy bien, sin problemas.

Al pie de la letra Exactamente, precisamente.

Al por mayor En gran cantidad. *En la fiesta había flores bonitas al por mayor.*

A viva voz En voz alta, gritando.

Comerse (una letra, un renglón, etc.) *Omitirlo al hablar o escribir.*

Como una fiera Muy enfadado, de muy mal genio.

Con las manos en la masa En el acto de cometer algún delito.

Costar un ojo de la cara Ser muy caro.

Dar a luz Parir, tener un bebé.

Dar en el clavo Acertar.

Dar gato por liebre Hacer algún trato o negocio en el que uno se beneficia grandemente a expensas de otro. *Voy a quejarme, porque creo que cuando compré este juego me dieron gato por liebre.*

Dar rabia Enfadar.

Dar rienda suelta No controlar en lo más mínimo. *Cuando uno le da rienda suelta a su imaginación, se le ocurren cosas verdaderamente fantásticas.*

Dar su brazo a torcer Admitir uno que ha hecho algún error. *Ella sabe que se ha equivocado, pero no quiere dar su brazo a torcer.*

Darle a uno lo mismo Serle indiferente.

Darle una mano a alguien Ayudarlo.

Darle vueltas (a un asunto) Preocuparse mucho por él. *Ya me duele la cabeza de darle tantas vueltas a este problema.*

De buenas a primeras De pronto, en muy poco tiempo. *De buenas a primeras, sin ninguna explicación, se levantó y se fue.*

De la noche a la mañana De pronto, en muy poco tiempo, repentinamente.

De lo lindo Mucho y bien. *Ayer fueron a una fiesta y disfrutaron de lo lindo.*

De par en par Completamente abierto.

De Pascuas a San Juan Con muy poca frecuencia. *Casi nunca lo vemos; nos visita de Pascuas a San Juan.*

Dejarlo a uno plantado No presentarse a una cita o no cumplir con algún compromiso.

Desde luego Por supuesto, claro que sí.

BRIGHT IDEA

Illustrating Idioms Students will appreciate both the usefulness and colorful nature of idioms when you involve them in illustrating an idiom's literal meaning.

Let groups create a computer that has been misprogrammed and takes everything literally. Students then write a sentence with an idiom and illustrate what the computer's screen or printout says it means.

Dejé a mi amigo plantado.

Echar a perder Malograr o inutilizar algo. *¡Derramaste la pintura y has echado todo a perder!*

Echar de menos Extrañar.

El día menos pensado Inesperadamente.

En el fondo En lo esencial.

En un abrir y cerrar de ojos Rápidamente, inesperadamente.

En un dos por tres Rápidamente, inesperadamente.

Estar en las nubes Estar uno abstraído o absorto en sus propios pensamientos.

Estar muy metido en algo Tener mucho interés en él y dedicarle mucho tiempo y esfuerzo.

Estar por las nubes Estar muy caro.

Haber gato encerrado Haber algo sospechoso que no es inmediatamente evidente. *Su explicación no me convence; aquí hay gato encerrado.*

Hacer buenas migas Llevarse bien. *Luisita y Dora no hacen buenas migas; siempre se están peleando.*

Hacer caso Escuchar, obedecer.

Hacer cola Hacer fila para conseguir algo.

Hacer juego Hacer buena mezcla, combinarse bien. *Esa camisa azul hace juego con estos pantalones de rayitas.*

Hacer papel de Actuar como, dar la impresión de ser.

Hasta por los codos Muchísimo, sin límites.

Llover a cántaros Llover mucho y violentamente.

Matar dos pájaros de un tiro Realizar dos objetivos de una vez.

Matar el tiempo Pasarlo sin provecho esperando por algo.

Meter la cuchara Entremeterse uno en lo que no le concierne. *No metas la cuchara, que eso no es asunto tuyo.*

Meterse con alguien Buscar problemas con alguien o dirigirse a él irrespetuosamente.

No darle a uno ni frío ni calor Serle indiferente.

No tener pelos en la lengua Expresarse libremente y con completa sinceridad.

Perder el hilo de algo No mantenerse al tanto de lo que ocurre.

Perder la cabeza Perder el control, dejarse llevar por la emoción.

Poner a uno al corriente Informarlo de todos los datos.

Poner el grito en el cielo Quejarse fuertemente. *Cuando le dije a mi papá lo que habían costado los patines, puso el grito en el cielo.*

Poner manos a la obra Comenzar a trabajar.

Quitarse un peso de encima Sentir alivio por haber salido de alguna preocupación.

Salirse uno con la suya Conseguir lo que quería, a pesar de la oposición de otros.

Seguirle la corriente a alguien Pretender uno simpatizar con sus opiniones sólo para evitar una discusión.

Tener algo en la punta de la lengua Estar a punto de recordarlo.

Tener los huesos molidos Estar muy cansado.

Tomar el pelo Engañar, burlarse de alguien.

Tomar medidas (contra algo) Actuar en contra de ello. *Las autoridades tomaron medidas para evitar que se repitieran los desórdenes.*

Y pico (Se usa con números.) Un poco más de. *Llegaron a la una y pico. Gastamos treinta y pico de dólares en el restaurante.*

PART 2

LA CULTURA

A compendium of things and people Hispanic, with an anthology of traditional Spanish children's folklore and literature

AQUÍ SE HABLA ESPAÑOL

Estados Unidos

Cuba

República Dominicana

Puerto Rico

México

Honduras

Guatemala

Nicaragua

El Salvador

Venezuela

Costa Rica

Colombia

Panamá

Ecuador

Perú

Bolivia

Paraguay

Chile

Argentina

Uruguay

España

COSITAS SUELTAS

*Here are some fascinating **facts about the Hispanic world.***

La bandera de Paraguay es la única bandera del mundo en la que un lado es distinto al otro. Un lado tiene el escudo de armas de la república; el otro tiene el emblema del Ministerio de Hacienda.

Argentina contiene el punto más alto y el punto más bajo de la América del Sur. El monte Aconcagua, de unos 22,800 pies de altura, es el punto más alto del hemisferio occidental. La península Valdés, a unos 130 pies bajo el nivel del mar, es el punto más bajo de la América del Sur.

El río Amazonas es más caudaloso que el Mississippi, el Nilo y el Yangtsé juntos.

La catarata Ángel, en el río Churún de Venezuela, es la más alta del mundo, con una caída vertical de 3,212 pies.

La Cordillera de los Andes, situada en América del Sur, tiene 54 picos mayores de 20,000 pies.

El Teatro Colón, en Buenos Aires, Argentina, es el teatro de ópera más grande del mundo.

Chile ocupa el segundo lugar en el mundo en la producción de cobre. Sólo Estados Unidos produce más.

Colombia ocupa el segundo lugar en el mundo en la producción de café. Sólo Brasil produce más.

Las cataratas del río Iguasú, que forma la frontera entre Argentina y Brasil, tienen una extensión de dos millas y media y una altura de 237 pies.

Argentina produce la mayor cantidad de carne de res del mundo hispano.

La Universidad de Buenos Aires, en la Argentina, es la más grande de América Latina, con más de 100,000 estudiantes.

La Universidad de Santo Domingo, fundada en 1538 y ubicada en la República Dominicana, es la más antigua del hemisferio occidental.

El pueblo de Ushuaia, situado en la porción argentina de Tierra del Fuego, es la población más sureña del mundo.

La Paz, en Bolivia, es la capital más alta del mundo, a 12,795 pies sobre el nivel del mar.

Ecuador exporta más bananas que cualquier otro país del mundo.

El Salvador tiene la población más densa de todos los países continentales del hemisferio occidental.

Perú tiene la mayor población de origen indígena del hemisferio occidental.

SIEMPRE LISTOS

Adjectives of National Origin Adjectives which denote national origin are known in Spanish as *gentilicios*. Here are the *gentilicios* for the countries shown on the map at left.

argentino	hondureño
boliviano	mexicano
chileno	nicaragüense
colombiano	panameño
costarricense,	paraguayo
costarriqueño	peruano
cubano	puertorriqueño,
dominicano	portorriqueño
ecuatoriano	salvadoreño
español	uruguayo
estadounidense	venezolano
guatemalteco	

El lago Titicaca, ubicado en el altiplano de la frontera entre Bolivia y Perú, tiene una altura de 12,500 pies y es el lago de mayor altura en el mundo en el cual se puede navegar.

El lago Maracaibo, ubicado en Venezuela, es el lago más grande de América Latina.

La costa del Pacífico de Colombia es el lugar que recibe la mayor cantidad de lluvia de todas las Américas.

México es el país con la mayor población de hispanoparlantes del mundo.

Cuba, la isla más grande de las Antillas, produce más azúcar que cualquier otro país del mundo hispano.

La población urbana de la Ciudad de México, unas 20 millones de personas en 1988, constituye la mayor concentración urbana del mundo.

México produce la mayor cantidad de plata del mundo.

México produce la mayor cantidad de petróleo de América Latina.

El área geográfica de Cuba representa más del 50% del área geográfica de las Antillas.

México dispone del mayor número de escuelas primarias del mundo hispano.

México produce más maíz que cualquier otro país hispano.

El Misti, volcán situado al oeste de la ciudad de Arequipa, Perú, tiene un cono casi perfectamente simétrico que se eleva a unos 19,100 pies de altura.

El volcán Paricutín, ubicado a unas 200 millas al oeste de la Ciudad de México, entró en erupción por primera vez en 1943 en un campo llano y creció a una altura de 450 pies en sólo una semana y a una altura de 1,000 pies en sólo dos meses.

España construye el mayor número de barcos del mundo hispano.

El volcán Cotopaxi, situado en el norte del Ecuador, es el volcán activo más alto del mundo, con una altura de 19,347 pies sobre el nivel del mar.

España tiene el mayor número de teatros y museos del mundo hispano.

El coquí, pequeña rana arbórea de Puerto Rico, es la rana arbórea más pequeña del mundo.

La cuenca de Puerto Rico, cerca de la isla del mismo nombre, es el punto más profundo del Océano Atlántico: unos 28,200 metros bajo el nivel del mar.

El pico Duarte, en la República Dominicana, es el punto más alto de las Antillas. Mide unos 10,400 pies de altura.

BRIGHT IDEA

Year-Long Map Project Students can use the facts given in this list to construct a map highlighting the varied marvels of the Hispanic world.

First, make an enlarged version of the map given on page 32, large enough to display on a bulletin board. One way to do this is to project the map (using an overhead projector) onto a piece of butcher paper and have students trace the outlines.

Then, perhaps as part of a calendar activity (see **Bright Idea** on page 39), present one interesting fact a week to your students. (Thirty-six facts are given in this list—enough for a whole year.) Have students find the spot on the map to which the fact refers and insert a brightly colored thumbtack to which a piece of yarn has been tied. They then stretch the yarn to an area outside the map and write the fact directly on the butcher paper or attach it on an index card, adding suitable illustrations. The thumbtack and yarn function as an arrow to point to the right spot.

CADA CUAL A SU MANERA

*Spanish is spoken in so many countries, it's no wonder that there is often more than one way to say the same thing. Here is just a taste of the **regional variety** that adds spice to Spanish. In the list below, if a word is followed by the name of a country or region, this indicates that its usage is peculiar to that country or region. Words without a country or region designator are either used throughout the Spanish-speaking world, or their usage is widely scattered.*

anger bronca (Argentina, Uruguay), ira

apron delantal, mandil

attic altillo, buhardilla, desván, guardilla, zarzo (Colombia)

baby bebé, guagua (Chile), nené

balloon globo, vejiga (Guatemala)

bean fréjol (Perú), frijol, fríjol, haba, habichuela (Puerto Rico), judía (España), poroto (Argentina)

binoculars anteojos (Cuba, Puerto Rico, Estados Unidos), binoculares, binóculos, gemelos, gemelos de campo, largavistas (Estados Unidos), prismáticos (España)

blanket coberto, cobija (México), colcha (Caribe), frazada

blond güero (México), rubio

boy chamaco (México), chaval (España), chavo (Guatemala), muchacho, niño, patojo (Guatemala), pibe (Argentina)

brown café, carmelita (Cuba), castaño, marrón

bus autobús, camión (México), colectivo, guagua (Puerto Rico, Cuba), ómnibus

bus stop parada, paradero (Perú)

butterfly chapola (Colombia), mariposa

buzzard buitre, urubú (Argentina), zopilote (México)

car auto, automóvil, carro, coche (España, México), máquina (Cuba)

chalk gis (México), tiza, yeso

cicada cigarra, chicharra (México, Caribe)

cold (illness) catarro, constipado, resfriado, resfrío

commotion algarabía, barullo, despiole (Argentina), embolate (Colombia), guirigay (España), jaleo, revolico, revolú (Puerto Rico)

container bote (México), envase, lata, tarro (Argentina)

corn abatí (Argentina), capi (América del Sur), cuatequil (México), maíz, mijo (España), millo (España), panizo, zara

cornfield maizal, milpa (México)

drawer cajón, gaveta (Cuba, Puerto Rico)

dried meat carne seca (México), charque, charqui (Argentina), tasajo

drive conducir (España), manejar

ear of corn choclo (América del Sur), elote (México), jilote (México), mazorca, panocha (Spain), panoja (Spain)

elevator ascensor, elevador (Estados Unidos, Caribe)

eyeglasses anteojos, espejuelos, gafas, lentes

frying pan paila (Paraguay), sartén

get mad enfadarse, enfogonarse (Puerto Rico), enojarse, ponerse bravo (Cuba)

grass grama (Venezuela), hierba, pasto (México, Puerto Rico), prado (Perú), yerba, zacate (México)

grasshopper chapulín (México), esperanza, grillo, saltamontes

Hello? (to answer telephone) ¿Adelante? (México), ¿Aló?, ¿Bueno?, ¿Diga?, ¿Hola?, ¿Oigo? (Cuba), ¿Sí?

hill colina, loma, jalda (Puerto Rico), monte

hut bohío (Caribe), cabaña, cancy (Colombia), chamizo (España), choza, jacal (México)

kite barrilete, cometa, chiringa, huila, papalote (Cuba, México), volantín

knapsack macuto (España), mochila, morral

manage arreglárselas, amañárselas (Nicaragua), apañárselas (España)

mat estera, petate (México)

match cerilla (España), cerillo (México), fósforo

monkey chango (México), mico, mono

opossum rabipelado (Venezuela), tlacuache (México), zarigüeya

party fiesta, jarana, juerga, pachanga (Cuba, Puerto Rico), reventón (México)

peach durazno, melocotón (Cuba, España)

peanut cacahuate (México), cacahuete (España), maní (Caribe, América del Sur)

pig cerdo, chancho (Argentina), cochino, marrano, puerco

pineapple ananás, piña

plaza plaza, zócalo (México)

pool alberca (México), piscina

potato papa, patata (España)

rope cabo, cabuya, cordel, cuerda, mecate (México), soga

rubber caucho, goma, hule (México), jebe (Perú)

sandals huaraches (México), sandalias

sandwich bocadillo (España), emparedado (Argentina), sándwich, torta (México)

short (person) bajito, chaparro (México), pequeño, petiso (Argentina)

sidewalk acera, banqueta (México), vereda (Argentina)

simpleton bobo, camote (Ecuador, México), memo, pánfilo, tilingo (México, Argentina), tonto

skirt falda, nagua (Nicaragua), pollera (Argentina, Uruguay), saya (Cuba)

socks calcetines, medias

split pea arveja (Argentina), arvejón, chícharo, guisante

stamp estampilla, sello, timbre

strawberry fresa, frutilla (Argentina)

stubborn cabeciduro (Cuba, Puerto Rico), cabezota, terco, testarudo, tetelque (Nicaragua), tozudo

NOTICIERO HISTÓRICO DEL MUNDO HISPANO

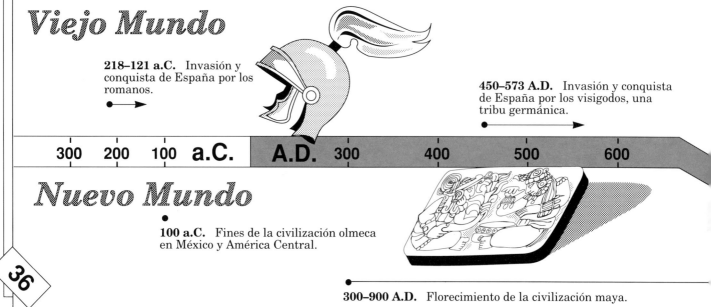

Viejo Mundo

218–121 a.C. Invasión y conquista de España por los romanos.

450–573 A.D. Invasión y conquista de España por los visigodos, una tribu germánica.

300 200 100 **a.C.** **A.D.** 300 400 500 600

Nuevo Mundo

100 a.C. Fines de la civilización olmeca en México y América Central.

300–900 A.D. Florecimiento de la civilización maya.

suitcase beliz (México), maleta, valija

sunflower acabual (México), gigante, girasol, mirabel, mirasol, tornasol

swimsuit bañador (España), calzoneta (América Central), malla (Argentina), traje de baño, trusa (Puerto Rico, Cuba)

swing balancín, columpio, hamaca (Argentina, Cuba), mecedor, trapecio

tadpole civori, renacuajo, tepocate (México)

ticket billete (España), boleto, pasaje, tiquete (Colombia)

tomato jitomate (México), tomate

turkey chumpipe (Guatemala), cócono, guajolote (México), guanajo (Caribe), pavo

ugly feo, fiero (Argentina)

waiter camarero, garzón (Argentina), mesero (México), mozo (Perú)

waste basket basurero, zafacón (Puerto Rico), bote de basura (México), papelera

woodpecker pájaro carpintero, picamaderos, picaposte

zipper cierre relámpago (Argentina), cierre zip, cremallera, rache (Venezuela), zíper

WORDWISE

Troubles with Regionalisms If you travel extensively through the Hispanic world—or if you deal with Hispanic students of diverse national origins—it pays to be aware of regional usages. Otherwise you risk not being understood or, worse, being severely misunderstood.

For example, throughout most of the Spanish-speaking world, a *banqueta* is a stool or bench; in Mexico, however, it is a sidewalk. *Camión* means "truck" to most Spanish speakers, but to Mexicans it means "bus." If you said the color of something was *carmelita*, most Spanish speakers would have no idea what you meant; Cubans, however, would know you meant "brown." *Guagua*, to most speakers of Spanish, is a totally meaningless word; in Cuba and Puerto Rico, however, everyone knows a *guagua* is a bus, and in Chile everyone knows a *guagua* is a baby.

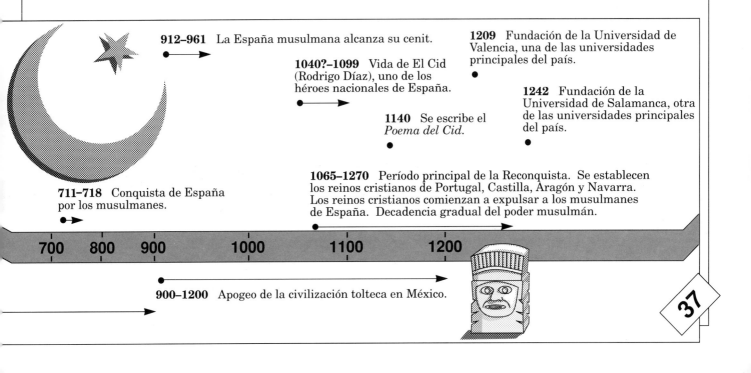

912–961 La España musulmana alcanza su cenit.

1040?–1099 Vida de El Cid (Rodrigo Díaz), uno de los héroes nacionales de España.

1140 Se escribe el *Poema del Cid.*

1209 Fundación de la Universidad de Valencia, una de las universidades principales del país.

1242 Fundación de la Universidad de Salamanca, otra de las universidades principales del país.

711–718 Conquista de España por los musulmanes.

1065–1270 Período principal de la Reconquista. Se establecen los reinos cristianos de Portugal, Castilla, Aragón y Navarra. Los reinos cristianos comienzan a expulsar a los musulmanes de España. Decadencia gradual del poder musulmán.

700 800 900 1000 1100 1200

900–1200 Apogeo de la civilización tolteca en México.

37

CELEBREMOS

*Here is a selection of some **special holidays** observed by Hispanics in the U.S.*

enero **1** *Año Nuevo* Se espera el Año Nuevo con fiestas, bailes y reuniones familiares. Hay personas que disparan armas de fuego al aire a medianoche. Los cubanos y los puertorriqueños tienen la costumbre de echar un cubo de agua fuera de la casa a medianoche, lo que se supone que trae suerte. Otra costumbre es comer doce uvas a medianoche. **6** *Los Reyes Magos* Familias recién llegadas a los Estados Unidos a menudo intercambian regalos de Navidad en este día, en vez del 25 de diciembre.

febrero *Carnaval* A fines de febrero o principios de marzo, antes de comenzar la Cuaresma, se celebra el carnaval. Áreas con grandes números de cubanos y puertorriqueños—como Miami y Nueva York—celebran con música, carrozas, desfiles, disfraces y bailes callejeros, como se hace en la zona del Caribe.

abril *Semana Santa* Se celebra a fines de marzo o principios de abril. En algunos pueblos de Texas los niños juegan al "cascarón": huevos se vacían, se decoran y se llenan con confeti; los niños se rompen los huevos en la cabeza unos a otros. **30** *Día del Niño* Se celebra en México, y muchas escuelas fronterizas en Texas han adoptado la costumbre.

mayo **5** *Cinco de Mayo* Los mexicanos celebran su victoria contra los invasores franceses en 1862. Se celebra con paseos, carrozas, y actos en las escuelas. **20** *Día de la Independencia (Cuba)* Los cubanos celebran el día en que Cuba se hizo república independiente en 1902. *Día de las Madres* Se celebra el segundo domingo de mayo.

junio *Día de los Padres* Se celebra el tercer domingo de junio.

julio **4** *Día de la Independencia (Estados Unidos)* Todos celebramos la independencia de nuestro país. **25** *Estado libre asociado* Los puertorriqueños conmemoran el día en 1952 cuando Puerto Rico se convirtió en estado libre asociado de los Estados Unidos.

septiembre **16** *Grito de Dolores* Los mexicanos celebran como su Día de Independencia el aniversario del Grito de Dolores, alzamiento revolucionario proclamado por Miguel Hidalgo en 1810.

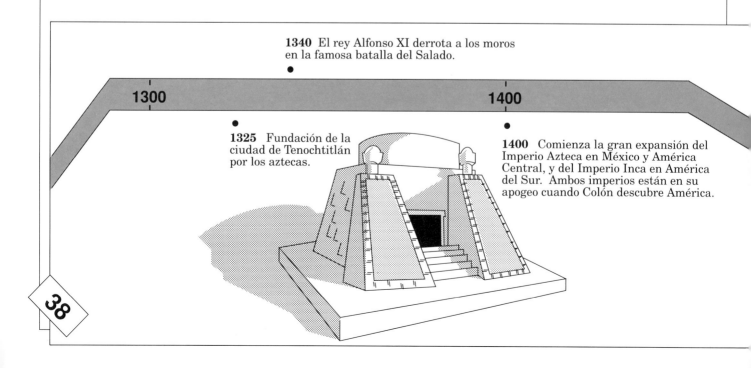

1340 El rey Alfonso XI derrota a los moros en la famosa batalla del Salado.

1300

1400

1325 Fundación de la ciudad de Tenochtitlán por los aztecas.

1400 Comienza la gran expansión del Imperio Azteca en México y América Central, y del Imperio Inca en América del Sur. Ambos imperios están en su apogeo cuando Colón descubre América.

octubre **10** *Grito de Yara* Los cubanos celebran el comienzo, en 1868, de su primera guerra de independencia.
12 *Día de la Raza* Se celebra el descubrimiento de América por Cristóbal Colón.

noviembre **1** *Día de los Muertos* Los mexicanos observan este día con reuniones y comidas sobre las tumbas de los antepasados. También se comen dulces y comidas en forma de calaveras y se hacen decoraciones con esqueletos. **5** *Día de la Independencia (El Salvador)* **19** *Día del Descubrimiento* Los puertorriqueños celebran el día en que Colón descubrió la isla en 1493.

diciembre **1** *Nuestra Señora de Guadalupe* Los mexicanos celebran el día de la patrona de México. En algunas iglesias se realiza la danza de los Matachines, una danza indígena. **16** *Las Posadas* Los mexicanos conmemoran la llegada de María y José a Belén con el niño Jesús. Hay representaciones públicas de los sucesos bíblicos. **24** *Nochebuena* Entre los hispanos, el 24 es el día de mayor celebración, en vez del 25. Se hace por lo general una gran cena y se reúnen muchos familiares. La comida tradicional entre los cubanos y puertorriqueños es lechón asado. Entre los mexicanos, tamales y "pan de polvo", unas galletitas especiales, son comidas favoritas de Nochebuena.

BRIGHT IDEA

Classroom Calendar Keeping a wall calendar can chronicle current and historical events, as well as bring special significance to students' cultural heritage. It is also an excellent opportunity for collaborative learning.

To start, invite the class to brainstorm the kinds of things they might record on their calendar. Some ideas: weather; holidays; students' birthdays; school or community events; ordinary events (the day Timoteo lost a tooth); accomplishments (the day Luci won the writing contest); special word for each week; sayings, poems, or words appropriate to the month (especially good for filling squares not used in a month).

Then let students decide on the size of their calendar and make a 7-column, 5-row grid for each month. (A good way to make grids for a large calendar is to prepare a master on a transparency, then project it onto butcher paper for students to trace. Copies of the small master work well for planning entries and illustrations.)

Put a different team in charge of each month's calendar. The members of the team should work together to plan and record entries, adding illustrations, stickers, or other decorations to complement the entries. For special days in their month, the team may also be in charge of sharing stories, songs, poems, skits, etc. during warm-up activities at the start of the day.

At the end of the year, bind the monthly pages in a Big Book for the school library, or reduce the pages on a photocopying machine for students to take home.

1469 Unificación de los reinos de Castilla y Aragón por medio del matrimonio de Isabel de Castilla y Fernando de Aragón.

1480 Comienzo de la Inquisición. Se establece una corte bajo los Reyes Católicos para castigar a los que no siguen la religión católica; dura unos 300 años.

1492 Bajo el patrocinio de la reina Isabel, Cristóbal Colón descubre las Américas. Los españoles conquistan el reino de Granada, último territorio moro en España.

1499 Se publica la primera novela española: *La Celestina* de Fernando de Rojas.

1500

1492 Colón descubre la isla de Cuba.

1493 Colón descubre la isla de Puerto Rico.

1508 Colonización de Puerto Rico por Ponce de León.

1511 Diego Velásquez emprende la colonización de Cuba.

APELLIDOS DE RENOMBRE

Here is a quick look at the origins and meanings of some common
Spanish surnames.

Acosta Procedente del pueblo de Acosta en España; que vive cerca de la costa.

Aguilar Parecido a un águila o que vive cerca de un nido de águilas.

Álvarez Hijo de Álvaro, que quiere decir "prudente".

Anaya De la palabra vasca que significa "hermano".

Ávila Procedente de la ciudad española de Ávila; del verbo *avilar*, que quiere decir "velar, vigilar".

Fernández Hijo de Fernando, que quiere decir "osado, aventurero". El apellido *Hernández* es una variante de *Fernández*.

González Hijo de Gonzalo, que procede de una palabra germánica que significa "pelear, vencer".

López Hijo de Lope o Lupe, nombres que proceden del latín *lupus*, que quiere decir "lobo".

SIEMPRE LISTOS

Histories of Surnames Names have histories just as countries and people do. Long ago, when villages were small and no one went very far from home, one name was all anyone needed. But life got too complicated for that, and surnames were added to first names to help people sort out who was who. People took their surnames from their surroundings (*Montes, Del Valle*) or from some physical characteristic (*Calvo, Delgado*) or from the work they did (*Herrero, Tejedor*). Or they identified themselves by their father's name, called a patronymic (*González: hijo de Gonzalo; Rodríguez: hijo de Rodrigo*). When surnames became hereditary, their original meanings became obscured. The following source will help you trace the original meanings of other Spanish surnames.

• Woods, Richard D. and Alvarez-Altman, Grace. *Spanish Surnames in the Southwestern United States: A Dictionary*. Boston: G.K. Hall, 1978.

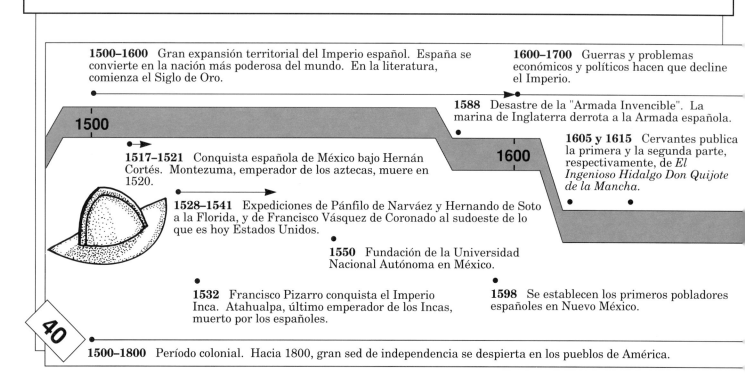

1500–1600 Gran expansión territorial del Imperio español. España se convierte en la nación más poderosa del mundo. En la literatura, comienza el Siglo de Oro.

1600–1700 Guerras y problemas económicos y políticos hacen que decline el Imperio.

1588 Desastre de la "Armada Invencible". La marina de Inglaterra derrota a la Armada española.

1500

1517–1521 Conquista española de México bajo Hernán Cortés. Montezuma, emperador de los aztecas, muere en 1520.

1600

1605 y 1615 Cervantes publica la primera y la segunda parte, respectivamente, de *El Ingenioso Hidalgo Don Quijote de la Mancha*.

1528–1541 Expediciones de Pánfilo de Narváez y Hernando de Soto a la Florida, y de Francisco Vásquez de Coronado al sudoeste de lo que es hoy Estados Unidos.

1550 Fundación de la Universidad Nacional Autónoma en México.

1532 Francisco Pizarro conquista el Imperio Inca. Atahualpa, último emperador de los Incas, muerto por los españoles.

1598 Se establecen los primeros pobladores españoles en Nuevo México.

40

1500–1800 Período colonial. Hacia 1800, gran sed de independencia se despierta en los pueblos de América.

Morales Hijo de Moral; que vive cerca de morales, es decir, parajes donde se cultivan moras.

Ochoa De la palabra vasca *otso*, que significa "lobo".

Pacheco Del latín *franciscus*, que quiere decir "hombre libre, hombre emancipado".

Pérez Hijo de Pero, que era una forma cariñosa de *Pedro*.

Quintana Procedente del pueblo de Quintana en España; que vive en o cerca de una quinta, hacienda campestre por la que había que pagar como renta un quinto de lo que se producía.

Ramírez Hijo de Ramiro, que quiere decir "sabio protector".

Rodríguez Hijo de Rodrigo, que quiere decir "caudillo o jefe ilustre".

Rojas Pelirrojo.

Rosales Que cultiva rosas o vive cerca de un rosal.

Sánchez Hijo de Sancho, que proviene del latín *sanctus* y quiere decir "santo, pío". Otras variantes son Sáenz, Sáez, Santos.

Santana Procedente de Santana (Santa Ana), ciudad de España. Ana proviene del hebreo *Hannah*, que significa "beneficial".

Torres Que vive en o cerca de un castillo o una torre.

Villarreal Que vive en o cerca de la villa real, es decir, un lugar donde habita el rey o la reina.

BRIGHT IDEA

Genealogy Genius Learning about surnames may spark an interest in genealogy. A family tree makes information about family relationships more manageable, gives a personal perspective to history and geography, and builds a sense of being part of a larger family.

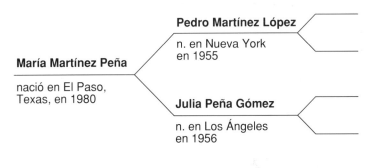

Pedro Martínez López
n. en Nueva York en 1955

María Martínez Peña
nació en El Paso, Texas, en 1980

Julia Peña Gómez
n. en Los Ángeles en 1956

Show students an example like the one above and let them trace their family tree back as far as possible. Allow plenty of time for them to consult relatives, even distant ones.

1700–1800 Expansión y exploración del Imperio en las Américas, pero varias guerras y conflictos con Inglaterra continúan debilitando a España.

1808–1813 Invasión de España por Napoleón. Guerra hasta que, aliados con Inglaterra, los españoles logran expulsar a los franceses in 1813. La mayoría de las colonias americanas se aprovechan de la guerra para declarar su independencia.

1700

1800

1769 Comienza la colonización española de California con la fundación de la primera misión por Junípero Serra.

1728 Fundación de la Universidad de La Habana.

1718 Fundación de San Antonio de Bexar, Texas.

1808–1824 La mayor parte de las colonias españolas en América se rebelan y obtienen su independencia. Entre los líderes de la independencia americana están Miguel Hidalgo y José María Morelos en México, y Simón Bolívar, José de San Martín, Antonio José de Sucre y Bernardo O'Higgins en América del Sur.

1810 Grito de Dolores: México proclama la independencia.

UN APLAUSO, POR FAVOR

*Hispanics have made significant contributions in many different fields of endeavor. The following is just a small sampling—the names of just a few **notable Hispanics** who, along with many others, can serve as positive role models for your students. Within each category we feature one person and give capsule descriptions of several others.*

Art

⭐ **JUDITH BACA** Nació y se crió en Los Ángeles. Después de graduarse de la universidad, obtuvo un empleo con el Departamento de Asuntos Culturales de la ciudad. Baca inició un programa mediante el cual se les ofreció a jóvenes hispanos del barrio pobre de East Los Angeles la oportunidad de pintar varios murales decorativos en su vecindario. El programa fue un éxito, y Baca supervisó la creación de muchos otros murales en la ciudad. Comenzando en 1976, su gran proyecto ha sido la creación de un monumental mural (más de una milla de largo) que rinde tributo a los distintos grupos étnicos que han contribuido al desarrollo de la ciudad. Judith Baca es conocida tanto por su talento artístico como por su conciencia social.

- **José Cuauhtémoc (Bill) Meléndez** Animador mexicano-americano que trabajó con el gran Walt Disney. Ha recibido los premios "Emmy" y "Peabody" por su animación de los personajes de la tira cómica "Peanuts".

- **Luis Jiménez** Destacado escultor modernista.

- **Marta Moreno Vega** Directora del Museo del Barrio, un museo de arte y artesanías hispanas en Nueva York.

A Special Tribute

⭐ **CÉSAR CHÁVEZ**
Fue uno de los primeros en dar expresión al orgullo y la alta estimación de cultura y tradición que florecen en la comunidad hispana hoy día. Chávez nació en Arizona en 1927. Con la fundación de lo que luego se convertiría en el *United Farmworkers of America*, Chávez se hizo líder del movimiento sindical de los trabajadores agrícolas mexicano-americanos del suroeste de los Estados Unidos. Hoy día su influencia alcanza más allá del movimiento sindical agrícola. Se ha convertido en un portavoz de los intereses y las aspiraciones de los hispanos en los Estados Unidos.

1834–1876 La época de las Guerras Carlistas. Se produce una serie de tres guerras con insurrecciones separatistas contra la monarquía.

1830

1836 Texas se separa de México y se constituye república independiente.

1846–1848 Guerra de México con los Estados Unidos. El tratado de Guadalupe Hidalgo pone fin a la guerra en 1848 y México pierde los territorios al norte del río Bravo y el Golfo de California, que comprenden los actuales estados de California, Nevada, Utah, Arizona y Nuevo México.

1854–1862 Se adopta la primera Constitución mexicana. Se llevan a cabo grandes reformas democráticas bajo el liderazgo de Benito Juárez (1806–1872), gran estadista y patriota mexicano.

1853 Nace José Martí (m. 1895), poeta y patriota cubano.

1864–1867 Francia establece a Maximiliano, un noble austriaco, como emperador de México. En 1867, los mexicanos expulsan definitivamente a los franceses y ejecutan a Maximiliano.

1862 Invasión francesa de México.

Business

⭐ **ROBERTO GOIZUETA** Goizueta nació en La Habana, Cuba, y estudió ingeniería química en los Estados Unidos, graduándose en 1953. De 1954 a 1960, fue director técnico de la compañía Coca-Cola en La Habana. En 1961, emigró a los Estados Unidos, donde continuó trabajando en la compañía. Ascendió a cargos de mayor y mayor importancia hasta por fin convertirse en presidente de la junta directiva. Goizueta representa la determinación y perseverancia que han impulsado a muchísimos hispanos al éxito en el mundo del comercio.

- **Bill Dávila** Presidente de los supermercados Vons y de los nuevos supermercados Tianguis, que ofrecen comidas y artículos hispanos.

- **Carolina Herrera** Famosísima diseñadora de modas, sus creaciones se venden internacionalmente.

- **Joseph Unanue** Presidente de Goya Foods, que ofrece una variedad de más de 700 productos comestibles, la mayoría hispanos.

Children's Literature

⭐ **ALMA FLOR ADA** Nacida en Cuba, la doctora Ada es una de las figuras más distinguidas en los Estados Unidos en los campos de educación bilingüe y literatura infantil en español. Como profesora universitaria y por medio de conferencias y seminarios que ha presentado por todos los Estados Unidos, ha contribuido inestimablemente a la formación de maestros y a la institución de programas efectivos de educación bilingüe. Es autora de un programa de lectura en español que se usa en muchas escuelas. Ha traducido varios libros de literatura infantil. Y sus creaciones originales para niños incluyen cuentos, libros de poesía, y canciones. Su libro *Encaje de piedra*, publicado en la Argentina, recibió en 1988 el destacado Premio Martha Salotti.

- **Pura Belpré** Escritora puertorriqueña. Muchos de sus cuentos tienen como protagonistas a niños puertorriqueños tratando de adaptarse a la vida en Nueva York.

- **Ernesto Galarza** Académico y experto en cuestiones sindicales que se interesó también en el desarrollo de materiales para la educación bilingüe. Autor de *Poemas pe-que pe-que pe-que-ñitos*.

- **Ana María Matute** Distinguida traductora y escritora española, ganadora de varios premios literarios.

- **Hilda Perera** Escritora que en más de una ocasión ha ganado el prestigioso premio Lazarillo con sus obras para niños. *Kike*, su novela más conocida, trata de un niño que viene de Cuba a los Estados Unidos.

- **María Puncel** Autora de *Abuelita Opalina* y muchísimos otros cuentos para niños. Entre sus premios literarios se hallan el codiciado Lazarillo y el Aro de Plata.

- **Eduardo Robles Boza (Tío Patota)** Célebre autor de *Los cuentos de Tío Patota*, este periodista y editor mexicano es ganador de varios premios nacionales e internacionales.

- **María Elena Walsh** Poetisa argentina, conocida por sus poemas humorísticos.

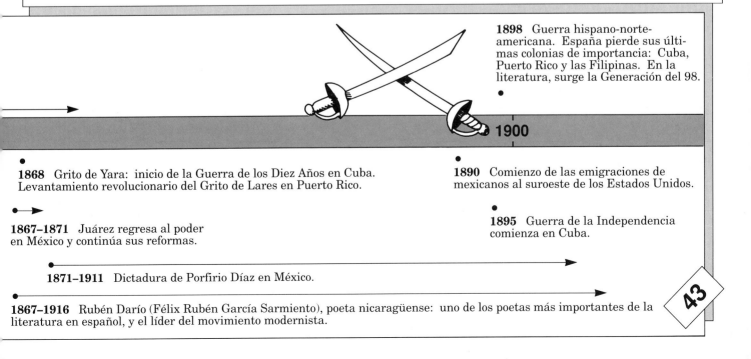

1898 Guerra hispano-norte-americana. España pierde sus últimas colonias de importancia: Cuba, Puerto Rico y las Filipinas. En la literatura, surge la Generación del 98.

1900

1868 Grito de Yara: inicio de la Guerra de los Diez Años en Cuba. Levantamiento revolucionario del Grito de Lares en Puerto Rico.

1890 Comienzo de las emigraciones de mexicanos al suroeste de los Estados Unidos.

1867–1871 Juárez regresa al poder en México y continúa sus reformas.

1895 Guerra de la Independencia comienza en Cuba.

1871–1911 Dictadura de Porfirio Díaz en México.

1867–1916 Rubén Darío (Félix Rubén García Sarmiento), poeta nicaragüense: uno de los poetas más importantes de la literatura en español, y el líder del movimiento modernista.

Education

⭐ **JAIME ESCALANTE**   Nacido en Bolivia en 1931, Escalante llegó a los Estados Unidos en 1964. Siendo maestro de matemáticas en la escuela secundaria Garfield, ubicada en Los Ángeles, Escalante motivó a un grupo de estudiantes hispanos a estudiar para tomar un examen avanzado de cálculo. Su devoción y sus esfuerzos fueron premiados con el gran éxito de sus estudiantes. La historia se relata en una película de 1988: *Stand and Deliver*. Escalante continúa hoy día sus esfuerzos por mejorar la educación de los estudiantes hispanos.

- **Raquel Báez**   Recipiente, en 1988, del primer premio anual Maestra Bilingüe del Año, otorgado por la National Association for Bilingual Education (NABE).

- **Rosa Guas-Inclán**   Figura sobresaliente en la educación bilingüe en la Florida, nombrada por la NABE una de las diez mujeres que han contribuido más a la educación bilingüe en los Estados Unidos.

- **Ramón Santiago**   Ex-presidente de la NABE y experto en la educación bilingüe que ha ayudado a implementar programas educacionales en muchas ciudades de los Estados Unidos.

Music

⭐ **JOAN BÁEZ**   Hija del físico mexicano-americano Albert Báez, Joan Báez nació en California. Desde muy joven se distinguió en sus estudios musicales. Después de que su familia se mudó a Boston, se interesó en la música tradicional que se había hecho popular en los cafés de esa ciudad. Se hizo cantante. Durante la década de 1960, su estilo sencillo y su purísima voz le trajeron fama nacional. Su envolvimiento en cuestiones de política le ha ganado admiradores y detractores, pero su talento musical es indiscutible. Como cantante y compositora, fue y continúa siendo una de las grandes figuras en la música popular y tradicional de los Estados Unidos.

- **Rubén Blades**   Popular cantante y artista de cine panameño que canta en inglés y en español.

- **Celia Cruz**   Cantante y bailadora cubana que por más de cuarenta años ha sido "la Reina de la Salsa".

- **Plácido Domingo**   Tenor operático de fama mundial.

Politics

⭐ **HENRY CISNEROS**   Al ser elegido alcalde de San Antonio, Texas, en 1981, Cisneros se convirtió en el primer mexicano-americano en hacerse alcalde de una ciudad principal de los Estados Unidos. Cisneros nació en San Antonio en 1947 y fue elegido miembro del concejo municipal en 1975. Ha alcanzado prominencia nacional en los Estados Unidos como vocero de los intereses de ciudadanos de origen hispano.

- **Polly Baca-Barragán**   Primera mujer de origen hispano elegida al senado estatal de Colorado.

- **Katherine Ortega**   Nombrada Tesorera por el presidente Reagan.

- **Xavier Suárez**   Primer cubano-americano en ser elegido al cargo de alcalde de una ciudad principal de los Estados Unidos (Miami).

1931   El rey Alfonso XIII se fuga de España y España se convierte en república.

1936–1939   Guerra Civil y comienzo de la dictadura del general Francisco Franco.

1939–1975   Dictadura de Franco.

ESPAÑA

1900

1902   Cuba realiza su independencia.

1911   Revolución mexicana, al mando de Francisco Madero.

1929   Fundación de LULAC (*League of United Latin American Citizens*), una organización dedicada a defender los intereses de ciudadanos de origen hispano en los Estados Unidos.

1960–1970   Gran emigración de cubanos a los Estados Unidos.

1959   Triunfo de la revolución castrista en Cuba. Comienzo de la dictadura de Castro.

1952   Se constituye por mutuo acuerdo el Estado Libre Asociado de Puerto Rico y se adopta la Constitución.

Science

⭐ **LUIS W. ÁLVAREZ** Nació en San Francisco, California en 1911 y estudió física en la Universidad de Chicago. Durante la Segunda Guerra Mundial, Álvarez trabajó con los mejores físicos norte-americanos en los proyectos de investigación que resultaron en el desarrollo del radar y de la bomba atómica. Después de la guerra, continuó sus investigaciones en el campo de la física nuclear y descubrió muchísimas de las llamadas "partículas subatómicas", trabajo que le valió el Premio Nobel de física en 1968. Su carrera científica ha dado fruto también en muchísimos otros inventos y teorías. En 1987, publicó su autobiografía: *Alvarez*.

• **Isabel Canet** Especialista en la vida de los camarones que desde hace muchos años dirige las investigaciones del prestigioso Smithsonian Institute en ese campo.

• **Franklin Chang-Díaz** Primer astronauta de origen hispano, empezó su asociación con la NASA en 1980.

• **Félix Soloni** Investigador en medicina en el Mount Sinai Medical Center de Miami Beach, en la Florida.

Sports

⭐ **ROBERTO CLEMENTE** Jugador del equipo Pittsburgh Pirates, Clemente fue una de las estrellas más brillantes del béisbol. Nacido en Carolina, Puerto Rico, en 1934, se interesó por los deportes a muy temprana edad. Murió en 1972 en un accidente de aviación que ocurrió mientras llevaba ayuda humanitaria a los damnificados de un gran terremoto en Managua, Nicaragua. En 1973, fue elegido al "Hall of Fame" del béisbol.

• **Nancy López** Jugadora profesional de golf de primera categoría, ha ganado varios torneos nacionales.

• **Alberto Salazar** Corredor cubano-americano de larga distancia, adquirió fama nacional al ganar los maratones de Nueva York y de Boston en 1982.

• **Fernando Valenzuela** Lanzador estrella de los Dodgers de Los Ángeles, el jugador más joven en ganar el premio "Cy Young".

Stage and Screen

⭐ **RITA MORENO** Nacida en Humacao, Puerto Rico, en 1931, Rita Moreno ha bailado desde que era niña. Después de varios papeles en Broadway, hizo su debut en el cine en 1950. Es la única persona que ha ganado los premios "Emmy", "Tony", "Grammy" y "Oscar", ganando este último por su actuación en la famosísima *West Side Story*. Sus apariciones en la serie infantil de televisión *Sesame Street* le han ganado el cariño de innumerables niños en los Estados Unidos.

• **Lourdes López** Bailarina principal con el Ballet de Nueva York.

• **Edward James Olmos** Actor de cine, teatro y televisión que se ha destacado también por sus esfuerzos por mejorar la educación de los jóvenes hispanos en los Estados Unidos.

• **Carmen Zapata** Actriz de teatro, cine y televisión que muchos niños conocen por su actuación en la serie infantil de televisión *Villa Alegre*.

1975 Se restablece la monarquía. Juan Carlos sube al trono e inicia una serie de drásticas reformas democráticas. España se convierte en una monarquía constitucional y democrática.

1978 España aprueba una nueva constitución.

1982 España se afilia a la Organización del Tratado del Atlántico Norte. Con la elección de Felipe González como primer ministro, España adquiere un gobierno socialista por primera vez desde la Guerra Civil.

2000

1988 Promulgación en los Estados Unidos de un acto legislativo que autoriza amnistía para ciertos inmigrantes que han entrado al país ilegalmente.

1968 Promulgación del Acto de Educación Bilingüe en los Estados Unidos.

1975–1985 Guerras civiles en El Salvador y Nicaragua hacen que muchos salvadoreños y nicaragüenses emigren a los Estados Unidos.

BRIGHT IDEA

Personal Inspiration As the lists on pages 42–45 show, there are plenty of Hispanics who, because of their talent, dedication, and achievement, can provide positive, inspiring role models for your students. But your students have to hear from them—or, at least, about them—first. This is where you can help.

- Make sure your students are familiar with Hispanics of national or international prominence. One way to do this is to feature a notable Hispanic once a week or so, perhaps as part of a calendar activity. During the course of the week, familiarize your students with the life and accomplishments of the person you select and encourage them to do further research about the person or topics associated with his or her career.

- Make sure that the messages of inspiration and encouragement addressed to Hispanic students by many notable Hispanics get to them. Blackline Master 5 on page 156, to be duplicated on card stock, provides some bookmarks with inspirational words from prominent Hispanics. There are also blank forms on which students can create additional bookmarks by soliciting inspirational words from local Hispanic leaders.

- Have Hispanic men and women who are respected and admired in your community come and talk to your students, discuss career opportunities, and offer encouragement and advice.

- Use the Hispanic organizations listed at right as resources any time you or your students need information on Hispanic topics. They can provide information about their activities and recommend speakers to invite to your class.

ALIADOS

*Here are some **organizations that promote Hispanic interests** in the U.S.*

League of United Latin American Citizens (LULAC) Foundation
400 First Street, Suite 721
Washington, D.C. 20001   (202) 628-8516

The League of United Latin American Citizens is the oldest and largest Hispanic organization in the U.S. The League serves to protect and defend the interests of the Hispanic community with regard to many issues. Local chapters exist in nearly every state.

Mexican-American Legal Defense and Educational Fund (MALDEF)
634 Spring Street, 11th Floor
Los Angeles, CA 90014   (213) 629-2512

The Mexican-American Legal Defense and Educational Fund is a national, nonprofit organization that promotes the rights of Hispanics through class-action litigation, community education, and leadership development.

National Association for Bilingual Education (NABE)
1201 16th Street N.W.
Washington, D.C. 20036   (202) 822-7870

The National Association for Bilingual Education is a nonprofit organization dedicated to recognizing, promoting, and publicizing educational excellence through bilingual education.

National Council of La Raza (NCLR)
Twenty F Street N.W.
Washington, D.C. 20001   (202) 628-9600

The National Council of La Raza seeks to improve the life opportunities for Americans of Hispanic descent and to strengthen Hispanic community-based organizations as a means to this end.

ASÍ CONTABA MI ABUELA

A collection of poems, rondas and games, tongue twisters, riddles, sayings, and other jewels from Spanish folklore and children's literature. Except as noted, these gems were mined from oral tradition.

DÁNDOLE TIEMPO AL TIEMPO

*It's about time for **poetry about time**! Here are some poems and songs about the months of the year, the days of the week, and the hours of the day.*

LOS MESES DEL AÑO

Andante

E - ne-ro, fe - bre - ro, mar-zo, a-bril y ma - yo son los cin - co me - ses pri - me-ros del a - ño.

UNO DE ENERO

Uno de enero,
dos de febrero,
tres de marzo,
cuatro de abril,
cinco de mayo,
seis de junio,
siete de julio . . .
¡San Fermín!

LOS SIETE DÍAS

Hay en la escuela
siete niñitos:
Primero el Lunes,
flojo y dormido.
Segundo el Martes,
bueno y activo.
Tercero el Miércoles,
pasa jugando.

Cuarto es el Jueves,
serio y callado.
Quinto es el Viernes,
tranquilo y tímido.
Sexto es el Sábado,
¡el más lucido!
Por fin, Domingo,
¡bello y querido!

—Oscar Jara Azócar

47

Many traditional poems and rhymes exist in different versions. Here are four versions of a rhyme about the hours of the day.

Cuando da la una,
sales de la cuna;
cuando dan las dos,
rezas a Dios.
Cuando dan las tres,
te mojas los pies;
cuando dan las cuatro,
te vas al teatro.
Cuando dan las cinco,
pegas un brinco.

In the game known as pídola *or* saltacabrillas, *one child stoops down while the others jump over his or her back. The children each say one line of a rhyme such as the following as they jump.*

A la una andaba la mula.
A las dos, la coz.
A las tres, los tres brinquitos de San Andrés:
    Pedro, Juan y Andrés.
A las cuatro, brinco y salto.
A las cinco, salto y brinco.
A las seis, cabeza de buey.
A las siete, salto y planto mi gran caperucete.
A las ocho, lo recojo.
A las nueve, empina la bota y bebe.
A las diez, borriquito, borriquito es.

A la una sale la Luna.
A las dos suena el reloj.
A las tres cojito es.
A las cuatro doy un salto.
A las cinco doy un brinco.
A las seis no me ves.
A las siete anda, vete.
A las ocho ten bizcocho.
A las nueve toma nieve.
Y a las diez, otra vez.

A la una como tuna.
A las dos me da la tos.
A las tres veo a Andrés.
A las cuatro voy al teatro.
A las cinco brinco y brinco.
A las seis merendaré.
A las siete soy Chapete.
A las ocho soy Pinocho.
De una, de dola, de tela canela,
zumbaca, tabaca, de vira virón.
¡Cuéntalos bien, que las once son!

48

CUENTA QUE TE CUENTA

*Here are some **poems about numbers** you can really count on.*

LA GALLINA PUMPUJADA

La gallina pumpujada
puso un huevo en la ramada:
puso uno,
    puso dos,
        puso tres,
puso cuatro,
    puso cinco,
        puso seis,
puso siete, puso ocho—
¡Guárdame este bizcocho
hasta mañana a las ocho!

*You can repeat this rhyme,
backwards and forwards, as
many times as you care to.*

UNO, DOS, TRES

Uno, dos, tres, el mundo
  al revés;
tres, dos, uno, al revés
  el mundo;
otra vez,
uno, dos, tres . . .

*This song can be continued
indefinitely. Just add more
elephants.*

LOS ELEFANTES

Un elefante
se balanceaba,
sobre la tela de una araña,
y como ésta
no se rompía,
fue a llamar
a otro elefante.

Dos elefantes . . ., etc.

LOS DIEZ PERRITOS

Yo tenía diez perritos. *(repita)*
Uno se cayó en la nieve.
Ya no más me quedan nueve, nueve, nueve,
  nueve, nueve.

De los nueve que tenía, *(repita)*
uno se comió un bizcocho.
Ya no más me quedan ocho, ocho, ocho, ocho, ocho.

De los ocho que tenía, *(repita)*
uno se golpeó su frente.
Ya no más me quedan siete, siete, siete, siete, siete.

De los siete que tenía, *(repita)*
uno se quemó los pies.
Ya no más me quedan seis, seis, seis, seis, seis.

De los seis que tenía, *(repita)*
uno se escapó de un brinco.
Ya no más me quedan cinco, cinco, cinco, cinco, cinco.

De los cinco que tenía, *(repita)*
uno se metió en un teatro.
Ya no más me quedan cuatro, cuatro, cuatro,
  cuatro, cuatro.

De los cuatro que tenía, *(repita)*
uno se cayó al revés.
Ya no más me quedan tres, tres, tres, tres, tres.

De los tres que tenía, *(repita)*
uno sufrió de una tos.
Ya no más me quedan dos, dos, dos, dos, dos.

De los dos que tenía, *(repita)*
uno se murió de ayuno.
Ya no más me queda uno, uno, uno, uno, uno.

A este uno que quedaba, *(repita)*
se lo llevó mi cuñada.
Ya no más me queda nada, nada, nada, nada, nada.

Cuando ya no tenía nada, *(repita)*
la perra parió otra vez.
Y ahora ya tengo otros diez, diez, diez, diez, diez.

ABECEDELICIAS

*These poems are as simple as **A-B-C** to learn.*

A E I O U

A, E, I, O, U.
Borriquito como tú.

A, E, I, O, U.
Más sabe el burro que tú.

A—El burro se va.
E—El burro se fue.
I—El burro está aquí.
O—El burro soy yo.
U—El burro eres tú.

A, E, I, O, U.
Arbolito de Perú.
Yo tengo _____ años.
¿Cuántos años tienes tú?

LA MARCHA DE LAS LETRAS

¡Que dejen toditos los libros abiertos!
Ha sido la orden que dio el general.
¡Que todos los niños estén muy atentos!
Las cinco vocales van a desfilar.

Primero verás
que pasa la *A*
con sus dos patitas
muy abiertas al marchar.

Ahí viene la *E*
alzando los pies:
el palo de en medio
es más chico como ves.

Le sigue la *I*
y luego la *O*:
una es flaca y otra es gorda
porque ya comió.

Y luego detrás
llegó la *U*
como la cuerda
con que siempre saltas tú.

—*Cri Cri*

ABC

A, Be, Ce, Che, De, E, ___ E - fe, Ge, Ha-che, *la – ré,*
E - ñe, O, Pe, Cu, E - re, E - rre, E - se, Te y U,

I, ___ Jo - ta, Ka, E - le, E - lle, E - me y E - ne;
Ve de va - ca, do - ble U, E-quis, Y, Ze - ta, *la – rú.*

JUEGOS CON LOS DEDOS

*Here are some rhymes used with **hand and finger games**.*

This rhyme is recited as you point to each finger of the hand, starting with the pinky.

Éste, chiquitito y bonito;
éste, el rey de los anillitos;
éste, tonto y loco;
éste se marchó a la escuela
y éste se lo come todo.

And this rhyme is for the toes.

Este chiquito
compró un huevito;
este flaco lo preparó;
este largote puso la mesa;
este tonto lo sirvió;
el gordote ¡se lo comió!

Recite these poems with a partner.

LA LUNA

Ahí viene la luna	*Form a crescent shape with your fingers.*
comiendo su tuna	*Pretend to eat.*
y echando las cáscaras	*Pretend to throw away the peelings.*
en esta laguna.	*Tickle your partner in the belly.*

LA VIEJITA

Ésta era una viejita	*Pat your partner's hand rhythmically.*
cortó este leñito.	*"Saw off" one finger.*
Cortó este otro;	*"Saw off" other fingers, one at a time.*
cortó este otro;	
cortó este otro;	
cortó este otro:	
chas—chas—chas.	
Hizo su carguita,	*Run your hand on your partner's forearm.*
se puso a hacer su lumbrita,	*Tickle the inside of the elbow.*
y luego vio una nube muy negra;	*Say these two lines slowly to build*
vino un aguacero	*anticipation.*
y corrió para su casita.	*Say this line very fast as you run your hand quickly up the arm and tickle your partner under the arm.*

LOS POLLITOS

Los pollitos dicen "pío, pío, pío"	
cuando tienen hambre,	*Touch your stomach.*
cuando tienen frío.	*Pretend to shiver.*
La gallina busca el maíz y el trigo.	*"Search" for corn with your hand.*
Les da la comida	*Touch your mouth.*
y les presta abrigo.	*Shelter your partner under your "wings."*
Acurrucaditos bajo las dos alas,	
hasta el otro día duermen los pollitos.	*Pretend to sleep.*

51

RONDAS

Rondas *is the name usually given to songs in rhyme, meant to be sung or recited by a group of children holding hands in a circle. The circle usually turns slowly as the children sing, and there may be other actions—such as squatting or raising the arms— performed at particular points in the song.* "La pájara pinta" *is one of the best-known rondas.*

LA PÁJARA PINTA

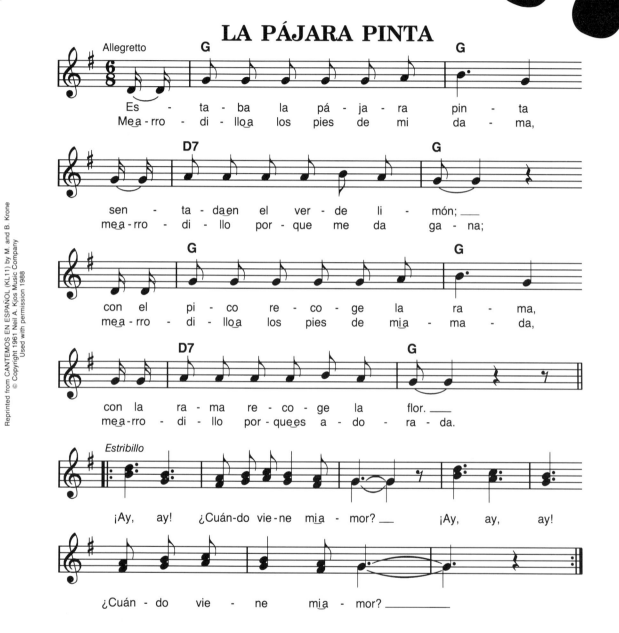

Es - ta - ba la pá - ja - ra pin - ta
Mea - rro - di - llo̲a los pies de mi da - ma,

sen - ta - da̲en el ver - de li - món; ___
mea - rro - di - llo por - que me da ga - na;

con el pi - co re - co - ge la ra - ma,
mea - rro - di - llo̲a los pies de mi̲a - ma - da,

con la ra - ma re - co - ge la flor. ___
mea - rro - di - llo por - que̲es a - do - ra - da.

Estribillo

¡Ay, ay! ¿Cuán - do vie - ne mi̲a - mor? __ ¡Ay, ay, ay!

¿Cuán - do vie - ne mi̲a - mor? _____

Reprinted from CANTEMOS EN ESPAÑOL (KL11) by M. and B. Krone
© Copyright 1961 Neil A. Kjos Music Company
Used with permission 1988

Here is another version.

Estaba la paloma blanca
sentada en el verde limón;
con el pico cortaba la rama,
con la rama cortaba la flor.
¡Ay, ay, ay!, ¿cuándo veré a mi amor?

Me arrodillo al pie de mi amante,
me levanto constante, constante.
Dame una mano, dame la otra;
dame un besito sobre la boca.
¡Ay, ay, ay!, ¿cuándo veré a mi amor?

"A la rueda, rueda" is another ronda *known throughout the Hispanic world.*

A LA RUEDA, RUEDA

A la rueda, rueda,
de pan y canela;
dame un besito
y ve para la escuela.
Si no quieres ir,
acuéstate a dormir.

For "El patio de mi casa," *the children in the circle squat down together on* agáchate *and* vuélvete a agachar.

EL PATIO DE MI CASA

El patio de mi casa
es muy particular:
se moja cuando llueve,
igual que los demás.
Agáchate, niña,
y vuélvete a agachar,
que las agachaditas
saben bailar.

H I J K L L Ll M A,
si tú no me quieres
otro amigo me querrá.

H I J K L L Ll M O,
si tú no me quieres
otro amigo tendré yo.

Another favorite ronda *is* "Arroz con leche."

ARROZ CON LECHE

Arroz con leche
me quiero casar
con una señorita
de este lugar.

Que sepa coser,
que sepa bordar,
que sepa las tablas
de multiplicar.

Con ésta, sí,
con ésta, no,
con esta señorita
me caso yo.

BRIGHT IDEA

Folklore Fest Involving students in an informal folklore study will develop their awareness of the richness of the oral tradition in Spanish.

Students working in cooperative/collaborative learning groups can select one or more favorite *rondas* and survey their neighborhood for:

- number, age, and gender of persons familiar with the *rondas*;
- different versions of the *rondas*;
- where each person first learned the *rondas*.

Invite students to present their findings in class.

To play "Naranja dulce," children form a circle and move around a child in the center, chanting the song. The child in the center chooses someone to hug and pulls him or her into the middle of the circle. Together they tap their feet to the music and shake hands as they sing the last lines (from adiós on). The child originally in the center then joins the circle while the child he or she selected remains inside the circle and the game repeats.

NARANJA DULCE

Moderato

1. Na-ran-ja dul-ce, li-món par-ti-do, da-me un a-bra-zo que yo te pi-do.

Naranja dulce, limón partido, dame un abrazo que yo te pido.
Si fueran falsos mis juramentos en algún tiempo se olvidarán.
Toca la marcha; mi pecho llora; adiós, señora, yo ya me voy.
A mi casita de sololoy; compro manzanas y no te doy.

In the ronda known as "San Severín," the children join hands and move in a circle as usual. When they get to the name of each occupation, they let go of each other's hands and pantomime the actions associated with it. For example, for panaderos, they pretend to be kneading dough; for carpinteros, they pretend to be sawing; etc. For a list of names of other trades and professions children might use, see page 95.

SAN SEVERÍN

Allegretto

San Se-ve-rín de la bue-na, bue-na vi-da,

ha-cen a-sí, a-sí
1. los pa-na-de-ros,
2. los car-pin-te-ros,
3. los za-pa-te-ros,

a-sí, a-sí, a-sí, a-sí me gus-ta a mí.

Reprinted from CANTEMOS EN ESPAÑOL (KL11) by M. and B. Krone
© Copyright 1961 Neil A. Kjos Music Company
Used with permission 1988

JUEGOS PARA MAYORCITOS

*There are plenty of **songs and games for older children**. To play "Matarile rile ró," the children form two parallel lines facing each other. The lines take turns skipping toward each other and back again as they sing each pair of verses. In verse 5, Line A chooses a player from Line B, naming an occupation for the player in verse 7. Verses 7 and 8 repeat until Line A hits upon an occupation that suits the player from Line B. At that point, line B responds with verse 9 instead of 8, and the entire group then sings the last verse. To continue the game, Lines A and B switch parts. (For a list of occupations that might be used in this game, see page 95.)*

MATARILE RILE RÓ

(1) LÍNEA A: Amó Ató.
Matarile rile rile.
Amó Ató.
Matarile rile ró.

(2) LÍNEA B: ¿Qué quería usted?
Matarile rile rile.
¿Qué quería usted?
Matarile rile ró.

(3) LÍNEA A: Yo quería un paje.
Matarile, *etc.*

(4) LÍNEA B: Escoja usted.
Matarile, *etc.*

(5) LÍNEA A: Escogemos a [María].
Matarile, *etc.*

(6) LÍNEA B: ¿Qué oficio le pondremos?
Matarile, *etc.*

(7) LÍNEA A: Le pondremos [cocinera].
Matarile, *etc.*

(8) LÍNEA B: Ese oficio no le agrada.
Matarile, *etc.*

(9) LÍNEA B: Ese oficio sí le agrada.
Matarile, *etc.*

(10) TODOS: Celebremos todos juntos.
Matarile rile rile.
Celebremos todos juntos.
Matarile rile ró.

In "La rueda de San Miguel," when the children get to the last line, they fill in the name of one of the players, who must then turn around and face the outside of the circle. The game continues until only two players are left facing the inside of the circle. These two then form an arch by joining hands and lifting them high over their heads. The other players pass through the arch and form the circle again, facing inward.

LA RUEDA DE SAN MIGUEL

♩=100

Rue - da, rue - da 'e San Mi - guel, San Mi - guel,

To - dos traen ca - mo - te y miel.

(*Hablado*: a lo maduro, a lo maduro, que se voltee [*nombre*] de burro.)

55

MARÍA BLANCA

To play this game, the children form a circle and select a girl to be María Blanca and a boy to be El viejo. María Blanca stands in the center of the circle, with El viejo outside. The other children move in a circle as the players sing or recite the lines above the asterisk. At the asterisked point, El viejo tries to break the circle. As he tries to separate the hands of any two players, the last two lines are spoken. The children name a weaker and weaker material with each successive try. When El viejo succeeds in breaking the circle, he chases María Blanca until he catches her. The children then choose another girl and boy to form a new pair, and the game continues.

LOS NIÑOS:	María Blanca está encerrada en pilares de oro y plata.
MARÍA BLANCA:	¿Quién anda alrededor de mi casa?
EL VIEJO:	El viejo tripón.
LOS NIÑOS:	¿Qué quería?
El VIEJO:	A María Blanca; ¡que se rompa un pilar!

✱

LOS NIÑOS:	¡Que lo rompa si puede!
EL VIEJO:	¿De qué es éste?
LOS NIÑOS:	De oro. [De cobre, De madera, De papel, etc.]

To play "A pares y a nones," you must have an odd number of children. Have the children form a circle and skip around as they say the rhyme. On uno and dos the children squat down together. On tres the circle breaks up and each child must rush to find a partner from the opposite side of the circle. The odd child out must pay a trivial penalty by fulfilling some silly task, like walking backwards all the way around the room.

A PARES Y A NONES

A pares y a nones vamos a jugar
y el que quede solo, ése perderá. —¡Uno!
A pares y a nones vamos a jugar
y el que quede solo, ése perderá. —¡Dos!
A pares y a nones vamos a jugar
y el que quede solo, ése perderá. —¡Tres!

To play "La tablita" one child serves as leader, and the other children line up in a row facing him or her. The leader recites the four lines of the first verse and then says the second verse, but without giving the sums. Instead, the leader points to children in the line, who must then give the sums. Any child who makes a mistake comes and stands in a row behind the leader. The game continues until there is only one child left in the original line. He or she becomes the leader of the next game.

LA TABLITA

Brinca la tablita.
Ya yo la brinqué.
Bríncala tú ahora,
que yo me cansé.

Dos y dos son cuatro.
Cuatro y dos son seis.
Seis y dos son ocho.
Y ocho dieciséis.

¿YA ESTÁ EL PAN?

*To start this game, children cross their arms and form a circle,
preferably sitting on the floor. One child is inside the circle. The
children in the circle say the first line, and the child inside the circle
says the second, pointing, after having done so, to one of the children
in the circle, who must then answer. The first two lines are repeated
before each question. The child in the center chooses different children
to take turns answering. After the last answer, the child in the center
feels each child's hands to see which are the warmest. The child with
the warmest hands gets to lead the next round.*

TODOS: Dormir, dormir, el pájaro pinto se quiere dormir.
NIÑO DEL CENTRO: ¿Ya está el pan?
RESPUESTAS:
No, el panadero apenas se va a levantar.
No, el panadero apenas se está poniendo los pantalones.
" " " " " " " los calcetines.
" " " " " " " los zapatos.
" " " " " " " la camisa.
" " " " " " " lavando la cara.
" " " " " " " peinando.
" " " " " " " desayunando.
" " " " " " " cepillando los dientes.
" " " " " " " lavando las manos.
" " " " fue a la cocina.
" " " " comenzó a amasar.
" " " " lo está poniendo en el horno.
No, todavía se está cociendo.
Ahora sí ya está.

*For this game, two children hold hands and lift their arms high above
their heads to form a bridge. The rest hold hands and form a circle
which constantly passes under the bridge as the song is sung. At the
end of the song, the children who form the bridge suddenly drop their
arms, trapping one of the players, who must then take the place of one
of the bridge children while the game continues.*

A LA VÍBORA DE LA MAR

A la víbora, víbora de la mar,
por aquí pueden pasar.
La de adelante corre mucho.
La de atrás se quedará.
Tras, tras, tras.
Una mexicana que fruta vendía,
ciruela, chabacano, melón y sandía.
Verbena, verbena, jardín de matatena,
verbena, verbena, jardín de matatena.

Campanita de oro, déjame pasar,
con todos mis hijos, menos el de atrás.
Tras, tras, tras.

57

Here are some miscellaneous, special-purpose rhymes for games.

This rhyme is used to start the game of "La gallinita ciega." To play, a paper bag is placed over a child's head so that he or she cannot see. (Leave the bottom open so there's plenty of ventilation.) The child must then try to touch one of the other players, who taunt him or her by coming as close as they dare.

—¿Qué busca la gallinita ciega?

—Una aguja y un dedal.

—Yo la tengo, yo la tengo,
   y no te la quiero entregar.

Any of these five rhymes can be used to choose a person at random—for example, to decide who will be "It" in a game. A child chants the rhyme rhythmically, emphasizing the stressed syllables (underlined). With each stressed syllable, the child points to a different player. The player on whom the last stressed syllable falls is "It."

Tin marín de don pingüé,
cúcara, mácara, títere fue.
El inglés sacó la espada
y mató a cuarenta y tres.

Un gato se cayó a un pozo,
las tripas hicieron gua,
arré moto piti, poto,
arré moto piti pa.

Una, dole,
tele, catole,
quile, quilete,
estaba la reina
en su gabinete;
vino Gil
y apagó el candil.
Gil, Gilón,
cuenta las veinte,
que las veinte son.

Don Pepito el verdulero,
se cayó en un sombrero.
El sombrero era de paja.
Se cayó en una caja.
La caja era de cartón.
Se cayó en un cajón.
El cajón era de pino.
Se cayó en un pepino.
El pepino maduró
y don Pepito se salvó.

En un rosal había tres rosas;
flor con flor, rosa con rosa,
la más florida y hermosa
que usted escoja.
Bucón, buquera, tarabique,
¡y afuera!

This rhyme is used in a game in which a child hides something that the other players then have to look for.

Tris, tras
por delante
y por detrás.
No lo ves,
ni lo verás.

Any of these rhymes can be used to start off the game of "Hide-and-Seek."

Ronda, ronda,
el que no se ha escondido,
que se esconda,
y el que sí,
que corra.

Punto y coma,
el que no está escondido
se embroma.

Aceitera, vinagrera,
trascordar,
amagar y no dar,
dar sin reír,
dar sin hablar,
pajaritos a esconder,
que va la liebre a pacer,
que va, que va, y que fue.

PARA BRINCAR LA CUERDA

*Here are a few **jump-rope rhymes**.*

UNA, DOS, PIMIENTO MORRÓN

Una, dos, pimiento morrón,
que pica, que rabia,
que toca la guitarra,
y empieza colección:
colección una,
colección dos,
colección tres,
colección cuatro,
colección cinco,
colección seis,
colección siete,
colección ocho,
colección nueve,
colección diez,
colección once y abretón,
colección doce y pisotón,
colección trece y volterón.

HOJAS DE TÉ

Hojas de té;
té de limón;
hojas y hojas
y nada de té.

EN EL PUENTE MARINERO

En el puente marinero
hay una niña brincando,
con su letra lo que dice:
"Soy la reina de los mares".
—Soy la reina de los mares,
ustedes lo van a ver,
tiro mi pañuelo al suelo
y lo vuelvo a recoger.
Si la cosa no se acaba,
la culpa la tienes tú,
por andar de parrandera
con tu vestidito azul.
Una, dos y tres,
sota, caballo y rey.

OSITO, OSITO

Osito, osito, toca el piso.
Osito, osito, da la media vuelta.
Osito, osito, da la vuelta entera.
Osito, osito, sal de la cuerda.

59

REQUETETRABALENGUAS

*Try these **tongue twisters** only if your tongue is in pretty good shape.*

Perejil, comí,
perejil, cené,
y de tanto comer perejil
me emperejilé.
Y ahora, ¿cómo me desemperejilaré?

En el monte hay una cabra hética,
perlética, pelambrética,
peluda, pelapelambruda.
Tiene sus hijos héticos,
perléticos, pelambréticos,
peludos, pelapelambrudos.
Si la cabra no fuera hética,
perlética, pelambrética,
peluda, pelapelambruda,
no tendría sus hijos héticos,
perléticos, pelambréticos,
peludos, pelapelambrudos.

Yo fui a Parangaricutirimícuaro,
ahí me emparangaricutirimicuarizaron.
El desemparangaricutirimicuarizador
que me desemparangaricutirimicuarice,
un buen desemparangaricutirimicuarizador
   será.

Una vieja, tecla, mecla,
chiririgorda, sorda y vieja,
tenía siete hijos, teclos, meclos,
chiririgordos, sordos y viejos.
Si la vieja no hubiera sido
tecla, mecla, chiririgorda, sorda y vieja,
los hijos no hubieran sido
teclos, meclos, chiririgordos, sordos
   y viejos.

El rey de Constantinopla
se quiere desconstantinopolizar;
el que lo desconstantinopolizara,
buen desconstantinopolizador sería.

Compadre, compre usted poca capa parda,
que el que poca capa parda compra
poca capa parda paga.
Yo, que poca capa parda compré,
poca capa parda pagué.

¿Cómo como?
Como como como.

Tres tristes tigres tragaban
tres gruesos trozos de grasa,
y tres hombres los buscaban
con ganas de darles caza.

Me han dicho un dicho
que han dicho que he dicho yo.
Ese dicho está mal dicho,
pues si lo hubiera dicho yo,
estaría mejor dicho
que el dicho que han dicho
que he dicho yo.

—Te conozco, mosco
—dijo el zancudo,
cuando la araña no pudo
soltarse de un nudo macanudo.

—Compadre, cómprame un coco.
—Compadre, no compro coco
porque como poco coco como,
poco coco compro.

Erre con erre, guitarra;
erre con erre, barril;
rápido corren los carros
cargados de azúcar
por ferrocarril.

María Chucena
techaba su choza.
Pasó un techador y le dijo:
—María Chucena,
¿por qué techas tu choza?
—No techo mi choza,
ni techo la ajena;
techo la choza
de María Chucena.

Paco Peco, chico rico,
insultaba como un loco
a su tío Federico,
y éste dijo: —Poco a poco,
Paco Peco, poco pico.

El cielo está encapotado.
¿Quién lo desencapotará?
El desencapotador que lo desencapotara,
buen desencapotador sería.

El cielo está enladrillado,
¿quién lo desenladrillará?
El desenladrillador que lo desenladrillara,
buen desenladrillador sería.

Pablito clavó un clavito.
Un clavito clavó Pablito.

El perro de San Roque
no tiene rabo
porque Ramón Ramírez
se lo ha robado.

ADIVÍNAME LO QUE ES

Can you guess these brain-teasing **riddles**? *If you can't, it's okay to look in the answer box.*

1 Vuelo y no tengo alas.
Ando y no tengo pies.
Y hablo y no tengo boca.

2 Dos arquitas de cristal
que abren y cierran sin rechinar.

In addition to a clever riddle, these adivinanzas *contain a rhyme.*

3 Fui al pueblo,
compré de ellas;
vine a mi casa
y lloré con ellas.

4 Subo siempre llena
y bajo vacía;
si no me apresuro,
la sopa se enfría.

5 En alto vive,
en alto mora,
en alto teje
la tejedora.

6 Siempre quietas,
siempre inquietas,
dormidas de día,
de noche despiertas.

8 En aquel lado,
en aquel otro,
relincha la yegua
y aparece el potro.

7 Soy Rey de imperio en toda nación,
tengo doce hijos de mi corazón,
de cada uno treinta nietos,
que son mitad blancos, y son mitad negros.

10 Chiquita como un ratón,
guarda la casa como un león.

9 Una vieja larga y seca
derritiendo la manteca.

11 Redondito, redondón;
no tiene tapa ni tapón.

BRIGHT IDEA

Rhyming Riddles It's fun for students to make up rhyming riddles. Give them a pair of rhyming words and ask them to create their own riddles. For instance, from the pair *tiene* and *viene*, the following riddle could be made: *Cuatro patas tiene, pero no va ni viene. (una mesa)* The list on pages 28–29 is a good resource of rhyming pairs.

12 Una cajita redonda,
blanca como el azahar,
se abre muy fácilmente,
y no se puede cerrar.

13 Dos hermanas, mentira no es,
la una es mi tía, la otra no lo es.

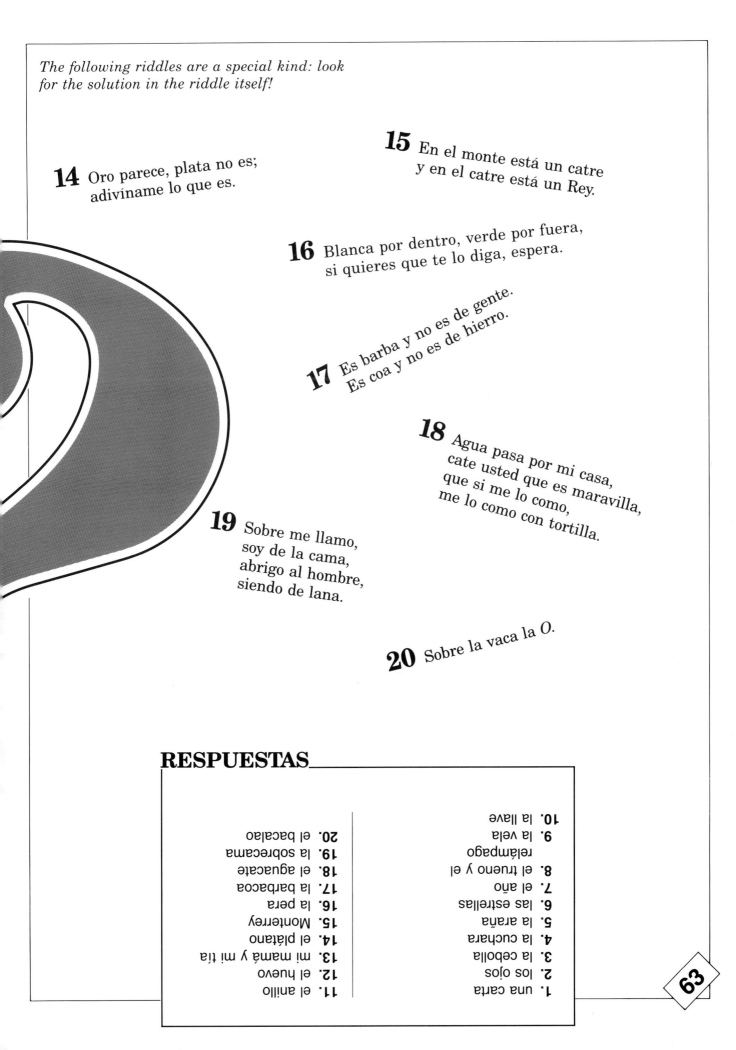

The following riddles are a special kind: look for the solution in the riddle itself!

14 Oro parece, plata no es;
adivíname lo que es.

15 En el monte está un catre
y en el catre está un Rey.

16 Blanca por dentro, verde por fuera,
si quieres que te lo diga, espera.

17 Es barba y no es de gente.
Es coa y no es de hierro.

18 Agua pasa por mi casa,
cate usted que es maravilla,
que si me lo como,
me lo como con tortilla.

19 Sobre me llamo,
soy de la cama,
abrigo al hombre,
siendo de lana.

20 Sobre la vaca la O.

RESPUESTAS

1. una carta
2. los ojos
3. la cebolla
4. la cuchara
5. la araña
6. las estrellas
7. el año
8. el trueno y el relámpago
9. la vela
10. la llave
11. el anillo
12. el huevo
13. mi mamá y mi tía
14. el plátano
15. Monterrey
16. la pera
17. la barbacoa
18. el aguacate
19. la sobrecama
20. el bacalao

DICHOS

*Here are some **proverbs** that are pearls of Hispanic folk wisdom.*

Camarón que se duerme, se lo lleva la corriente.

Con hambre no hay mal pan.

De lo dicho a lo hecho, hay mucho trecho.

De tal palo tal astilla.

Del plato a la boca, se pierde la sopa.

Dime con quién andas, y te diré quién eres.

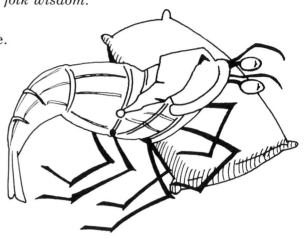

El que espera, desespera.

El que nace para tamal, del cielo le caen las hojas.

El que no oye consejo, no llega a viejo.

El que se fue a la villa, perdió su silla.

En boca cerrada no entran moscas.

En lunes ni las gallinas ponen.

En tierra de ciegos, el tuerto es rey.

Entre menos burros, más elotes.

Hablando del rey de Roma, y en eso se asoma.

Más vale malo conocido que bueno por conocer.

Más vale pájaro en mano que ciento volando.

Más vale solo que mal acompañado.

Más vale tarde que nunca.

No dejes para mañana lo que puedas hacer hoy.

No es tan bravo el león como se pinta.

No le busques ruido al chicharrón.

Ojos que no ven, corazón que no siente.

Panza llena, corazón contento.

Quien mucho abarca, poco aprieta.

Quien sabe dos lenguas vale por dos.

Fractured Proverbs To have some fun with proverbs, try this. First, familiarize students with several Spanish proverbs, so that they get a feel for the clipped, condensed style and the metaphorical language. Then post the first part of a well-known proverb on the bulletin board and invite students to write their own humorous or unusual endings for it. For example:

> *El que espera . . .*
> *no es manzana.*
> *llega tarde.*
> *echa raíces.*
> *tiene tiempo para revisar*
>   *su tarea.*
> *que se siente o se cansará.*

REPERTORIO CLÁSICO

*From here to page 69 you will find a few **classics from Spanish folklore** and literature for children.*

MI MUÑECA

Tengo una muñeca
vestida de azul,
con su camisita
y su canesú.

La saqué a paseo,
se me resfrió;
la metí en la cama
con mucho dolor.

Esta mañanita
me dijo el doctor
que le dé jarabe
con un tenedor.

2 y 2 son 4,
4 y 2 son 6,
6 y 2 son 8
y 8, 16.

Y 8, 24
y 8, 32.
Ya verás muñeca
si te curo yo.

TENGO TENGO TENGO

Tengo, tengo, tengo.
Tú no tienes nada.
Tengo tres ovejas
en una cabaña.

Una me da leche,
otra me da lana
y otra me mantiene
toda la semana.

Caballito blanco,
llévame de aquí;
llévame hasta el pueblo
donde yo nací.

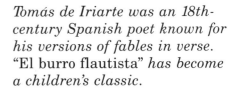

Tomás de Iriarte was an 18th-century Spanish poet known for his versions of fables in verse. "El burro flautista" has become a children's classic.

EL BURRO FLAUTISTA

Esta fabulilla,
salga bien o mal,
me ha ocurrido ahora
por casualidad.

Cerca de unos prados
que hay en mi lugar,
pasaba un borrico
por casualidad.

Una flauta en ellos
halló que un zagal
se dejó olvidada
por casualidad.

Acercóse a olerla
el dicho animal,
y dio un resoplido
por casualidad:

En la flauta el aire
se hubo de colar,
y sonó la flauta
por casualidad.

—¡Oh! —dijo el borrico.—
¡Qué bien sé tocar!
¿Y dirán que es mala
la música asnal?

Sin reglas del arte
borriquitos hay
que una vez aciertan
por casualidad.

—*Tomás de Iriarte*

DE COLORES

De colores,
de colores se visten los campos en la
     primavera;
de colores, de colores son los pajarillos
     que vienen de afuera;
de colores, de colores es el arco iris
     que vemos lucir
y por eso los grandes amores, de muchos
     colores, me gustan a mí.

Canta el gallo,
     canta el gallo con el kiri kiri,
     kiri kiri kiri, kiri kiri kiri;
la gallina, la gallina con el cara cara,
     cara cara cara, cara cara cara;
los polluelos, los polluelos con el pío pío,
     pío pío pío, pío pío pi.
Y por eso los grandes amores de muchos
     colores me gustan a mí.

LA TIJERA DE MAMÁ

Cuando me recorta el pelo
la tijera de mamá,
va diciendo en su revuelo:
chiqui-chiqui-chiqui-chá . . .

Aletea,
viene y va,
y a mi oído cuchichea:
chiqui-chiqui-chiqui-chá . . .

Cuando el pelo me recorta
la tijera de mamá,
charla más de lo que corta:
chiqui-chiqui-chiqui-chá . . .

—*Germán Berdiales*

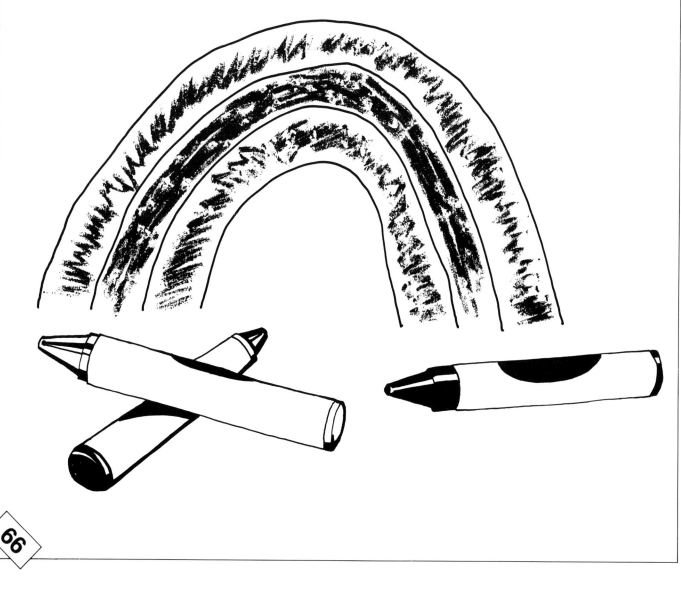

TARA, TARA, LA GUITARRA

En la feria de San Juan
yo compré una guitarra,
tara, tara, tara, la guitarra.

Coro: Vaya usted, vaya usted,
a la feria de San Juan.

En la feria de San Juan
yo compré un clarinete,
nete, nete, nete, el clarinete,
tara, tara, tara, la guitarra.

Coro

En la feria de San Juan
yo compré un violín,
lin, lin, lin, el violín,
nete, nete, nete, el clarinete,
tara, tara, tara, la guitarra.

Coro

LA VOZ DE LOS ANIMALITOS

Tengo una gatita
que sabe maullar:
¡miau, miau, miau!,
tengo dos perritos
que saben ladrar:
¡gua, gua, gua!,
tengo tres pollitos
que saben piar:
¡pío, pío, pío!,
cuatro borreguitos
que saben balar:
¡be, be, be!
y cinco ranitas
que saben croar:
¡croa, croa, croa!

—*A.L. Jáuregui*

PATITO, PATITO

—Patito, patito,
color de café,
¿por qué estás tan triste?,
quisiera saber.

—Perdí mi papito,
color de café.
Por eso estoy triste.
Y triste estaré.

—Tu papá yo vi,
muy lejos de aquí,
con otro patito,
color de café.

Patito, patito,
color de café,
¿por qué estás tan triste?,
quisiera saber.

 **BRIGHT IDEA**

Sound Words That Sound Like Fun   The poems on these pages are an excellent springboard for some "ears-on" experience in creating onomatopoeias.

- How many animals can your students name? After you brainstorm a good list, challenge them to come up with words for how the animals sound, and then use their lists to create new verses for *"La voz de los animalitos."*

- Try the same idea with musical instruments and continue the song *"Tara, tara, la guitarra."* Then divide the students into pairs, assign one instrument to each pair, and perform the song as a choral reading.

- Encourage students to name other actions that *chiqui-chiqui-chiqui-chá* could represent—a train, for example. Then help them create a new poem following the pattern of *"La tijera de mamá."*

See page 26 for a variety of words that stand for common sounds.

EN LA CIUDAD DE ROMA

Ésta es la ciudad de Roma,
en la cual hay una puerta.
Esta puerta da a una calle
y la calle va a una plaza.
En la plaza hay una casa;
dentro de la casa, un patio;
en el patio, una escalera:
la escalera va a una sala.
Esta sala da a una alcoba;
en la alcoba hay una cama;
junto a la cama, una mesa;
sobre la mesa, una jaula;
dentro de la jaula, un loro,
que cantando pide a todos:
Que lo saquen de la jaula,
que está encima de
    la mesa,
que está al lado de
    la cama,
que está dentro de
    la alcoba,
que está al lado de la sala,
adonde va la escalera,
que sube desde ese patio,
que está dentro de la casa,
la casa que está en
    la plaza,
a la que va aquella calle,
a la cual da aquella puerta,
que hay en la ciudad
    de Roma.

QUE LLUEVA

Moderato

Que llue - va, que llue - va, la Vie - ja de la cue - va.

Los pa - ja - ri - tos can - tan, la ma - dre se le -

Fine

van - ta. Que sí, que no, ¡que llue-va un cha-pa - rrón!

A - gua, San Mar - cos, rey de los char - cos.

Después de repetirse cinco veces, D.C. al Fine

Pa - ra mi tri - gui - to que es - tá muy bo - ni - to;

Para mi cebada que está granada;
Para mi melón que ya tiene flor;
Para mi sandía que ya está florida;
Para mi aceituna que ya tiene una.

68

SEÑOR DON GATO

Estaba el señor don Gato
en silla de oro sentado,
calzando medias de seda
y zapatito bordado,
cuando llegó la noticia
que había de ser casado
con una gatita parda,
con una pinta en el rabo.
El gato, con la alegría,
se ha caído del tejado.
Se rompió siete costillas
y la puntita del rabo.
Llamaron al curandero,
médicos y cirujanos;
mataron siete gallinas
y le dieron de aquel caldo.
Le llevaron a enterrar
por la calle del pescado,
y ni al olor de las sardinas
el gato ha resucitado.
Aunque tiene siete vidas,
las siete, al fin, ha entregado;
ninguno de los doctores
ha podido remediarlo.
Sobre la cajita iban
siete ratones bailando,
al ver que se había muerto
aquel enemigo malo.

EL CARACOL

Aquel caracol
que va por el sol,
en cada ramita
besaba una flor.

Que viva la vida,
que viva el amor,
que viva la gracia
de aquel caracol.

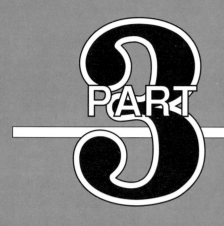

PART 3

VOCABULÁLOGO

A resource of instructional words for reading and writing, as well as the content areas

LA LISTA

Here is the Hampton-Brown list of **words most frequently used in Spanish basal reading programs** *in the U.S.*

What It Is

The Hampton-Brown Spanish-Reading Word List ("LA LISTA"), which appears on pages 71–73, is a high-frequency vocabulary list for use in primary-grade bilingual language-arts instruction. It has been culled from all words found in the first- and second-grade readers of the four leading Spanish basal reading series used in the United States. They are:

- Harcourt Brace Jovanovich, *HBJ Lectura,* © 1987, Levels 1–7.
- Houghton Mifflin Company, *Programa de lectura en español,* © 1987, Levels PP1–2/2.
- Macmillan Publishing Company, *Campanitas de oro,* © 1987, Levels 1–7.
- Scott, Foresman and Company, *Scott, Foresman Spanish Reading,* © 1987, Levels 2A–6.

How It Is Organized

LA LISTA is made up of two parts.

- **Core Vocabulary** This part presents those function words, verbs, adjectives, and adverbs which appear in greatest frequency in the basal series. These 210 words are presented first in a combined Grades 1 and 2 List and then according to the level—low first grade, high first grade, and second grade—in which they appear with high frequency.

- **Common Nouns** This part contains the most frequently encountered nouns across Grades 1 and 2.

How It Was Developed

Every word to be read by the students in the Pupil Text of the four series was input into a computerized system. The words were then sorted both alphabetically and in order of frequency. Numbers, foreign words, proper nouns, and onomatopoetic words (such as *auuuu, guauguau,* etc.) were deleted. In addition, certain decisions were made to combine entries. These decisions can be summarized as follows:

1. All forms of nouns and adjectives (including diminutives) were counted under the singular, masculine, "dictionary" form. For example, *ositas* and

blancas were counted under *oso* and *blanco,* respectively. This was not done, of course, in cases where masculine and feminine forms are completely different words: *vaca* was not counted under *toro.*

2. Adverbs formed regularly from adjectives by the addition of *-mente* were counted under the adjectives from which they were formed.

3. All forms of regular verbs were counted under the infinitive of the verb (e.g., *mirar, llegar,* etc.), as were predictable "irregular" verbs (such as *sentarse, querer,* etc.).

4. Irregular tenses of highly variable verbs were counted as separate words, while the regular tenses of the same verbs were counted under the infinitive. For example, the verb *dar* is mostly regular, except in the first-person present tense *(doy).* Therefore, all forms of *dar* except *doy* were counted under *dar,* and *doy* was counted as a separate entry. The list

of verb forms that were not counted under their infinitives follows:

caigo (from *caer*)	*sal* (from *salir*)
conozco (from *conocer*)	*sigo* (from *seguir*)
digo (from *decir*)	*soy* (from *ser*)
doy (from *dar*)	*sigue* (from *seguir*)
eres (from *ser*)	*siguen* (from *seguir*)
es (from *ser*)	*sigues* (from *seguir*)
estoy (from *estar*)	*somos* (from *ser*)
ha (from *haber*)	*son* (from *ser*)
hago (from *hacer*)	*sonríe* (from *sonreír*)
han (from *haber*)	*ten* (from *tener*)
has (from *haber*)	*tengo* (from *tener*)
hay (from *haber*)	*traigo* (from *traer*)
he (from *haber*)	*va* (from *ir*)
hemos (from *haber*)	*vamos* (from *ir*)
oigo (from *oír*)	*van* (from *ir*)
pon (from *poner*)	*vas* (from *ir*)
pongo (from *poner*)	*ven* (from *ir*)
ríe (from *reír*)	*vengo* (from *ir*)
ríes (from *reír*)	*veo* (from *ver*)
río (from *reír*)	*voy* (from *ir*)
sé (from *saber*)	

5. In cases where an accent changes the function of a word but not its basic meaning (e.g. interrogative *quién* versus relative *quien*), both forms were counted under the unaccented form.

CORE VOCABULARY
Combined List for Grades 1 and 2

a	bien	creer	empezar	grande	listo
abrir	bonito	cuando	en	gritar	lo
ahí	bueno	dar	encontrar	gustar	los
ahora	buscar	de	enseñar	haber	luego
al	cada	deber	entonces	hablar	llamar
algo	caer	decir	entrar	hacer	llegar
alguno	caminar	dejar	eres	hacia	llevar
allí	cantar	del	es	hasta	más
alto	cerco	dentro	esconder	hay	me
amarillo	claro	desde	ese	ir	mejor
antes	comer	después	esperar	jugar	meter
aprender	como	don	estar	junto	mi
aquí	comprar	donde	este	la	mientras
arriba	con	dormir	estoy	largo	mirar
así	contar	dos	feliz	le	mismo
ayudar	contento	el	feo	leer	mucho
bailar	contestar	él	fuerte	lejos	muy
bajar	correr	ella	ganar	levantar	nada
bajo	crecer	ellos	gordo	lindo	nadar

nadie	pero	regresar	sí	tiempo	van
necesitar	pintar	rojo	siempre	tirar	vas
ni	poco	saber	sin	tocar	ven
no	poder	sacar	sobre	todavía	vender
nos	poner	salir	solo	todo	venir
nuevo	por	saltar	son	tomar	veo
nunca	porque	se	sonreír	trabajar	ver
o	preguntar	sé	soy	traer	vez
oír	primero	seguir	su	tres	viejo
otro	pronto	sentar	subir	triste	vivir
para	pues	sentir	también	tu	volar
parecer	que	señor	tan	un	volver
pasar	quedar	señora	tanto	usar	voy
pedir	querer	señorita	te	usted	y
pensar	quien	ser	tener	va	ya
pequeño	rápido	si	tengo	vamos	yo

List of Low-First-Grade Words

a	decir	grande	más	querer	tomar
ahora	el	gustar	me	saltar	tu
al	en	hacer	mi	se	un
aquí	es	jugar	mirar	señor	va
ayudar	ese	la	no	ser	vamos
bueno	estar	le	otro	sí	ver
comer	este	lindo	para	su	voy
con	feliz	lo	poder	tener	y
correr	gordo	los	que	todo	yo
de					

List of High-First-Grade Words

allí	del	ir	pensar	salir	tengo
así	después	llegar	pequeño	sé	van
bien	don	llevar	pero	sentar	ven
bonito	donde	mucho	poner	si	venir
buscar	ella	muy	por	son	vez
caer	encontrar	nuevo	preguntar	subir	vivir
como	gritar	oír	rojo	también	volar
cuando	haber	pasar	saber	te	ya
dar	hay				

List of Second-Grade Words

abrir	arriba	claro	dejar	enseñar	fuerte
ahí	bailar	comprar	dentro	entonces	ganar
algo	bajar	contar	desde	entrar	hablar
alguno	bajo	contento	dormir	eres	hacia
alto	cada	contestar	dos	esconder	hasta
amarillo	caminar	crecer	él	esperar	junto
antes	cantar	creer	ellos	estoy	largo
aprender	cerco	deber	empezar	feo	leer

lejos	nadar	poco	seguir	soy	tres
levantar	nadie	porque	sentir	tan	triste
listo	necesitar	primero	señora	tanto	usar
luego	ni	pronto	señorita	tiempo	usted
llamar	nos	pues	siempre	tirar	vas
mejor	nunca	quedar	sin	tocar	vender
meter	o	quien	sobre	todavía	veo
mientras	parecer	rápido	solo	trabajar	viejo
mismo	pedir	regresar	sonreír	traer	volver
nada	pintar	sacar			

COMMON NOUNS
Combined List for Grades 1 and 2

abuelo/a	cuerda	lobo	pregunta
agua	cuidado	lugar	pueblo
algo	chivo	luna	rama
amigo/a	día	luz	rana
animal	dibujo	mamá	rato
año	elefante	mano	ratón
árbol	escuela	mañana	rey
arco	estrella	mar	río
ardilla	familia	mariposa	rosa
ave	fiesta	mesa	ruido
barco	fin	miedo	sapo
bicicleta	flor	música	semilla
bosque	gallina	nada	sol
bota	ganso	nadie	sombrero
burro	gato	narrador/a	sorpresa
caballo	gente	niño/a	tarde
cabeza	globo	noche	tiempo
caja	gracias	nube	tierra
calle	granjero	ojo	tío/a
cama	hermano/a	oso	títere
camino	hijo/a	oveja	todo
campo	hoja	pájaro	tortuga
casa	hombre	palo	trabajo
cerco	hormiga	pan	vaca
cielo	hoy	papá	ventana
ciudad	huevo	papel	verdad
cola	idea	parte	vez
color	jardín	pato	viento
comida	lado	pelota	voz
conejo	lechuza	perro	zapato
cosa	letrero	piedra	zorro
coyote	libro	pintura	
cuarto			

SIEMPRELISTOS

Gender Agreement When gender agreement for nouns beginning with *a* or *ha* distresses you, just remember this simple rule about stress:

- Masculine articles are used with feminine nouns beginning with *a* or *ha* **only when the initial syllable is stressed.**

  un hambre   *una hamaca*
  el águila **but** *la aguja*

More tips:

- This rule applies only to articles immediately before feminine **nouns**. If other words intervene, feminine articles are used.

  el águila   la enorme águila

- Feminine articles are used even if an intervening adjective begins with stressed *a*.

  la alta colina

- *Using el* or *un* with a feminine noun does not alter the gender of the noun, so adjectives that follow are feminine.

  un hambre tremenda
  el águila blanca

SILABARIO SABELOTODO

*The following list of **syllables and sample words** will be useful if you are following a syllabic approach to teaching decoding and phonics skills in Spanish. All words are appropriate to auditory-discrimination practice. Words containing the syllable in initial position are listed first, followed by words containing the syllable in medial or final position. The vast majority of the words chosen can be easily drawn, so that they are appropriate for practices involving pictures. Words in **boldface** are appropriate for reading exercises with controlled vocabulary because they contain only the syllable under which they are listed and other previously listed syllables. For an overview of the syllabic sequence followed in this Silabario, see the box at right.*

Vowels

a	e	i
abanico	elefante	idea
abeja	embudo	iglesia
águila	enano	iglú
ala	enfermera	igual
ancla	escalera	iguana
anillo	escoba	imán
árbol	escuela	importante
arete	espejo	insecto
avestruz	espuma	ir
avión	estrella	isla

o	u
ocho	último
oficina	unicornio
ojal	uniforme
ojo	unir
ola	uno
olla	uña
once	urraca
oreja	usar
oso	útil
oveja	uva

Syllabic Sequence

a	e	i	o	u
ma	me	mi	mo	mu
pa	pe	pi	po	pu
sa	se	si	so	su
ta	te	ti	to	tu
la	le	li	lo	lu
da	de	di	do	du
na	ne	ni	no	nu
ba	be	bi	bo	bu
fa	fe	fi	fo	fu
ña	ñe	ñi	ño	ñu
va	ve	vi	vo	—
ha	he	hi	ho	hu
ca	—	—	co	cu
—	que	qui	—	—
ra	re	ri	ro	ru
rra	rre	rri	rro	rru
ya	ye	—	yo	yu
ga	—	—	go	gu
lla	lle	lli	llo	llu
cha	che	chi	cho	chu
—	ge	gi	—	—
—	gue	gui	—	—
ja	je	ji	jo	ju
za	—	—	zo	zu
—	ce	ci	—	—
dra	dre	dri	dro	dru
tra	tre	tri	tro	tru
bla	ble	bli	blo	blu
bra	bre	bri	bro	bru
fla	fle	fli	flo	flu
fra	fre	fri	fro	fru
gla	gle	—	glo	glu
gra	gre	gri	gro	gru
pla	ple	pli	plo	plu
pra	pre	pri	pro	pru
cla	cle	cli	clo	
cra	cre	cri	cro	cru

Diphthongs: ia, ie, io, iu, ai, ei, oi,
ui, ua, ue, uo, au, eu

Open Syllables With Single Consonants

ma	**me**	**mi**	**mo**	**mu**
madera	**me**	**mi**	modo	**mu**
mágico	mecánico	**mí**	mojado	muchacho
mago	medalla	micrófono	molino	mucho
maleta	médico	milla	moneda	mudo
mamá	mesa	mimar	mono	mujer
mami	México	mina	moto	muleta
mano		minuto		mulo
mañana				muñeca
mapa	americano	**mío**	**amo**	muro
mariposa	come	mira	como	museo
	número		famoso	música
	plomero	amigo	humo	
ama	plumero	camino	limonada	
amarillo	teme	dominó	ramo	comunidad
cama		hormiga	remo	comunión
espuma			tomo	
goma				

pa	**pe**	**pi**	**po**	**pu**
palo	pelo	pico	poco	**púa**
paloma	pelota	pido	polo	pudo
papa	pepino	pila	pollo	**puma**
papá	pera	piñata	pone	puño
para	perro	pito	pozo	puro
pasa	peso			
paso		cepillo	chapoteo	apuro
	papeles	pepino	mariposa	empujar
mapa	tapete	repita	sapo	
ropa	trompeta		tipo	
sepa			topo	
sopa				
tapa				

sa	**se**	**si**	**so**	**su**
sabe	**se**	**si**	soga	**su**
saca	**sé**	**sí**	solo	subir
sala	seda	siga	sonido	sucio
sale	semana	sigue	**sopa**	sudor
sano	seña	silla		**suma**
sapo	**sepa**	sitio	famoso	sumar
	serio		**oso**	
gusano		**así**	**paso**	ensuciar
masa	clase	casi	**peso**	resumen
mesa	**ese**	casita	**piso**	sesudo
pasa	José	música	**puso**	
pesa	**pasé**	osito		
pisa	**puse**			

ta	**te**	**ti**	**to**	**tu**
taco	**te**	**ti**	tocino	**tu**
tablero	tela	tímido	todo	**tú**
tamaño	teléfono	tina	**toma**	tubo
tapa	**tema**	**tío**	**tomate**	tulipán
tapete	**temo**	**tipo**	**tomo**	tuna
tarro	tesoro	títere	**topo**	
			toro	aceituna
bota	bate	gelatina		altura
lata	bote	**matita**	bonito	estudiar
maleta	botella	metido	gato	montura
mata	jinete	patito	foto	octubre
meta	machete	tortilla	**pato**	pintura
nata	**mete**		**pito**	
nota	**tapete**		zapato	
pata	tomate			
pelota				

la	**le**	**li**	**lo**	**lu**
la	**le**	libre	lo	lucero
lado	leche	libro	lobo	luna
lago	lechuga	**lima**	lodo	lunar
laguna	**lee**	limonada	**loma**	lunes
lápiz	leña	**lío**	loro	**lupa**
lata	**leo**	**liso**	**losa**	
		litro		iluminar
ala	dale		**elote**	peluca
cola	dile	California	**malo**	peludo
fila	**maleta**	colina	**palo**	**pelusa**
mala	**mole**	delicado	**paloma**	saludo
pila	**paleta**	felicidad	**pelo**	
pupila	teléfono	**palito**	**pelota**	
sala		**solito**	**solo**	

da	**de**	**di**	**do**	**du**
da	**de**	**día**	doblar	ducha
dado	debe	dibujo	doce	**duda**
dale	décimo	dicho	dólar	**dúo**
dama	decir	digo	domingo	duque
dame	dedo	**dile**	dominó	duro
	derramar	**dime**	dorado	
manada		dinamita		educación
moneda	adelante	dinero	**lado**	maduro
nada	cadena		**lodo**	producir
pedazo	**idea**	cerdito	**mido**	reducir
seda	**mide**	jardines	**modo**	
toda	**pide**	medicina	**pido**	
vida	**pude**	médico	sábado	
		perdido	**saludo**	
		rodilla	**todo**	

na	**ne**	**ni**	**no**	**nu**
nabo	neblina	**ni**	**no**	nube
nada	necesitar	**nido**	noche	**nudo**
nadar	negro	niña	nopales	número
naranja	**nena**	niño	**nota**	
nariz	**nené**		notar	**lanudo**
nave		animal		llanura
	cine	bonito	camino	manubrio
banana	cocinero	granizo	**enano**	**minuto**
cuna	chinela	ranita	gusano	monumento
laguna	enero	**sonido**	**mano**	
lana	granero		**molino**	
limonada	**moneda**		**mono**	
luna	**pone**		**pepino**	
pena			**pino**	
tina				

ba	**be**	**bi**	**bo**	**bu**
banana	**bebé**	bicicleta	**bobo**	búfalo
baño	beber	bigote	boca	búho
base	besar	billete	**boda**	buque
bata	**beso**		**bola**	burro
bate		gabinete	**boleto**	buzo
batido	abeja	hábito	**bonito**	buzón
	debe	hebilla	**bota**	
daba	**nube**	**lobito**	bote	aburrido
debajo	**sabe**	rubí		fabuloso
escoba	**sube**		cubo	tribu
guayaba			**lobo**	
sábado			**nabo**	
sábana			**subo**	

fa	**fe**	**fi**	**fo**	**fu**
fabuloso	**fe**	ficha	foca	**fulano**
fama	**fea**	figura	foco	fumar
famoso	**feo**	fija	fogata	fusil
faro	fecha	**fila**	**foto**	
favorito	feliz	**filo**		perfume
		fino	micrófono	
búfalo	café		**teléfono**	
jefa	diferente	difícil	zafo	
jirafa	jefe	suficiente		
rifa		tráfico		
sofá				
zafa				

ña	**ñe**	**ñi**	**ño**	**ñu**
ñame	arañe	**bañito**	ñoño	ñu
ñato	**bañe**	**leñito**		
	enseñe	**niñito**	año	
araña	muñeca		baño	
caña			cariño	
leña			**daño**	
mañana			**moño**	
montaña			**niño**	
niña			**otoño**	
peña			**paño**	
piña			pequeño	
piñata			**puño**	
puñado			señora	
uña			señorita	

va	**ve**	**vi**	**vo**	
va	ve	vi	vocal	
vaca	**vela**	**vía**	voces	
vacaciones	**veleta**	**vida**	volar	
vale	**velo**	**visita**	votar	
vaso	venado	**vitamina**	**voto**	
	veo	**viva**		
eleva	**vete**	**vive**	bravo	
lava		**aviso**	chivo	
uva	**ave**	evitar	**favorito**	
viva	**avenida**	**movía**	**lavo**	
	nave	**todavía**	**pavo**	
	nieve		**vivo**	

ha	**he**	**hi**	**ho**	**hu**
habla	hebilla	hígado	hocico	**humano**
hacer	hecho	higo	hoja	humedad
hacia	**helado**	hijo	**hola**	**humo**
hacha	herido	hilera	hora	humor
hada	héroe	**hilo**	hoyo	
hamaca	herradura	**hipopótamo**		
	herramienta	hizo	ahogo	
rehacer			ahora	
		ahí	**búho**	
		bahía		

ca	**co**	**cu**	**que**	**qui**
cada	cocina	cubo	que	químico
cadena	coco	cuchillo	qué	quitar
cae	codo	cuna	quedar	quiso
café	cola	cuña	quemar	
caja	cono	cuñado	queso	aquí
calle	coma			chiquito
cama	comida	ocupar	aquella	equipaje
camino	como		buque	equipo
camisa	conejo		dique	esquina
caña	corona		duque	máquina
canica	cosa		paquete	poquito
capa			pequeño	vaquita
carro	abanico			
casa	chocolate			
casi	foco			
caso	médico			
cayo	pico			
	poco			
acá	saco			
boca	taco			
foca				
hamaca				
mágica				
muñeca				
música				
pica				
saca				
vaca				

ra	**re**	**ri**	**ro**	**ru**
rábano	regaño	rico	roce	rubí
rabo	reí	rima	roer	rudo
rama	remar	río	ropa	ruso
rana	remo	risa	rosa	ruta
rápido	repetir	risotada	roto	
raqueta				oruga
rata	arena	americano	caro	
ratón	derecho	cariño	corona	
rayo	moreno	favorito	dinero	
	pareja	harina	duro	
cara	puré	herida	faro	
mira	sirena	lorito	miro	
para	títere	marido	número	
pera	torero	marinero	oro	
pirata		mariposa	puro	
pura		zapatería	seguro	
rara			tesoro	
			toro	

79

rra	rre	rri	rro	rru
agarra	**arreglo**	**aburrido**	**arroyo**	serrucho
ahorra	**barre**	**arriba**	**barro**	
barra	**borre**	**burrito**	**burro**	
gorra	**carreta**	**carrito**	**carro**	
herradura	**carretera**	**corrido**	charro	
narra	**carrera**	**derrite**	chorro	
perra	**corre**	**perrito**	gorro	
tierra	**narre**	terrible	hierro	
urraca	**terremoto**		jarro	
	terreno		**perro**	
	torre			

ya	ye	yo	yu
ya	yegua	**yo**	**yuca**
yagua	**yema**	**yoyo**	yugo
yate	**yeso**		**yute**
		bayoneta	
joya	oye	**cayo**	**ayuda**
maya		**cayó**	**desayuno**
payaso		**hoyo**	
vaya		**mayo**	
		suyo	
		tuyo	

ga	go	gu
gabinete	golondrina	**gusano**
galope	**goma**	
gallina	**gorila**	aguja
gallo	**gorra**	**laguna**
gana	**gota**	ninguno
ganado	gozar	orgullo
gato		
	amigo	
amiga	**apago**	
apaga	**digo**	
bodega	**hago**	
diga	**higo**	
miga	**lago**	
paga	**mago**	
pega	**pago**	
regalo	**pego**	
siga	**sigo**	
soga	trigo	
tortuga		

BRIGHT IDEA

Syllable Practice Pictures and printed syllables can be valuable resources for decoding practice. Blackline Masters 6–9 on pages 157–164 provide for a variety of practice formats.

- Duplicate the sheets as they appear. Glue each page of pictures on one side of an 8½″ × 11″ piece of oaktag, and the corresponding page of syllables on the other. Then cut along the dotted lines to create a set of picture cards, each with the corresponding syllable on the back. These cards are useful for introducing sound-syllable correspondence. To make larger cards, merely duplicate the Blackline Masters on a photocopier with a magnification feature.

- Just the syllables can be enlarged on a photocopier and made into flashcards. By trimming the cards close to the letters, you can amass sets of syllables that students can use to build words and sentences in pocket charts.

- Flashcards useful for blending two syllables into a word can be made as shown below.

lla	**lle**	**lli**	**llo**	**llu**
llama	llegada	allí	llorar	lluvia
llamada	llegar	bellísimo	llorón	lluvioso
llamar	lleno	gallina		
llano	llevar	pollito		
llave			amarillo	
	ballena		aquello	
allá	caballero		caballo	
aquella	calle		cabello	
botella	galleta		camello	
callado	valle		gallo	
cebolla			maravilloso	
halla			pollo	
hebilla			rollo	
milla			sello	
olla				
orilla				
silla				

cha	**che**	**chi**	**cho**	**chu**
chaleco	anoche	chico	chocolate	chupar
chapoteo	coche	chillar	chofer	chupete
chaqueta	leche	chimenea	choque	churro
chayote	machete	chino	chorro	
	noche	chivo	choza	lechuga
cuchara	peluche			lechuza
ducha	puchero	cochino	derecho	pechuga
fachada		cuchillo	dicho	
fecha		enchilada	hecho	
flecha		salchicha	muchacho	
lucha			mucho	
muchacha			ocho	
			pecho	
			serrucho	
			techo	

ge	**gi**	**gue**	**gui**
gelatina	gigante	guerra	guía
gemelo	girar	guerrero	guiño
general	girasol	hormiguero	guisado
generoso	gitano	juguete	guiso
genio		llegue	guitarra
	lógico	pague	
dirige	mágico	sigue	águila
escoge	página		aguinaldo
ligero	rugido		amiguito
recoge	zoológico		seguido
vegetales			

ja	je	ji	jo	ju
jabón	jefa	jinete	jota	jugo
jalapeño	jefe	jirafa	joven	juguete
jamón	jerigonza		joya	julio
jarra		ají	joyero	junio
	agujero	cajita		jurado
abeja	ajedrez	hijito	abajo	
caja	dije	hojita	ajo	bejuco
hija	eje	rojizo	bajo	brújula
hoja	garaje	tejido	conejo	
paja	relojero		dibujo	
pájaro	teje		hijo	
teja			ojo	
vieja			rojo	

za	zo	zu	ce	ci
zanahoria	zócalo	zumo	cebolla	cigüeña
zapatería	zona		ceja	cima
zapatero	zoológico	azúcar	cena	cine
zapato	zorrillo	azuloso	cepillo	cita
	zorro	pezuña	cera	
cabeza				cocina
calabaza	brazo		aparece	hocico
caza	granizo		cacerola	medicina
ceniza	hizo		conoce	oficina
cereza	lazo		doce	policía
lechuza	pedazo		lucero	vecino
plaza	pozo		nace	
taza	rizo		necesita	

Open Syllables With Consonant Blends

dra	dre	dri	dro	dru
dragón	adrede	golondrina	dromedario	madrugada
	ladre	ladrillo		
cuadra	madre	madrina	cuadro	
cuadrado	padre	padrino	ladrones	
ladra	pudre	podrido		

tra	tre	tri	tro	tru
trabajo	trébol	tribu	trono	truco
trae	trece	triciclo	tropa	trucha
tráfico	trecho	trigo	trotar	
traje	trenes	trineo	trozo	
trapo	trepar	trío		
			dentro	
letra	atreve	estribo	metro	
retrato	estrella	nutritivo	otro	
	postre	potrillo	potro	

bla	**ble**	**bli**	**blo**	**blu**
habla	cable	neblina	bloque	blusa
poblano	doble	público		
tabla	noble	tablita	establo	
	roble		hablo	
	tablero		pueblo	
	terrible			

bra	**bre**	**bri**	**bro**	**bru**
bravo	breve	brillante	brocha	bruja
brazo		brillar	broche	brújula
	abre	brillo	broma	bruto
cabra	febrero	brisa	brotar	
cebra	hombre		brote	
libra	libre	abrigo		
palabra	nombre	colibrí	abro	
sobra	pobre	fábrica	hombro	
	sobre	librito	libro	
	timbre	sobrino	miembro	

fla	**fle**	**fli**	**flo**	**flu**
flaco	fleco	afligido	flojo	fluye
flamenco	flecha	chiflido	florero	
flaquito	flechazo		flores	
			Florida	
chiflado	reflejo		flota	
inflado	rifle			
			aflojar	
			chiflo	
			inflo	

fra	**fre**	**fri**	**fro**	**fru**
fracaso	freír	frijoles	frotar	fruta
fragante	freno	frío		frutero
frágil	fresa	frito		
frase				disfrutar
frazada	cofre	africano		
	ofrece	enfríar		

gla	**gle**	**glo**	**glu**
gladiolo	iglesia	globo	iglú
		glotón	
arregla			
regla		arreglo	
		siglo	

gra	**gre**	**gri**	**gro**	**gru**
gracia	alegre	grillo	negro	grúa
grado	cangrejo	grito	ogro	grulla
granero	regresar			grupo
granizo	sangre	lágrima		
grano	**tigre**			agrupar
grasa	**vinagre**			
agrada				
fotografía				
negra				

pla	**ple**	**pli**	**plo**	**plu**
planear	**pleno**	aplicación	**plomero**	**pluma**
planeta		multiplicar	**plomo**	**plumero**
plano	cumpleaños	**soplido**		
plata	**empleo**	suplicar	ejemplo	desplumado
plátano	repleto			
platicar	simple			
plato				
playa				
plaza				

pra	**pre**	**pri**	**pro**	**pru**
pradera	precioso	**primavera**	probar	prudente
prado	preferir	**primero**	**profesora**	
	pregunta	**primo**	**promesa**	
compra	premio	**prisa**	proteger	
temprano	preparar			
	presidente	**aprisa**		
	apresurar			
	expresar			
	representar			
	siempre			

cla	**cle**	**cli**	**clo**
claridad	**bicicleta**	**clima**	**cloro**
clarinete	**bucle**	**clínica**	
claro	**chicle**		**triciclo**
clase		**inclinado**	
clave			
clavel			
clavo			
ancla			
mezcla			
tecla			

cra	cre	cri	cro	cru
cráneo	crecer	crimen	croqueta	crucigrama
cráter	creer	crines		**crudo**
	crema		**acróbata**	cruzar
		describir		
		escribir		

Diphthongs

(**Note**: At this point all words are considered decodable.)

ia	io	oi	ue
copia	cambio	boina	abuelo
demasiado	diccionario	oigo	bueno
familia	espacio		cigüeña
feria	furioso	**ui**	cuello
gracias	indio	buitre	cuero
hacia	julio	cuidado	cueva
historia	junio	cuidar	dueño
iglesia	medio	güiro	fuego
lluvia	mencionar	juicio	juego
media	negocio	ruido	nueve
piano	patio		nuevo
viaje	precioso	**ua**	pueblo
	radio	agua	rueda
ie	violento	antigua	sueño
cielo		averiguar	
hielo	**iu**	cuatro	**uo**
hierro	viuda	estatua	antiguo
miedo	viudo	lengua	continuo
nadie		suave	
nieve	**ai**		**au**
pie	aire		astronauta
piedra	baile		ausente
pieza	caigo		auto
serie	caimán		autor
siete	paisaje		flauta
tiene	traigo		jaula
tierra			
viejo	**ei**		**eu**
viene	peine		deuda
	pleito		eucalipto
	reina		Europa
	reino		reuma

HABLANDO CON ACENTO

The lists and rules on these two pages will help you give just the right emphasis to lessons on **syllabication and accent.**

Palabras agudas

Son las que llevan la fuerza de pronunciación en la última sílaba.

animal	caer	comerás	honor	pared
arroz	café	corazón	león	quizás
ataúd	caminar	dominó	nivel	reloj
azafrán	capitán	dormilón	papel	sofá
baúl	colibrí			

Palabras llanas

Son las que llevan la fuerza de pronunciación en la penúltima sílaba.

actúa	canto	chocolate	lápiz	tenía
álbum	cárcel	días	nenúfar	tijeras
automóvil	cariño	era	orden	turista
azúcar	césped	fénix	río	útil
azucena	coro	huésped		

Palabras esdrújulas

Son las que llevan la fuerza de pronunciación en la antepenúltima sílaba.

albóndiga	cándido	eléctrico	mayúscula	rábano
apóstoles	cáustico	esdrújula	médico	simpático
árabe	ciénaga	lógico	pétalo	síntoma
árbitro	cómico	matemáticas	psicólogo	teléfono
bárbaro	crímenes			

Palabras sobresdrújulas

Son las que llevan la fuerza de pronunciación en una sílaba anterior a la antepenúltima. Se forman cuando se le añade el sufijo -mente a una palabra llana o esdrújula o cuando se le añaden enclíticos a un verbo.

difícilmente	devuélvenosla
enérgicamente	díganselo
fácilmente	pónganmelo
lógicamente	tráigamela
trágicamente	tírenselos

Syllabication and Accentuation Here's a quick refresher course in the rules for syllabication and written accent in Spanish.

SYLLABLES

- A consonant between two vowels belongs with the second vowel:

    ca-fé   co-ro

- When there are two consonants between two vowels, one consonant goes with each vowel, except in the case of the blends *bl, cl, fl, gl, pl, tl, br, cr, dr, fr, gr, pr,* and *tr,* which act as a single consonant:

    can-to hués-ped **but**   ma-dre i-glú

- When there are three or more consonants between two vowels, a blend will always be involved: an *l* or *r* blend from the list above, or one of the following—*bs, ds, ns*—or both. All of these blends should be treated as single consonants:

    es-cri-bir obs-truc-ción trans-mi-tir

    Note: When *bs, ds,* or *ns* appear as the *only two* consonants between vowels, they follow the general rule given above: *pren-sa, ob-se-sión.*

- Vowels are divided into two groups: *strong* vowels—*vocales fuertes*: *a, e, o*—and *weak* vowels—*vocales débiles*: *i, u.* When a weak vowel and a strong vowel, or two weak vowels, appear together, they form a diphthong and belong in the same syllable. Otherwise, vowels that appear together belong in different syllables.

    hé-ro-e ma-re-a pei-ne ciu-dad rui-na

- An accent on the *weak* vowel of what would otherwise be a diphthong breaks the diphthong and separates the vowels:

    te-ní-a ba-úl **but** co-mió far-ma-céu-ti-co

ACCENT

- Words of one syllable normally have no written accent, except to distinguish between two different meanings or two different functions. For example, *mi* = my; *mí* = me. Others to watch out for are:

cuál/cual	sé/se
dé/de	sí/si
él/el	té/te
qué/que	tú/tu

- In general, *palabras agudas* have a written accent only if they end in *n, s,* or a vowel:

    café león **but**   arroz animal

- *Palabras llanas* have a written accent only if they *don't* end in *n, s,* or a vowel:

    cárcel lápiz **but**   chocolate tijeras

- *Palabras esdrújulas* and *sobresdrújulas* always have a written accent.

- Notwithstanding the general rules given above, a written accent is used on the weak vowel of a diphthong whenever necessary to show correct pronunciation:

    ba-úl (to show that it is not pronounced /baul/)
    te-ní-a (to show that it is not pronounced /te-nia/)

PALABRA POR PALABRA

*These specific **alternatives to broad, overused words** will put precision and sparkle into your students' writing.*

Instead of *decir*, have them choose

admitir	comentar	enumerar	mentir	proponer
advertir	comunicar	exclamar	murmurar	quejarse
afirmar	conceder	explicar	musitar	razonar
alabar	confesar	exponer	narrar	recordar
alardear	contestar	expresar	negar	refunfuñar
alegar	corregir	gritar	notificar	regañar
amonestar	cotorrear	gruñir	opinar	responder
anunciar	criticar	indicar	precisar	revelar
añadir	cuchichear	informar	predecir	rogar
asegurar	chillar	insinuar	preguntar	señalar
asentir	declamar	insistir	preguntarse	soltar
aseverar	declarar	intimar	proclamar	soplar
avisar	dejar escapar	jactarse	proferir	subrayar
balbucir	denunciar	jurar	prometer	sugerir
berrear	desahogarse	lanzar	pronunciar	susurrar
citar	elogiar	mencionar	propagar	vociferar

Instead of *bueno* or *bonito*

acertado	caritativo	estupendo	hábil	primoroso
adecuado	clemente	excelente	honrado	prodigioso
admirable	compasivo	excepcional	impresionante	que es una
afable *(person)*	conveniente	exquisito *(food)*	incomparable	delicia *(food)*
agradable	delicioso *(food)*	extraordinario	inolvidable	sabroso *(food)*
alegre	de rechupete	fantástico	inteligente	sensacional
amable *(person)*	*(food)*	favorable	magnánimo	sin par
apropiado	deseable	fenomenal	magnífico	sublime
bárbaro *(slang)*	divertido	fino	maravilloso	súper *(slang)*
bello	eficaz	formal	óptimo	único
benévolo	especial	formidable	perfecto	valioso
benigno	espléndido	generoso	pintiparado	virtuoso
bondadoso	estimable	gustoso	portentoso	*(person)*

Instead of *malo* or *feo*

abominable	desafortunado	escandaloso	inicuo	nocivo
bajo	desastroso	falso	lamentable	penoso
calamitoso	desdichado	fastidioso	maldito	pérfido
catastrófico	desgraciado	feroz	maléfico	perjudicial
culpable	deshonesto	funesto	maligno	pernicioso
dañino	despiadado	inadecuado	malintencionado	ruin
dañoso	detestable	indigno	mezquino	siniestro
deficiente	enfadoso	infame	miserable	tenebroso
deplorable	enojoso	infausto	molesto	torvo
	equivocado	infeliz	monstruoso	travieso
	errado	ínfimo	nefando	vil

Instead of *hacer*

acabar	echarse a	formar
armar	efectuar	fundar
causar	ejecutar	llevar a cabo
concluir	elaborar	obrar
confeccionar	emprender	ocasionar
construir	establecer	producir
crear	fabricar	realizar
darse a	forjar	

Instead of *poner*

acomodar	estacionar	plantar
colocar	fijar	sentar
depositar	instalar	situar
descansar	meter	ubicar
establecer	montar	

Instead of *estar*

andar por	mantenerse
encontrarse	seguir
habitar	tener su domicilio
hallarse	vivir

Instead of *gustar*

agradar	deleitar	hacer gracia
atraer	divertir	halagar
complacer	encantar	hechizar
contentar	entretener	placer
dar gusto	gratificar	satisfacer

Instead of *mirar* or *ver*

acechar	divisar	observar
advertir	echar la vista	ojear
atisbar	encima	percibir
avistar	echar un vistazo	presenciar
contemplar	entrever	reconocer
curiosear	escudriñar	reparar
descubrir	espiar	vigilar
distinguir	notar	vislumbrar

Instead of *ir* or *irse*

abandonar	caer *(slang)*	encaminarse	llegarse	presentarse
acudir	caminar	entrar	marcharse	recorrer
alejarse	coger la calle	escabullirse	partir	salir
alzar velas	comparecer	estirarse	pasar a	salir disparado
andar	darse una	evaporarse	peregrinar	subir
aparecer	vuelta por	huir	ponerse en	trasladarse
arrancar	deslizarse	largarse	camino	vagar
asistir	dirigirse	liar el petate		
bajar	echarse a correr			

SEÑALES DE TRÁNSITO

*There are certain words and phrases that act as signposts in a piece of writing, signaling to the reader the general drift or flow. Mastery of these **transitional words and phrases** will help your students become both better readers and better writers.*

Amplification or explanation/ Amplificación o aclaración
además
aun
en otras palabras
en otros términos
en términos más sencillos
es decir
o sea
pues bien
también
y

Concession/Concesión
admitiendo que
a pesar de que
aun cuando
aunque
dado que
si bien
suponiendo que

Contrast/Contraste
al contrario
a pesar de que
aun cuando
aunque
no obstante
no . . . sino
pero
por el contrario
por una parte . . . por otra
por un lado . . . por otro
por . . . que sea
sea lo que sea
si bien . . . también
sin embargo

Insistence/Insistencia
de todas maneras
de todos modos

Recapitulation/ Recapitulación
en conclusión
en fin

Result or consequence/ Resultado o consecuencia
así pues
así que
con el resultado de que
conque
de aquí
de forma que
de manera que
de modo que
en consecuencia
por consiguiente
por eso
por esto
por lo tanto
por tanto
puesto que
ya que

Sequence/Secuencia
anteriormente
antes
antiguamente
desde que
después
en cuanto
enseguida
en tanto que
finalmente
hasta ahora
luego
mientras
por último
posteriormente
primero
segundo

Similarity/Semejanza
así mismo
de la misma manera
del mismo modo
igualmente

BRIGHT IDEA

Practice with Transitional Words   Once you have discussed transitional words and phrases with your students, you can develop cloze paragraphs like the following to give them more of a feel for how these important devices work. Students copy the paragraph, filling in the blanks with suitable choices from lists you display.

Julio quería comprarse un tocadiscos. Pero no quería un modelo barato. _____(contraste)_____, quería uno que costaba $200, _____(resultado)_____ se consiguió un empleo cortando céspedes los fines de semana. _____(concesión)_____ sabía que le tomaría bastante tiempo ahorrar el dinero, _____(insistencia)_____ estaba decidido a hacerlo. _____(recapitulación)_____, en unos cuantos meses, pudo comprarse el tocadiscos.

MINIGLOSARIO EDUCACIONAL

*Proper terminology is essential in any instructional context. On the following pages you will find the **Spanish equivalents for some English terms commonly encountered in several content areas.** To facilitate its use, this miniglossary has been divided into content areas—Science, Social Studies, and Math—with several subtopics within each content area.*

CIENCIAS

The human body/ El cuerpo humano

anvil yunque
aorta aorta
appendix apéndice
aqueous humor
  humor ácueo
arteries arterias
auditory canal
  conducto auditivo
auditory nerve
  nervio auditivo
auricle pabellón
bile bilis
blood sangre
brain cerebro
canine teeth caninos
cartilage cartílago
cerebellum cerebelo
cheek mejilla
chest pecho
circulatory system
  circulación
cochlea caracol
cornea córnea
cranium cráneo
Eustachian tube
  trompa de Eustaquio
eardrum tímpano
esophagus esófago
eye ojo
forearm antebrazo
gums encías
hammer martillo
heart corazón
heel talón
hips caderas
incisors incisivos
index finger dedo índice

inner ear oído interno
iris iris
jaw mandíbula
joint conyuntura
kidney riñón
knee rodilla
labyrinth laberinto
large intestine
  intestino grueso
larynx laringe
lens cristalino
little finger
  dedo meñique
liver hígado
lung pulmón
middle ear oído medio
middle finger
  dedo de en medio
molars molares
muscle músculo
nail uña
navel ombligo
optic nerve
  nervio óptico
outer ear oído externo
palate paladar
pupil pupila
retina retina
ribs costillas
ring finger dedo anular
saliva saliva
shoulder hombro
skeleton esqueleto
skin piel
small intestine
  intestino delgado
sole of foot
  planta del pie
spinal column
  columna vertebral

spleen bazo
stirrup estribo
stomach estómago
taste buds papilas
  gustativas
thigh muslo
throat garganta
thumb dedo gordo,
  pulgar
tissue tejido
tonsils amígdalas
vitreous humor
  humor vítreo

Cell biology/ Biología celular

algae algas
amoeba ameba
bacteria bacteria
cell célula
cell division
  división celular
cell membrane
  membrana celular
chloroplast cloroplasto
cytoplasm citoplasma
embryo embrión
fungus hongo
microbe microbio
nucleus núcleo
organism organismo
paramecium paramecio
protozoon protozoo
virus virus
yeast levadura

Ecology/Ecología

amphybian anfibio
biosphere biosfera
carbohydrate
   carbohidrato
carnivore carnívoro
cold-blooded
   de sangre fría
community comunidad
decompose
   descomponerse
evolution evolución
extinct extinto
fat grasa
habitat hábitat
hardy resistente
herbivore herbívoro
herd rebaño
life cycle ciclo vital
mammal mamífero
metamorphosis
   metamorfosis
migration migración
mutualism mutualismo
nymph ninfa
omnivore omnívoro
parasite parásito
photosynthesis
   fotosíntesis
predator predador
prey presa
protein proteína
reproduce reproducirse
reptile reptil
rodent roedor
seed semilla
shelter abrigo
species especie
spore espora
starch fécula
warm-blooded
   de sangre caliente

Plant biology/ Biología de las plantas

annual anual
anther antera
aquatic acuático
bark corteza
bud yema
cambium cámbium
chlorophyll clorofila
cotyledon cotiledón
dicot dicotiledóneo
egg óvulo
embryo embrión,
   germen
evergreen siempreverde
fertilizer fertilizante,
   abono
filament filamento
geotropism geotropismo
monocot
   monocotiledóneo
ovary ovario
perennial perenne
petal pétalo
petiole peciolo
phloem líber
phototropism
   fototropismo
photosynthesis
   fotosíntesis
pistil pistilo
pollen polen
pollination polinización
primary root
   raíz principal
secondary root
   raíz secundaria
sepal sépalo
stamen estambre
stoma estoma
style estilo
xylem xilema

General astronomy/ Astronomía general

autumnal equinox
   equinoccio de otoño
axis eje
black hole
   agujero negro
comet cometa (el)
elliptical elíptico
Great Bear Osa Mayor
heavenly body
   cuerpo celeste
Little Bear Osa Menor
light year año de luz
Milky Way Vía Láctea
magnitude magnitud
meteor meteoro
meteorite meteorito
North Star
   estrella polar
nebula nebulosa
orbit órbita
radiotelescope
   radiotelescopio
revolution revolución
revolve girar
rotation rotación
satellite satélite
summer solstice
   solsticio de verano
supergiant supergigante
telescope telescopio
vernal equinox
   equinoccio vernal
winter solstice
   solsticio de invierno

Planets/Planetas

Earth Tierra
Jupiter Júpiter
Mars Marte
Mercury Mercurio
Neptune Neptuno
Pluto Plutón
Saturn Saturno
Uranus Urano
Venus Venus

Sun and Moon/ El Sol y la Luna

corona corona
crater cráter
eclipse eclipse
first quarter (waxing)
  cuarto creciente
full moon luna llena
nucleus núcleo
photosohere fotosfera
solar eruption
  erupción solar
solar spot mancha solar
third quarter (waning)
  cuarto menguante

Space travel/ Vuelo espacial

astronaut astronauta
booster rocket
  cohete acelerador
gravity gravedad
rocket cohete
space shuttle
  transbordador espacial

Sound/Sonido

acoustics acústica
decibel decibel
echo eco
frequency frecuencia
intensity intensidad
medium medio
receiver receptor
sonic wave onda sonora
stethoscope estetoscopio
supersonic supersónico
transmitter emisor
ultrasonic ultrasónico
vacuum vacío
vibrate vibrar

Light/Luz

angle ángulo
concave mirror
  espejo cóncavo

convex mirror
  espejo convexo
focal point punto focal
focus foco
lense lente
mirage espejismo
opaque opaco
prism prisma
refraction refracción
shade sombra
translucent translúcido
transparent
  transparente

States of matter/ Estados de la materia

boil hervir
boiling point
  punto de ebullición

Celsius Celsio
centigrade centígrado
condensation
  condensación
contract contraerse
crystal cristal
degree grado
dissolve disolver
evaporate evaporar
expand expandirse
Fahrenheit Fahrenheit
freezing point
  punto de congelación
gas gas
gaseous gaseoso
liquid líquido
melt fundirse, derretirse
solid sólido
solution solución
steam vapor
thermometer
  termómetro

BRIGHT IDEA

Film Strips And Whirligigs Two important concepts in science are sequence and cause-and-effect. Here are a couple of fun ideas.

To demonstrate sequence, students will enjoy making "filmstrips." For the showing, they can use Blackline Master 10 on page 165 and glue it on oaktag or heavy cardboard, cutting slits as shown. The master serves as the holder for the "film strip," a long series of pages that have been glued or taped together. The pages contain drawings that show the different phases of a sequence. They could show the stages of a plant growing from seed to fruit-bearing tree. Or they could illustrate the sequence from the sprouting of a wheat seed to bread on the table.

Cause-and-effect can be graphically shown by cards pasted to the end of craft sticks or tongue depressors. On one side of the card a student may illustrate and label an effect, such as *Hay día y noche.* On the other side would appear a drawing of the earth and *La tierra gira sobre su eje.* These "whirligigs" could be used in independent study or in a cooperative-learning pair as flashcards.

ESTUDIOS SOCIALES

Geography/ Geografía

antarctic antártico
arctic ártico
axis eje
basin cuenca
bay bahía
beach playa
canyon cañón
coast costa
conservation
    preservación
continent continente
crater cráter
desert desierto
dune duna
Earth's crust
    corteza terrestre
earthquake terremoto
erosion erosión
fault falla, quebrada
fertile fértil
forest bosque
frigid zone zona glacial
glacier glaciar
gulf golfo
hemisphere hemisferio
hill loma, colina
island isla
isthmus istmo
jungle selva
lake lago
latitude latitud
longitude longitud
magma magma
mantle manto
mountain montaña
mountain chain
    cordillera
nucleus núcleo
peninsula península
plains llanura
pole polo
prairie pradera
river río

steppe estepa
swamp pantano
temperate zone
    zona templada
terrain terreno
tropical zone
    zona tropical
volcano volcán

Maps/Mapas

antarctic circle
    círculo antártico
arctic circle
    círculo ártico
atlas atlas
border frontera
cardinal directions
    puntos cardinales
city map plano de
    una ciudad
compass rose rosa de
    los vientos, rosa náutica
Equator ecuador
east este, oriente
globe globo terráqueo
key clave
latitude latitud
longitude longitud
North Pole Polo Norte
north norte
prime meridian
    primer meridiano
South Pole Polo Sur
scale escala
south sur
state capital
    capital estatal
symbol símbolo
Tropic of Cancer
    Trópico de Cáncer
Tropic of Capricorn
    Trópico de Capricornio
west oeste, occidente

Concept Maps Another way to reinforce both vocabulary and concepts in the content areas is through the use of concept maps. General directions for conducting a concept-map brainstorming appear on pages 98–99, and several examples appear on pages 108–126. (Particularly good examples for the content areas are the ones for **Animales**, pages 108–109, **País**, pages 118–119; and **Plantas**, pages 120–121.)

Government/ Gobierno

chief executive
    mandatario
citizen ciudadano
city council
    concejo municipal
city council member
    concejal
city hall ayuntamiento
congress congreso
constitution constitución
county condado
democracy democracia
dictatorship dictadura
election elección
governor gobernador
house of representatives
    cámara de diputados,
    cámara de
    representantes
mayor alcalde, alcaldesa
political party
    partido político
president presidente
representative
    representante, diputado
republic república
senate senado
senator senador
supreme court corte
    suprema, tribunal
    supremo

The community/ La comunidad

airport aeropuerto
apartment building
 edificio de apartamentos
bakery panadería,
 dulcería
bank banco
barbershop peluquería,
 barbería
church iglesia
clinic clínica
firehouse cuartel o
 estación de bomberos
hospital hospital
laundry tintorería
movie theater cine
museum museo
neighborhood barrio
office building
 edificio de despachos
park parque
pharmacy farmacia
police station cuartel o
 estación de policía
post office
 oficina de correos
railroad station
 estación de ferrocarril
repair shop
 taller de reparaciones
restaurant restaurante
school escuela
shoe store zapatería
shop tienda
skyscraper rascacielos
supermarket
 supermercado
synagogue sinagoga
theater teatro
warehouse almacén

Professions/ Profesiones

accountant contador
actor actor
actress actriz
architect arquitecto
artist artista
baker panadero
banker banquero
barber barbero,
 peluquero
bookkeeper tenedor
 de libros
business person
 negociante
carpenter carpintero
cashier cajero
chef cocinero
chemist químico
coach entrenador
cowboy vaquero
dentist dentista
dietician dietista
doctor médico
draftsperson dibujante
driver chofer
editor redactor
electrician electricista
engineer ingeniero
farmer agricultor,
 campesino
fireman bombero
flight attendant
 aeromoza
forest ranger
 guardabosque
furniture maker
 ebanista
gardener jardinero
geologist geólogo
grocer abarrotero,
 bodeguero (Cuba)
housewife ama de casa
jeweler joyero
journalist periodista
judge juez
lawyer abogado,
 licenciado
librarian bibliotecario

lifeguard salvavidas
mail carrier cartero
marine biologist
 biólogo marítimo
mason albañil
mechanic mecánico
medical assistant
 asistente médico
musician músico
nurse enfermero
oceanographer
 oceanógrafo
painter pintor
pharmacist boticario,
 farmacéutico
photographer fotógrafo
plumber plomero
professor profesor
real estate agent
 agente de bienes raíces
reporter reportero
scientist científico
sculptor escultor
secretary secretario
shoemaker zapatero
social worker asistente
 social, trabajador social
surgeon cirujano
teacher maestro
treasurer tesorero
truck driver camionero
typographer tipógrafo
veterinarian veterinario
waiter mesero, camarero
writer escritor

Professional Fun A fun way
to teach the names of professions to young children is
through the song game *"San
Severín."* Instructions and a
score appear on page 54.

The family/La familia

ancestor antepasado
aunt tía
brother hermano
children hijos
cousin primo, prima
daughter hija
father padre
goddaughter ahijada
godfather padrino
godmother madrina
godson ahijado
granddaughter nieta
grandfather abuelo
grandmother abuela
grandson nieto
great-granddaughter biznieta
great-grandfather bisabuelo
great-grandson biznieto
great-grandmother bisabuela
husband esposo, marido
mother madre
nephew sobrino
niece sobrina
parents padres
relatives parientes
sister hermana
son hijo
uncle tío
wife esposa, mujer

The home/El hogar

attic desván
basement sótano
bathroom baño
bedroom recámara, cuarto
dining room comedor
garage garaje
hallway corredor, pasillo
kitchen cocina
living room sala

MATEMÁTICAS

General vocabulary/Vocabulario general

arithmetic aritmética
average promedio
borrow tomar prestado
calculate calcular
carry over llevar
check comprobar
column columna
compare comparar
compass compás
count contar
decimals decimales
equation ecuación
estimate calcular aproximadamente
even number número par
exponent exponente
fraction fracción
group agrupar
hundreds centenas
hundredths centésimas
increase aumentar
lessen disminuir
measure medir
millions millones
odd number número impar
ones unidades
operation operación
pair aparear
place colocar (verb), lugar (noun)
position posición
probability probabilidad
random al azar
replace sustituir
round off redondear
solve resolver
square root raíz cuadrada
take away quitar
tens decenas
tenths décimas
thousands millares
thousandths milésimas

Addition/Suma

add sumar, añadir
addend sumando
plus más
sum suma

Subtraction/Resta

difference diferencia
minuend minuendo
minus menos
subtract restar
subtrahend substraendo

Multiplication/Multiplicación

associative property propiedad asociativa
distributive property propiedad distributiva
factor factor
factoring factorización
least common multiple mínimo común múltiplo
multiple múltiplo
product producto
times por

Division/División

divide dividir
divided by entre
dividend dividendo
divisible divisible
divisor divisor
maximum common divisor máximo común divisor
quotient cociente
remainder residuo
whole division división de números enteros

Geometry/Geometría

angle ángulo
area área
circle círculo
cone cono
cube cubo
cylinder cilindro
diagonal diagonal
diameter diámetro
hexagon hexágono
line línea
parallel paralelo
parallelogram paralelogramo
pentagon pentágono
perimeter perímetro
point punto

polygon polígono
protractor transportador
quadrilateral cuadrilátero
radius radio
rectangle rectángulo
right angle ángulo recto
sphere esfera
square cuadrado
triangle triángulo

Computers/ Computadoras

character carácter
command instrucción, orden
cursor cursor
data datos, información

data processing informática
digit dígito
disk disco
edit revisar, corregir
file archivo, fichero
hardware "hardware"
input entrada
key tecla
keyboard teclado
library biblioteca
memory memoria
output salida
printer impresora
process tratar
program programa
software software
storage almacenamiento
terminal terminal
update actualizar

SIEMPRE LISTOS

Classroom Vocabulary There are vocabulary problems that are not content-area-related! What do you call a VCR in Spanish? *Bi-ci-ar*? So you "talk around it," calling it perhaps *la máquina* or even *esa cosa*. We hope this list, although far from complete, will enrich your classroom vocabulary in Spanish.

bandage curita, venda
binder carpeta
block bloque
bookcase librero, estante
brad puntilla
bulletin board tablón de anuncios
cabinet alacena, armario, gabinete
cart carretilla
cassette recorder grabadora de "cassettes"
chalk tray borde o repisa del pizarrón
chart stand portacarteles
clothes rack percha, perchero
computer computadora
construction paper papel de colores
counter top mostrador
craft stick paleta
crayon lápiz de color, creyón
earphones audífonos
easel caballete
faucet pila, llave
first-aid kit botiquín de primeros auxilios
folder cuaderno

glue pegadura, goma de pegar
hole punch perforadora
light switch interruptor
listening post puesto de escucha
movie projector proyector (de películas)
overhead projector retroproyector
paint brush pincel, brocha
paper clip presilla, sujetapapeles
paper cutter cortapapeles, guillotina
paper towel toalla de papel, papel absorbente
paste engrudo
pin alfiler
projection screen pantalla
record player tocadiscos
rug alfombra
shelf (boards) anaqueles, repisas
sink fregadero, lavamanos
slide projector proyector de transparencias
sponge esponja
staple grapa
stapler engrapadora
string hilo *(thread-like)*, cuerda *(cord)*
tagboard cartulina
tape cinta adhesiva
tape dispenser dispensador de cinta adhesiva
thermostat termostato
VCR videograbadora
wall outlet enchufe, tomacorriente
watercolors acuarela
yarn estambre

PART 4

TEMAS HASTA POR GUSTO

Some good ideas for implementing a theme-oriented approach to teaching, and ten fruitful themes that can get you started

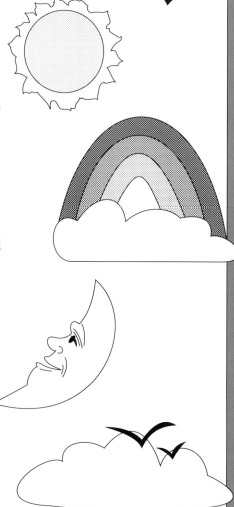

Start with *sky*. With your class, brainstorm a list of words, phrases, topics, titles, and names that you associate with *sky*. Break your list into categories and use them to make a concept map like those on pages 108–127. Add new items to the map as they occur to the group. When you have finished, you will probably have covered every writing surface in your classroom! *Sky* is a big subject.

Big, yes, but it demonstrates clearly how students might explore a single theme across many content areas. Such a thematic approach is one of the best ways of implementing a whole-language program or generating extension activities within a conventional curriculum.

The advantages of organizing lessons and activities around a theme are that the theme provides a rich context for learning sessions and gives a common purpose to a variety of activities. Themes also allow for purposeful collaborative learning and can accommodate individual differences without singling out individual students. They offer many alternatives for organizing time, materials, and resources. So how do you begin?

First, select a theme that fits your students' ages and interests. A good way to motivate exploration of a theme is to involve students in reading a fine literature selection or previewing content-area books that establish the theme. For younger students, read aloud a suitable book. The ten terrific themes highlighted on pages 108–127 include bibliographies of books guaranteed to create interest. (See **Siempre Listos** on page 149 for a listing of the major companies from which fine Spanish-language children's literature is available.)

Once students are motivated, brainstorm a concept map with the class. Prompt and encourage students as needed so that your concept map is at least as broad as those given on pages 108–127. Then, using the subcategories, plan how the theme can be developed across a wide range of subject areas.

Next, select theme-related books to read aloud to your students, and/or for your students to read independently. The Listening and Speaking section of the **Bright Idea** on pages 102–107 offers a wealth of ideas for oral-interpretation activities to do with the books recommended in the bibliography for each theme.

Most important, get familiar with the theme yourself. Review basic concepts and make sure you've got a good handle on all the essential terminology, in Spanish. Encyclopedia articles usually present a good basic review of subject-area topics. For Spanish terminology, consult a good Spanish-English dictionary, or Spanish textbooks (which may be available from subject-area teachers in your school).

In the ten sample theme planners presented on pages 108–127, we have done some of this preliminary work for you, giving a sample concept map, listing some theme-related books, and providing special vocabulary or teaching ideas for the theme.

Whether you take advantage of these themes or brainstorm ones of your own, the **Bright Idea** on pages 102–107 will help you plan theme-related activities in any subject area. Just put on your thinking cap and read down the list of activities, keeping your theme in mind. This process will spark one theme link after another, and soon you'll have an enviable chain of creative, theme-related activities. The "Theme Links" provided give just a few specific applications for the ten themes highlighted on pages 108–127. The Quick-Reference Chart that appears on pages 100–101 will help you find specific activity ideas for any of our ten themes in any of the subject areas listed. Simply look up the key word or words from the chart in the alphabetically ordered listings under the subject area. The "Theme Link" for that entry will contain a specific suggestion for that theme.

Once you have planned your theme and its cross-curriculum activities, schedule time and provide resources for the activities. This may seem difficult if you are tied to a set textbook, but you might begin by infusing the theme into each subject area at least once a week. Allow the theme to become the focus for storytime, a writing assignment, a science experiment, or a math activity. You may also wish to set up learning stations where individuals, partners, or teams can engage in theme-related projects during scheduled blocks of time. A good way of giving unity and structure to a thematic approach is to have students work toward a culminating activity: a class fair, an exhibit, an open house during parents' week, or a performance, for example.

How the theme is incorporated into the curriculum remains up to you. A theme is such a versatile learning tool, ideas for ways to use it will just keep coming. In fact, the sky's the limit!

99

QUICK-REFERENCE CHART FOR THEME-RELATED ACTIVITIES

THEMES	ART	LANGUAGE ARTS	MATH

1. Animales	• flip books
	• modeling clay
	• paper and paper-carton structures
		R: • syllable rhymes
		    • word games
		L/S: • oral interpretation
		W: • a day in the life . . .
		    • conversations
		    • word pictures
			• graphs and charts
			• measurements
			• money
			• time

2. Arquitectura	• collage
	• paper and paper-carton structures
		L/S: • oral interpretation
		W: • a day in the life . . .
		    • biographical fiction
		    • mystery stories
		    • public notices
			• graphs and charts
			• measurements
			• money

3. Comunicación	• modeling clay
	• paper and paper-carton structures
		R: • word games
		L/S: • oral interpretation
		W: • a day in the life . . .
		    • biographical fiction
		    • mystery stories
		    • public notices
			• graphs and charts
			• money
			• time

4. Dentro	• flip books
	• paper and paper-carton structures
		R: • word games
		L/S: • oral interpretation
		W: • a day in the life . . .
		    • mystery stories
		    • word pictures
			• graphs and charts
			• money
			• time

5. Noche	• collage
	• flip books
		L/S: • oral interpretation
		W: • biographical fiction
		    • conversations
		    • public notices
		    • word pictures
			• graphs and charts
			• measurements
			• money

6. País	• collage
	• flip books
	• modeling clay
	• paper and paper-carton structures
		R: • word games
		L/S: • oral interpretation
		W: • a day in the life . . .
		    • biographical fiction
		    • mystery stories
			• measurements
			• money
			• time

7. Plantas	• flip books
	• modeling clay
	• paper and paper-carton structures
	• spatter painting
		L/S: • oral interpretation
		W: • a day in the life . . .
		    • biographical fiction
		    • word pictures
			• measurements
			• time

8. Sentidos	• spatter painting	L/S: • oral interpretation
		W: • conversations
		    • mystery stories
		    • public notices
		    • word pictures
			• estimating
			• measurements

9. Tiempo	• flip books
	• paper and paper-carton structures
	• spatter painting
		L/S: • oral interpretation
		W: • a day in the life . . .
		    • mystery stories
		    • word pictures
			• estimating
			• time

10. Yo	• collage
	• spatter painting
		R: • word games
		L/S: • oral interpretation
		W: • a day in the life . . .
		    • conversations
		    • public notices
		    • word pictures
			• estimating
			• graphs and charts
			• measurements
			• money
			• time

How To Use This Chart: Look up each key word under the subject-area head in the listings on pages 102–107 to find the specific activity. In the Language Arts section, R=Reading, L/S=Listening and Speaking, W=Writing.

MUSIC & DANCE	SCIENCE	SOCIAL STUDIES	THEMES
• fingerplay • *rondas* • unusual instruments	• field trips • habitats and ecosystems • observing and recording	• campaign or fund-raising drive • career-information day • maps • time lines, time spirals	**1. Animales**
• unusual instruments	• field trips • habitats and ecosystems • problem solving	• campaign or fund-raising drive • maps • pen pals • time lines, time spirals	**2. Arquitectura**
• *rondas*	• health and nutrition • observing and recording • problem solving	• campaign or fund-raising drive • career-information day • pen pals • time lines, time spirals	**3. Comunicación**
• unusual instruments	• field trips • health and nutrition • observing and recording	• career-information day • pen pals • time lines, time spirals	**4. Dentro**
• fingerplay	• field trips • health and nutrition • problem solving	• career-information day • maps	**5. Noche**
• expressive or interpretive dancing	• health and nutrition • problem solving	• pen pals • time lines, time spirals	**6. País**
• unusual instruments	• field trips • habitats and ecosystems • observing and recording • "smell-a-rama"	• campaign or fund-raising drive • career-information day • maps	**7. Plantas**
• expressive or interpretive dancing	• health and nutrition • observing and recording • "smell-a-rama"	• campaign or fund-raising drive • pen pals	**8. Sentidos**
• fingerplay • *rondas*	• field trips • habitats and ecosystems • observing and recording	• campaign or fund-raising drive • career-information day	**9. Tiempo**
• unusual instruments	• health and nutrition • observing and recording • "smell-a-rama"	• maps • pen pals • time lines, time spirals	**10. Yo**

BRIGHT IDEA

Theme Teaching in the Subject Areas Use this inventory of activities in Art, Language Arts, Math, Music, Science, and Social Studies as an idea source for planning theme-related activities across the curriculum. The "Theme Links" give suggestions on how the activities may be related to some of the themes highlighted on pages 108–127: Animales, Arquitectura, Comunicación, Dentro, Noche, País, Plantas, Sentidos, Tiempo, Yo. Theme names appear in boldface.

ART

- cloth puppets/*títeres de tela* ◊ Stitch together two identical pieces of cloth shaped like a three-fingered glove. Turn the cloth inside out and press seams. Add felt hands. Glue or sew on scraps of cloth and trim to make the puppet face and clothing.

- collage/*collage* ◊ Students create mixed-media pictures using buttons, cloth, photographs, etc.

Theme Link *Collage offers a technique for impressionistic portrayals. For **Arquitectura,** try original interpretations of ancient buildings; for **Noche,** interpretations of the night sky; for **País,** of traditional costumes; for **Yo,** a self-portrait.*

- construction paper puppets/ *títeres de papel de colores* ◊ Fold a sheet of 8" x 12" construction paper into three equal parts; then fold again as shown in

Step 2. Fold the two new edges down as shown in Step 3. Students paint, color, or glue on facial details. Then they make their puppet talk by slipping four fingers into the top open space, and the thumb into the bottom.

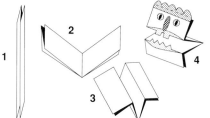

- costumes/*trajes o disfraces*
- diorama/*diorama*
- drawings—pen, pencil/ *dibujos—a pluma, a lápiz*
- egg decorating/*decorar huevos*
- face painting/*pintarse la cara*
- finger painting/*pintar con los dedos*
- finger puppets/*títeres de dedos* ◊ Cut two identical felt shapes, large enough to slip over a child's finger. Stitch the shapes together. Sew on facial and body details.

- flip books/*libros animados* ◊ Students draw each movement of an action on a separate page and put them in sequence—as in animated art. Students staple the pages together, then flip them to see the illusion of motion.

Theme Link *Children will flip over flip books! For **Animales,** try a running animal; for **Dentro,** moving gears; for **Noche,** the phases of the moon; for **País,** a waving flag; for **Plantas,** a blossoming flower; for **Tiempo,** a tree losing its leaves in autumn.*

- gourd craft/*artesanías hechas con güiras*
- kites/*cometas o papalotes*
- masks/*máscaras*
- mobiles/*móviles*
- modeling clay/*plastilina*

Theme Link *Consider using modeling clay for making these objects or replicas: for **Animales** or **Plantas,** fossil prints; for **Comunicación,** clay tablets with messages; for **País,** artifacts of a primitive culture, or topographical maps.*

- murals/*murales*
- paper and paper-carton structures/*estructuras de papel o cartón*

Theme Link *For **Animales** or **Plantas,** model dioramas of natural environments; for **Arquitectura** or **Dentro,** make doll houses and furniture; for **Arquitectura** or **País,** model dioramas of buildings or other living environments; for **Comunicación,** make televisions; for **País,** make paper dolls; for **Tiempo,** make windmills.*

- paper-bag puppets/ *títeres de bolsas de papel* ◊ Students place fingers in the bottom of a small paper bag and, by moving the folded bottom up and down, can make the bag talk! Paint a face on the bag as shown. The fold becomes the dividing line of the mouth.
- papier-mâché/*papier-mâché*
- pasta jewelry/*joyas hechas con pastas* ◊ Students string painted pieces of pasta on yarn.
- piñatas/*piñatas*

- plastic-foam puppets/*títeres de plástico* ◊ Sharpen the end of a dowel or craft stick, coat the sharpened end with glue, and stick it into a plastic-foam ball. Glue or color facial details on the plastic-foam ball. Tie a cross stick to the craft stick for arms. Use cloth scraps to dress the puppet.

- pop-up books/*libros tridimensionales* ◊ See publishing ideas on pages 138–141.
- posters/*carteles*
- potato prints/ "*papagrabados*" ◊ Students carve designs on the flat surface of a cut potato and print them on paper using ink or tempera paints of different colors.
- seed paintings/*diseños hechos con semillas* ◊ Students "paint" with glue, then sprinkle seeds over the wet glue to create textured designs or pictures.
- sock puppets/*títeres de calcetines* ◊ Cut a slit across the foot of the sock as shown. Then stitch a band of felt around the inside of the slit to make the puppet's mouth. Stitch eyes and hair onto the heel of the sock.

cut

felt insert

- spatter painting/*diseños hechos salpicando pintura*

Theme ⎯⎯⎯⎯⎯

Link *Spatter painting and finger painting are good for illustrating such evocative themes as: for* **Plantas** *or* **Tiempo,** *the seasons; for* **Sentidos** *or* **Yo,** *reactions to a piece of music or other sensory experiences; for* **Tiempo,** *a stormy sky, or wind and water; for* **Yo,** *moods or feelings.*

- "stained glass"/*"vidrio de color"* ◊ Students use an iron to press flowers or colored tissue paper between sheets of wax paper, and hang the papers in a sunny window.
- stick puppets/*títeres de paleta* ◊ Students draw and color puppet figures on heavy paper, cut out the figures and glue them to craft sticks.
- "tapestries"/*"tapices"* ◊ Students make pictures by gluing or sewing yarn and cloth to sheets of paper.
- wreaths/*guirnaldas o coronas* ◊ Students cut circles out of the centers of paper plates. They lace-stitch dried grasses and leaves to the doughnut-shaped plates and attach ribbons, acorns, etc.
- yarn paintings/*diseños hechos con estambre*

LANGUAGE ARTS

See Part 5, pages 128–149, for a wide range of Language Arts activities. The following ideas are especially suitable for theme-based curricula.

Reading

- book fairs/*ferias de libros*
- book talks/*charlas de libros*
- collaborative projects/*proyectos que requieren colaboración* ◊Students form groups to discuss ideas, themes, novels, poems, or short stories; to recreate story episodes by turning them into short stories or dramatic theater; to research theme-related subtopics; or to work on graphic displays. Groups report back to the whole class.
- comparisons of facts and fictionalizations/*comparaciones de hechos y ficcionalizaciones* ◊ Students compare the facts of a historical event or a natural process with fictionalized, imaginative versions.

- comparisons of versions/*comparaciones de versiones* ◊ Students discuss different versions of a familiar tale.
- research/*investigación* ◊ Children research a topic in the library, individually or in groups. The product may be a written report, an oral presentation, a dramatization, etc.
- shared retelling/*narración en grupo* ◊ Students select a favorite story and retell it as a group with the teacher acting as scribe.
- syllable rhymes/*rimas silábicas*

Theme ⎯⎯⎯⎯⎯

Link *Theme-related rhymes that are easy to memorize can help beginning readers remember phonetic elements. In* **Animales,** *for example, try rhymes like this one:*

   for o: Oso, oso,
       no seas celoso.
For a resource of rhyming words, see pages 28–29.

- word collections/*colecciones de palabras* ◊ See **Bright Idea** on page 25.
- word games/*juegos de palabras*

Theme ⎯⎯⎯⎯⎯

Link *For* **Animales,** *students could invent names for new animals created by genetic engineering—for example, an animal that's half* cocodrilo *and half* hipopótamo *might be called a* cocopótamo *or* hipodrilo; *for* **Comunicación,** *students could make up acronyms for special groups, for example,* ACTO: Asociación Central de Teatros Originales; *for* **Dentro,** *you could try a word search in which students look for short words inside a longer word, for example, in* maravilla: mar, villa, a, vi, ara; *for* **País** *and* **Yo,** *students could create a crossword puzzle based on their heritage or personal history.*

Listening and Speaking

See pages 142–145 for a catalog of listening and speaking activities. It is easy to relate these activities to any theme. In addition, you might use the theme-related books listed on pages 108–127 to develop **oral-interpretation** activities.

Theme

Link For **Animales,** you might have students do an oral interpretation of Nadarín. Students make a set of felt fish in different colors and sizes to match those of the book. Then they take turns retelling the story as they move the fish on, off, and around the felt board.

For **Arquitectura,** have students make a plastic-foam puppet (see page 103) of the main character of El tesoro de Azulín, and simple props to retell the story and make up new adventures.

For **Comunicación,** have students make two stick puppets (see page 103)—one from newsprint, one from blank paper—of the paper man in El hombrecillo de papel. Students can also make other stick puppets, perhaps resembling themselves, for the kids in the crowd scenes of the book. Personal photographs work well for the faces.

For **Dentro,** help students adapt the text of Lanzaderas espaciales to make it into a TV documentary. Copy pictures from the book, paste them on a roll of butcher paper, and "scroll" them through a TV screen made from a box.

For **Noche,** you might make your students into stars for an interpretation of La noche más oscura del mundo. Have students make paper-plate masks: one for the moon, one for the comet, and the rest for the stars. Students wear their masks as each recites one page of the book. Each star might even have a reversible mask: one side shiny, one dull.

For **País,** students might memorize and recite poems from ABC de Puerto Rico.

For **Plantas,** use shadow puppets (see page 116) to retell the story of El chivo en la huerta. Make the goat's back legs movable so it can kick on cue.

For **Sentidos,** all you need is a few cardboard props and an imaginary elephant for an interpretation of Tommy y el elefante. One student reads the narration as the others act out the parts and chime in with dialogue.

For **Tiempo,** students might make scenery and costumes, and dramatize the wonderful Tajín y los siete Truenos.

For **Yo,** students might make sock puppets (see page 103) of the main characters of Los seis deseos de la jirafa, El patito feo, or El dragón y la mariposa. The puppets may be used to accompany dramatic readings of the tales or to make up new adventures for the animals.

Making puppet stages offers additional opportunites to explore the themes of **Arquitectura** and **Dentro.**

Writing

No writing project is complete until it is published. Creative ideas for publishing what students write are listed in Part 5 of El Sabelotodo, pages 138–141.

- a day in the life of . . ./un día típico en la vida de un . . .

Theme

Link For **Animales,** try a day in the life of a lonesome beaver; for **Arquitectura,** of a train station; for **Comunicación,** of an overworked disc jockey; for **Dentro,** of a coal miner; for **País,** of a child in a foreign country; for **Plantas,** of a neglected house plant; for **Tiempo,** of a cloud; for **Yo,** of a personal (and favorite) article of clothing.

- biographical fiction/ficción biográfica

Theme

Link Have students write a first-person narrative in which they pretend to be the friend, acquaintance, or servant of a famous person. For **Arquitectura,** try Antonio Gaudí; for **Comunicación,** Alexander Graham Bell; for **Noche,** Cheherezada (the heroine of the Arabian Nights or Las mil y una noches); for **País,** Benito Juárez or Simón Bolívar; for **Plantas,** Luther Burbank.

- conversations/conversaciones

Theme

Link For **Animales,** students could write a conversation between a bear and a fox; for **Noche,** between the sun and the moon; for **Sentidos,** between an ear and an eye; for **Yo,** between one's present self and one's future self.

- fictional diaries/*diarios fictivos* ◊ Students assume a persona and write fictional diaries such as *Diario de un taxista.*
- letters/*cartas* ◊ Students could write letters expressing their feelings about wildlife preserves, curfew, Winter Olympics, etc., to the editor of the daily newspaper.
- magazines/*revistas* ◊ Students combine their writing efforts to produce a theme-related magazine.
- mystery stories/*cuentos de misterio*

  Theme

  Link *For **Arquitectura** or **Dentro**, make it a mystery that involves a building with secret passages and rooms; for **Comunicación**, one that involves a secret code; for **País**, the loss of a national treasure; for **Sentidos**, a mysterious scent; for **Tiempo**, a "dark and stormy night."*

- name game/*juego de nombres* ◊ Students create new names for known things.
- picture captions/*pies o leyendas de fotos* ◊ Students write one or more sentences about a picture or series of pictures.
- poetry/*poesía* ◊ Students write theme-related poems.
- pourquoi tales/*leyendas explicativas* ◊ See discussion on page 129.
- public notices/*avisos al público*

  Theme

  Link *For **Arquitectura**, invite students to write a public notice urging people to save a public site or building; for **Comunicación**, a notice urging them to listen to or watch a favorite broadcast; for **Noche**, to play it safe at night; for **Sentidos**, to quit smoking; for **Yo**, to clean up the school yard. See also "campaigns and fund-raising drives" under Social Studies activities.*

- travel folders/*panfletos turísticos* ◊ Students write travel folders that focus on sites related to the theme.
- word pictures/*dibujos con palabras*

  Theme

  Link *After thoroughly researching the topic, students use the research to write a word picture or description. For **Animales**, it might be a description of a chipmunk's burrow; for **Dentro** or **Sentidos**, of the inside of a refrigerator; for **Noche**, of a city street at night; for **Plantas** or **Tiempo**, of a garden in the winter; for **Sentidos**, of a special dessert; for **Yo**, of a favorite friend or relative.*

MATH

- estimating/*estimar*

  Theme

  Link *Don't underestimate your students' ability to make accurate guesses. For **Sentidos**, have them estimate distances or the weights and sizes of objects in a "touch box"; for **Tiempo**, temperature; for **Yo**, the cost of feeding and caring for themselves for one month.*

- graphs and charts/*gráficas y tablas*

  Theme

  Link *Students can make graphic records of survey results about many different topics: for **Animales**, try surveys about the most popular pets; for **Arquitectura**, about preferred styles of architecture; for **Comunicación**, favorite TV shows; for **Dentro** or **Yo**, the most looked-for qualities in a friend; for **Noche**, people's bedtimes.*

- measurements—length, area, volume, weight, speed, time/*medidas—longitud, área, volumen, peso, velocidad, tiempo*

  Theme

  Link *Students have to measure to compare things. For **Animales**, try comparing animal speed records or life spans; for **Arquitectura**, building heights and areas; for **Noche**, distances between various stars and planets; for **País**, speeds of different modes of transportation between cities; for **Plantas**, germination times for different seeds; for **Sentidos** or **Yo**, reaction times.*

- money/*dinero*

  Theme

  Link *Students' money sense will increase as they engage in the following activities. For **Animales**, they could research the costs of owning different pets; for **Arquitectura** or **Dentro**, tour a bank; for **Comunicación**, participate in a fund-raising drive or compare costs of commercial air-time; for **Comunicación** or **Noche**, compare day and night telephone rates; for **Dentro** or **Sentidos**, identify coins by touch; for **País**, chart weekly foreign-exchange rates; for **Yo**, they could play store.*

- problem solving/*resolver problemas*
- scale models/*modelos a escala*
- tangram/*rompecabezas geométrico chino* ◊ This is a puzzle formed from seven geometric shapes. Students use all the shapes, without cutting or overlapping them, to make recognizable pictures.

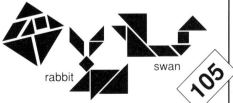

rabbit   swan

BRIGHT IDEA

- time measurement, time schedules, time telling/*medir el tiempo, horarios, leer el reloj*

  Theme ——————
  Link *Students will have a good time exploring these timely topics: for **Animales**, **Plantas**, or **Tiempo**, seasonal clocks; for **Comunicación**, broadcast-programming schedules; for **Dentro**, clockworks; for **Dentro** or **Yo**, body rhythms and circadian clocks; for **País**, time zones; for **Yo**, favorite unusual timepieces, such as metronomes, cuckoo clocks, sundials, stopwatches, hourglasses, water clocks, etc.*

MUSIC & DANCE

- background music/*música de fondo* ◊ Students play or select background music for choral readings, pantomimes, or dramatic presentations.
- expressive or interpretive dancing/*baile expresivo o interpretativo*

  Theme ——————
  Link *For **País**, create new dance steps to a traditional folk melody; for **Sentidos**, dance to sounds from nature.*

- fingerplay/*juegos con los dedos* ◊ See Part 2, page 51, for some examples of finger games.

  Theme ——————
  Link *For **Animales**, you can use "Los pollitos"; for **Noche**, "La luna"; for **Tiempo**, "La viejita"; all on page 51.*

- homemade musical instruments/*instrumentos musicales caseros*
- lip-sync a recording/*doblar un disco*
- marching to music/*marchar al son de música* ◊ Students make drill-team formations to march music.

106

- music fair/*feria musical* ◊ Students share ethnic songs, dances, recordings, and musical instruments.
- nature sounds/*sonidos de la naturaleza* ◊ Students record nature sounds. The sounds can be inserted into choral readings or songs.
- *rondas* and other traditional children's songs/*rondas y otras canciones infantiles tradicionales* ◊ See Part 2, pages 47–69.

  Theme ——————
  Link Rondas *and other children's songs can often be linked to a given theme. Considering just the songs given in Part 2: for **Animales**, you could use "Los elefantes" (page 49), "Los diez perritos" (page 49), and "La pájara pinta" (page 52); for **Comunicación**, you could use "Matarile rile ró" (page 55); for **Tiempo**, you could use "Que llueva" (page 68).*

- singing telegram/*telegrama musical*
- unusual instruments/*instrumentos raros*

  Theme ——————
  Link *You can give your students a sound start with unusual instruments. For **Animales**, they could practice with bird calls and bird whistles; for **Arquitectura** or **Dentro**, they could practice making sounds with interior surfaces, such as walls, floors, doors, windows, etc.; for **Plantas**, students could make gourd drums and maracas; for **Yo**, they could transform their own bodies into instruments by clapping, slapping, clicking, snapping, tapping, thumping, stomping, whistling, etc.*

- wind chimes/*carillón de viento* ◊ Students make musical chimes using twigs, shells, etc.

SCIENCE

- categorizing/*categorizar*
- classifying/*clasificar*
- dissecting/*disecar*
- extrasensory experiments/*experimentos extrasensoriales* ◊ Students conduct experiments to test the validity of theories of extrasensory perception. For example, students may try to communicate "telepathically" a number they are thinking of or a card they are holding.
- field trips/*excursiones*

  Theme ——————
  Link *Go "on site" to see the sights. For **Animales**, visit an animal shelter; for **Arquitectura**, a construction site; for **Dentro**, a film-developing lab; for **Noche**, a planetarium; for **Plantas**, an arboretum or a nursery; for **Tiempo**, a weather station.*

- habitats and ecosystems/*habitáculos y ecosistemas*

  Theme ——————
  Link *Transform a carton, cage, jar, or aquarium into a specialized environment, such as: for **Animales**, a straw skep (beehive); for **Arquitectura**, a hamster playground; for **Tiempo** or **Plantas**, a solar-heated hothouse.*

- health and nutrition/*salud y nutrición* ◊ Students make nutritious menus and recipes.

  Theme ——————
  Link *Serve up some tasty assignments, such as: for **Comunicación**, reviewing a cooking show; for **Dentro**, experimenting with substitute ingredients; for **Noche**, creating healthy bedtime snacks; for **País**, researching how recipes reflect a nation's crops and climate; for **Sentidos** or **Yo**, exchanging ethnic recipes.*

- magnification/*magnificación*
  ◊ Students use magnifying glasses or microscopes to view common objects.
- nature walks/*caminatas al aire libre*
- observing and recording/ *observar y llevar registros*

Theme———————
Link *For **Animales** or **Dentro**, students will gain insights as they observe terrariums, aquariums, ant farms, worm jars, etc.; for **Comunicación**, they can observe body language; for **Plantas** or **Tiempo**, the effects of sunlight on plants; for **Sentidos** or **Yo**, the effects of sounds and colors on emotions.*

- problem solving/*resolver problemas*

Theme———————
Link *Explore possible solutions to theme-related problems, such as: for **Arquitectura**, ways to create space in a small room; for **Comunicación**, new ways to communicate with people who are speech- or hearing-impaired; for **Noche**, ways to improve sleeping environments; for **País**, new ways to use natural resources.*

- skeletons/*esqueletos* ◊ Students use tagboard and brads to make skeletons with movable parts.
- "smell-a-rama"/*"aromálogo"*

Theme———————
Link *These activities will exercise your students' scent sense. For **Plantas** or **Sentidos**, students can make potpourris; for **Sentidos**, they can try to identify various scents with their eyes closed, or to distinguish between various scents in a bakery, garden, etc.; for **Yo**, they can try using scented candles to create moods or settings.*

SOCIAL STUDIES

- campaign or fund-raising drive/ *campaña publicitaria o para reunir fondos*

Theme———————
Link *There are countless drives you can launch, if you're really driven. For **Animales**, students might launch a drive to promote the humane treatment of animals; for **Arquitectura**, to restore a local historical building or to promote equal access for the handicapped; for **Comunicación**, students could join a local arts-and-crafts festival to raise funds for a needed project; for **Plantas**, they could plant a public garden of local native plants; for **Sentidos**, they could launch a drive to reduce land, water, air, or noise pollution; for **Tiempo**, a drive to promote awareness of safety procedures and community services during weather emergencies.*

- career-information day/*día de información sobre las carreras y oficios* ◊ The musical game *"San Severín"* may be used to teach trades and professions. An explanation of the game appears on page 54. A list of trades and professions appears on page 95.

Theme———————
Link *Students write job descriptions, such as: for **Animales** or **Plantas**, a conservationist; for **Comunicación** or **Tiempo**, a TV weather forecaster; for **Dentro**, a computer programmer; for **Noche**, an astronomer.*

- field trips/*excursiones*
- films/*películas*
- maps/*mapas* ◊ Start with a map of your neighborhood or city. Use an overhead projector to enlarge the area you wish to use.

Then overlay a grid to help students copy the area.

Theme———————
Link *For **Animales**, maps may show bird-watching sites; for **Arquitectura**, a real-estate tour or a "heritage trail"; for **Noche**, safe nighttime routes; for **Plantas**, a garden tour; for **Yo**, routes from house to school.*

- pen pals/*amigos por correo*

Theme———————
Link *For **Arquitectura**, **País**, or **Yo**, suggest that students exchange photographs with their pen pals; for **Comunicación**, they could exchange taped or filmed messages; for **Dentro**, each student could write a personality profile of his or her pen pal; for **País** or **Tiempo**, students could follow weather conditions in the pen pal's country; for **Sentidos**, they could exchange recipes with pen pals.*

- photographs/*fotografías*
- public-opinion polls/*encuestas sobre la opinión pública*
- questionnaires/*cuestionarios*
- slide shows/*presentaciones de transparencias*
- talks by guest speakers/*charlas presentadas por invitados*
- time lines, time spirals/ *cronologías gráficas*

Theme———————
Link *Time lines and spirals are excellent for showing the evolution, progression, or sequence of events of many subjects. For **Animales**, a time line or spiral could show the age of dinosaurs; for **Arquitectura**, various architectural periods; for **Comunicación**, the growth of communications technology; for **Dentro**, the birth of a volcano; for **País**, the dates of explorations, discoveries and famous lives; for **Yo**, a personal history.*

Animales

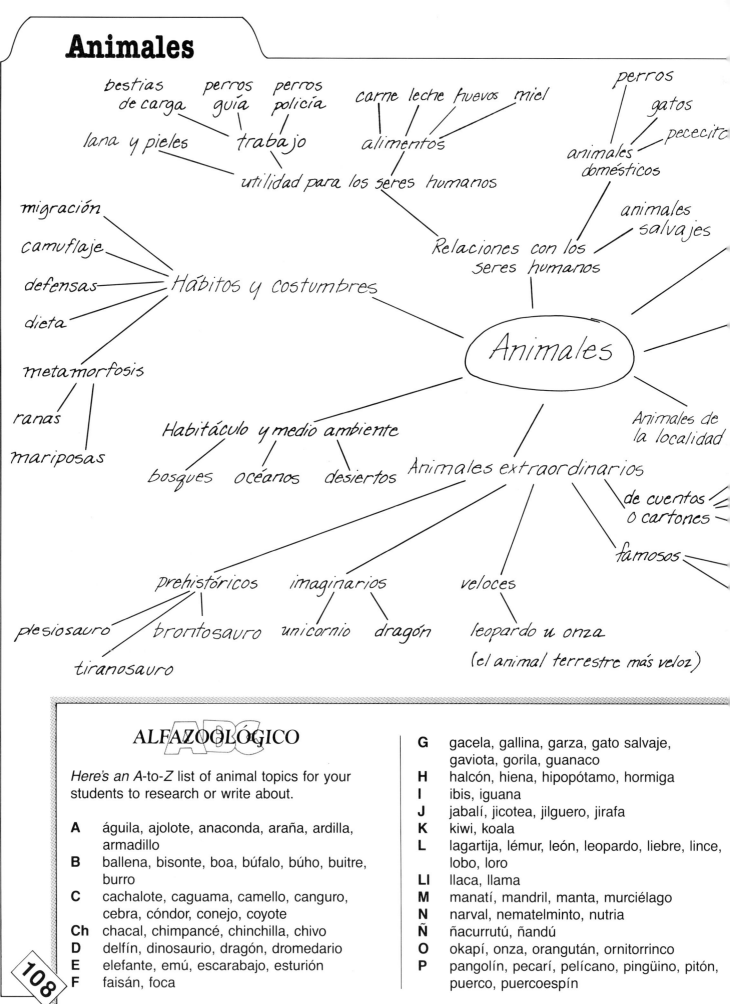

bestias de carga

perros guía

perros policía

lana y pieles

trabajo

utilidad para los seres humanos

carne   leche   huevos   miel

alimentos

perros

gatos

pececito

animales domésticos

animales salvajes

Relaciones con los seres humanos

migración

camuflaje

defensas

dieta

metamorfosis

ranas

mariposas

Hábitos y costumbres

Animales

Habitáculo y medio ambiente

bosques   océanos   desiertos

Animales extraordinarios

Animales de la localidad

de cuentos o cartones

famosos

prehistóricos

imaginarios

veloces

plesiosauro

brontosauro

tiranosauro

unicornio

dragón

leopardo u onza

(el animal terrestre más veloz)

ALFAZOOLÓGICO

Here's an A-*to-*Z *list of animal topics for your* students to research or write about.

A	águila, ajolote, anaconda, araña, ardilla, armadillo
B	ballena, bisonte, boa, búfalo, búho, buitre, burro
C	cachalote, caguama, camello, canguro, cebra, cóndor, conejo, coyote
Ch	chacal, chimpancé, chinchilla, chivo
D	delfín, dinosaurio, dragón, dromedario
E	elefante, emú, escarabajo, esturión
F	faisán, foca

G	gacela, gallina, garza, gato salvaje, gaviota, gorila, guanaco
H	halcón, hiena, hipopótamo, hormiga
I	ibis, iguana
J	jabalí, jicotea, jilguero, jirafa
K	kiwi, koala
L	lagartija, lémur, león, leopardo, liebre, lince, lobo, loro
Ll	llaca, llama
M	manatí, mandril, manta, murciélago
N	narval, nematelminto, nutria
Ñ	ñacurrutú, ñandú
O	okapí, onza, orangután, ornitorrinco
P	pangolín, pecarí, pelícano, pingüino, pitón, puerco, puercoespín

antílope gigante   canguro rojo   tigre

Animales en peligro de extinción

murciélago

mamíferos — ballena

serpiente

reptiles — cascabel

boa

Clasificación

anfibios — rana

pingüino

aves

avestruz

Mickey Mouse

Lassie

Carlota (la araña de
      Las telarañas de Carlota,
      de E.B. White)

Platero

Laika (el primer animal en viajar
      al espacio)

Koko (el gorila que habla por señas)

Q	quetro, quetzal
R	rana, ratón, rinoceronte, ruiseñor
S	salamandra, salmón, sapo, serpiente cascabel, sinsonte, sunsún
T	tapir, tecolote, tiburón, tlacuache, topo, tortuga, tucán
U	unicornio
V	vaca, venado, víbora, vicuña
W	wombat
Y	yac, yegua
Z	zarigüeya, zopilote, zorrillo, zorro

A good resource of animal photos is the Life Nature Library *(New York: Time-Life Books).*

THEME-RELATED BOOKS

Armellada, Fray Cesáreo de. *El cocuyo y la mora: Cuento de la tribu pemón.* Caracas: Ekaré, 1980. Legend which illustrates life cycles of firefly and blackberry. **1:RA/2–3:IR***

Belpré, Pura. *Santiago.* New York: Frederick Warne, 1969. Story of Puerto Rican boy's nostalgia for a pet chicken he has had to leave behind when he moves to New York. **2:RA/3–4:IR**

Clark, Mary Lou. *Dinosaurios.* Trans. Lada Kratky. Chicago: Childrens Press, 1984. About dinosaurs and their disappearance. **3–4:IR**

García Sánchez, J.L. and Pacheco, M.A. *El zoo fantástico.* Madrid: Altea. Collection includes *El avestruz, El búho, El camello, El canguro, El cocodrilo, El elefante, El gorila, El hipopótamo, La jirafa, El león, El lobo, El oso, El tigre,* and *El zorro.* **K–1:RA/2:IR**

Lionni, Leo. *Nadarín.* Trans. Ana María Matute. Barcelona: Lumen, 1981. Story about ocean life, illustrated in collage. **K:RA/1–2:IR**

Marzot, Janet and Livio. *Las liebres blancas.* Barcelona: Lumen, 1981. A sensitive story about how a rabbit helps a dejected artist rediscover his craft. **3:RA/4–6:IR**

Rimas y Risas. Carmel: Hampton-Brown, 1989. Series of four Big Books with repetitive, predictable stories that feature animals as their protagonists. Includes *Los seis deseos de la jirafa, Sale el oso, El chivo en la huerta,* and *La gallinita, el gallo y el frijol* **K:RA/1:IR**

White, E.B. *Las telarañas de Carlota.* Barcelona: Noguer, 1988. The Spanish version of this classic tells of a friendship between a spider and a pig. **2:RA/3–5:IR**

See also *El río de los castores,* p. 111; *Julie y los lobos* and *El dolor de muelas de Alberto,* p. 113; *El oso más elegante,* p. 115; *Frederick,* p. 123; *El Búho en su casa,* p. 125.

*****K, 1, 2,** etc., refer to grade level;
RA = Read Aloud; **IR** = Independent Reading

Arquitectura

metal

plástico

cemento

cristal

manufacturados

Edificio "Empire State"

Taj Mahal

Alhambra

Torre Eiffel

Obras famosas

estadios

ayuntamientos

museos y teatros

Edificios públicos

Materiales

naturales

adobe

madera

piedra

Arquitectura

Arquitectos famosos

Frank Lloyd Wright

Antonio Gaudí

Christopher Wren

Carreras y oficios

albañil

arquitecto

carpintero

plomero

Estilos de arquitectura

griego

romano

asiático

español del suroeste de E.E.U.U.

VOCABULARIO ARQUITECTÓNICO

These are some of the words that may come up during your discussion of this theme.

Estilos de arquitectura
barroco, churrigueresco, gótico, moderno, mudéjar, ojival, románico

Términos técnicos
arcada, arco, arquitrabe, basa, bóveda, columna, cornisa, cúpula, fachada, nave, pilastra, pináculo, portada

Materiales
adobe, cemento, hormigón armado, ladrillo, madera, mampostería, mármol, piedra

Casas de animales
acuario, colmena, corral, cueva, cubil, guarida, hormiguero, jaula, madriguera, nido

Estructuras
casa, chalé, choza, fuente, edificio, gazebo, hospital, hotel, iglesia, mansión, pagoda, palacio, patio, puente, rascacielos, teatro, templo, torre

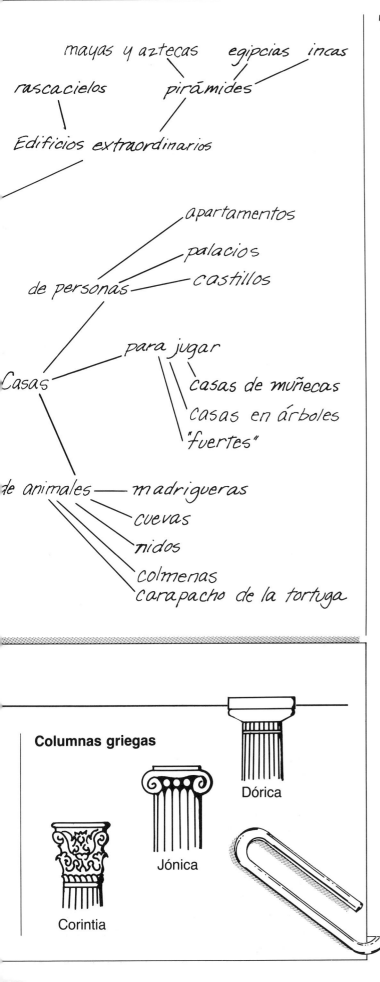

mayas y aztecas   egipcias   incas

rascacielos   pirámides

Edificios extraordinarios

de personas —— apartamentos
                 palacios
                 castillos

Casas —— para jugar
         casas de muñecas
         casas en árboles
         "fuertes"

de animales —— madrigueras
               cuevas
               nidos
               colmenas
               carapacho de la tortuga

Columnas griegas

Dórica

Jónica

Corintia

THEME-RELATED BOOKS

Kurusa. *La calle es libre.* Caracas: Ekaré, 1981. The children of this neighborhood have no park to play in. Their parents join together to make them one. **1–2:RA/3–4:IR***

Martínez Gil, Fernando. *El río de los castores.* Madrid: Noguera, 1985. Beavers are one of the great builders of nature. In this story, they must protect their river and homes against humans. **4:RA/5–6:IR**

McKissack, Pat. *Los incas* and *Los mayas.* Trans. Robert Franco. Chicago: Childrens Press, 1987. Information about these cultures' civilization and architecture, with full-color photos. **1–3:IR**

Montserrat, Salvador. *El arte de hacer cometas de papel.* Barcelona: Labor, 1985. Basic guide to building a paper kite. Children learn from experience the requirements of seeing a construction through from conception to completion. **2:IR**

Poulet, Virginia. *El tesoro de Azulín.* Chicago: Childrens Press, 1988. Trans. Lada Kratky. A little blue bug, Azulín, finds objects of various shapes and constructs something special from them. **K:RA/1:IR**

Puncel, María. *El círculo y sus cosas.* Madrid: Altea. Part of a series about the adventures of some common shapes. Other books in the series: *El cuadrado y sus cosas, El rectángulo y sus cosas, El triángulo y sus cosas.* **K:RA**

Puncel, María. *El viejo teatro.* Madrid: Altea, 1981. Neighborhood children learn how theaters are constructed as they search for one of their friends who has gotten trapped inside a space under the stage. **K:RA/1–2:IR**

Sales, Francesc. *Hansel y Gretel.* Barcelona: Hymsa, 1987. Retelling of the Grimms' story of the children who outsmart the witch who lives in a gingerbread house. **1–2:RA/3–4:IR**

See also, *Clara y el caimán,* p. 115.

---

*K, 1, 2, etc., refer to grade level;
RA = Read Aloud; **IR** = Independent Reading

Comunicación

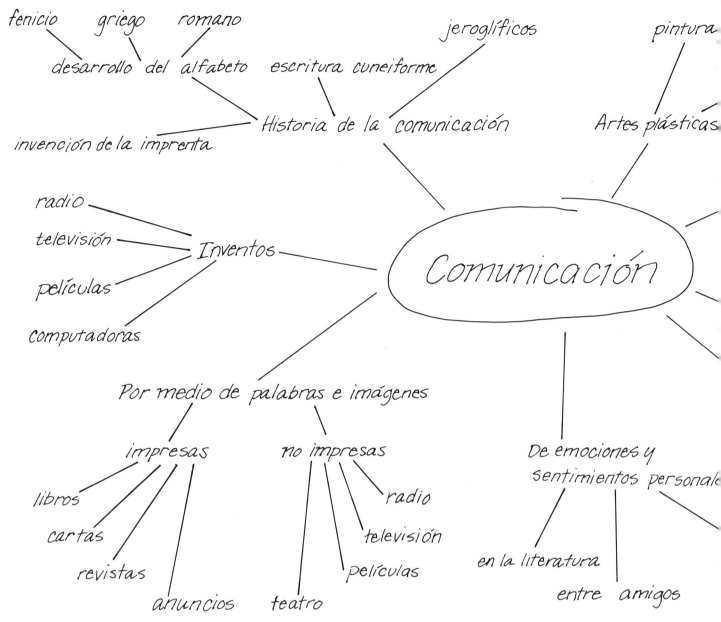

fenicio griego romano

desarrollo del alfabeto escritura cuneiforme jeroglíficos pintura

invención de la imprenta Historia de la comunicación Artes plásticas

radio

televisión Inventos Comunicación

películas

computadoras

Por medio de palabras e imágenes

impresas no impresas De emociones y sentimientos personales

libros radio

cartas televisión en la literatura

revistas películas entre amigos

anuncios teatro

112

BRIGHT IDEA

Codes Codes *(cifras* or *claves)* are a good way to create interest in this theme because they involve students in the essence of communication—sending, receiving, and understanding messages.

Select a code at the appropriate difficulty level (some examples follow) and show students how it works. Then encode *(cifrar)* some secret messages *(mensajes en clave)* and let the group decipher *(descifrar)* them. Students will soon be creating codes on their own.

- A simple code, suitable for very young children, is to use random word spacing. The message ME VOY MAÑANA, for example, might be written: MEVO YMAÑ ANA.

- More complicated is the system that divides the letters of a message into groups, ignoring word spacing, and then reverses the order of the letters in each group. With this system, the message ME VOY MAÑANA might first be divided into MEVOYM AÑANA, and then reversed: MYOVEM ANAÑA.

- For older students, try alphabetic codes. Numbers 1 to 28 can simply be assigned to the letters of the alphabet in order, forward ($1 = A$, $28 = Z$) or backward ($1 = Z$, $28 = A$), and then

escultura   arquitectura

Onomatopeyas —— Véase la lista de la página 26.

danza de las abejas

canto de las ballenas

En los animales

ruidos de los delfines

Sin palabras —— gestos

banderas de señales

señales de humo

escritura pictográfica

dibujos en las paredes de las cuevas

entre miembros de la familia

substituted for the letters in a message. Or, a chart like this one can be created to establish each letter's number. Here, for example, *G* is 23 (the combination of row 2 and column 3. As with the other codes, encoding messages without regard for word spacing makes them more challenging.

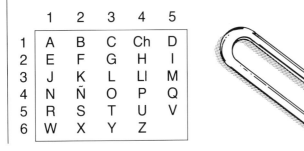

	1	2	3	4	5
1	A	B	C	Ch	D
2	E	F	G	H	I
3	J	K	L	Ll	M
4	N	Ñ	O	P	Q
5	R	S	T	U	V
6	W	X	Y	Z	

THEME-RELATED BOOKS

Alonso, Fernando. *El hombrecillo de papel.* Valladolid: Miñón, 1978. A little man made of newspaper communicates the values of brother-hood and life, in contrast to the headlines on the newspaper he is made of. **K–1:RA/2–3:IR***

Carballido, Emilio. *El pizarrón encantado.* Mexico City: CIDCLI, n.d. Humorous story in which a boy finds a magic chalkboard on which he writes words which cause strange things to happen. **4–5:IR**

George, Jean Craighead. *Julie y los lobos.* Madrid: Alfaguara, 1980. Julie, an Eskimo girl, gets lost in the tundra. She learns how to sur-vive by imitating the wolves she observes. A touching story of interspecies communication. **5–6:IR**

Joslin, Sesyle. *¿Qué se dice, niño?* New York: Young Scott, 1966. Humorous book on good manners in any situation. Illustrated by Maurice Sendak. **K–1:RA/1–2:IR**

Vázquez-Vigo, Carmen. "La gata" in *Animales charlatanes.* Madrid: Noguer, n.d. A little cat who goes out adventuring learns that there's more to communication than just words. **2– 3:RA**

Williams, Barbara. *El dolor de muelas de Alberto.* Trans. Alma Flor Ada. New York: Dutton, 1977. Because turtles don't have teeth, Albert's family won't believe him when he says he has a toothache. Finally, with a little communication, his grandmother discovers the problem. **K–1:RA/2–3:IR**

See also *El cocuyo y la mora: Cuento de la tribu pemón* and *Santiago,* p. 109; *El chivo en la huerta* and *¡Manzano, manzano!* p. 121; *Tommy y el elefante,* p. 123; *Tajín y los Siete Truenos, El Búho en su casa,* and *Historia de una nube que era amiga de una niña,* p. 125; *Harquin, el zorro que bajó al valle, Elefantito y Gran Ratón, Kalamito,* and *¿Tienes tiempo, Lidia?,* p. 127.

---

*K, 1, 2, etc., refer to grade level;
RA = Read Aloud; **IR** = Independent Reading

Dentro

lava   magma

terremotos   volcanes   núcleo de la Tierra

geología

túneles

minas

cuevas

oleoductos y gasoductos

tubos de un órgano

acueductos

ferrocarriles subterráneos

De la Tierra

Tubos y tuberías

de un edificio

de una planta

de un insecto

Sección transversal

Dentro

¿Cómo funciona un reloj? — Mecanismos

¿Cómo funciona un motor?

¿Cómo funciona una computadora?

Del ser humano

enfermedades   funcionamiento

De carteras o bolsos

dinero

tarjetas de crédito

tarjetas de identidad

pasaportes

sentimientos

sistema nervioso

alegría   tristeza

DENTRO DE MUCHO

Here's a list of research topics on which your students can get the inside information.

- ¿Qué ocurre dentro de una arteria cuando hay un ataque al corazón?

- ¿Cómo funciona una computadora? . . . un automóvil? . . . una bomba de agua?

- ¿Cómo pueden las serpientes tragarse enteros animales mucho más grandes que ellas?

- ¿Cómo pueden los gatos sacar y meter las uñas?

- ¿Cómo es el interior de un ciclón? . . . de un tornado?

- ¿Qué hacen los canguritos dentro del marsupio del canguro?

- ¿Cómo sería un viaje al centro de la Tierra?

- ¿Se forma el pollito de la clara o de la yema del huevo?

- ¿Cómo es el interior de la Estatua de la Libertad?

- ¿Sería posible vivir en el interior de una ballena?

- ¿Cómo es un hormiguero por dentro? ¿Cómo es una colmena?

índice y organización
/
/ encuadernación
/ /
De un libro —————— imprenta

zarigüeyas   koalas   canguros
/   /   /
-Animales marsupiales o didelfos

pasadizos secretos
/
e edificios ____ el interior de una pared
\ (detalles de construcción)
\
Cómo son las fábricas
por dentro

stema circulatorio ———— sistema digestivo
\
una expedición por todo
el cuerpo humano en una nave
pequeñísima que viaja
por el sistema circulatorio

And here are some story starters fit to spark some "core" literature.

- Después de la lluvia del otro día, me fijé en un charco y vi a una pulga buceando en el centro. . . .

- Me caí en un hueco que va de un lado a otro de la Tierra. . . .

- En el interior de la cueva, todo estaba oscuro. De pronto, tropecé con un . . .

- Moví la pequeña estatua y el librero rodó hacia un lado, revelando un pasadizo secreto que—estaba segura—me llevaría al tesoro del conde Telur. . . .

THEME-RELATED BOOKS

Barbot, Daniel. *Un diente se mueve.* Caracas: Ekaré, 1980. When Clarisse discovers a first loose tooth inside her mouth, her imagination runs wild. **K–1:RA/2–3:IR***

Blocksma, Mary. *Chirrinchinchina, ¿qué hay en la tina?* Trans. Lada Kratky. Chicago: Childrens Press, 1988. Predictable book about the many toys a boy can fit inside his bathtub. **K–1:RA/1:IR**

Blocksma, Mary. *El oso más elegante.* Trans. Alma Flor Ada. Chicago: Childrens Press, 1986. Predictable book about a bear who gets inside the perfect set of clothes—almost. **K–1:RA/1:IR**

Felix, Monique. *Historia de la ratita encerrada en un libro.* Caracas: María de Mase, 1981. A little mouse who has been shut up in a book makes her way into the world. **K–1:Wordless Picture Book**

Friskey, Margaret. *Lanzaderas espaciales.* Trans. Lada Kratky. Chicago: Childrens Press, 1984. Describes life inside a space shuttle and how it operates. **3–5:IR**

Puncel, María. *Clara y el caimán.* Madrid: Altea, 1983. Adventures of a pet alligator that goes down the toilet and gets stuck inside the city pipes. **4:RA/5–6:IR**

Robles Boza, Eduardo (Tío Patota). *Rollito.* Mexico City: Trillas, 1983. Rollito the caterpillar is Xóchitl's friend. Rollito wraps himself in a cocoon to await metamorphosis. Will Xóchitl see him again? **3:RA/4:IR**

Solé Serra, Luz. *La pelota.* Barcelona: Hymsa, 1985. A soccer ball gets tired of being shut up inside a closet every night, escapes, gets thrown into the trash, and is rescued by a poor boy. **3:RA/4–5:IR**

See also *El viejo teatro,* p. 111; *El dolor de muelas de Alberto,* p. 113; *El chivo en la huerta,* p. 121; *El Búho en su casa,* p. 125.

***K, 1, 2,** etc., refer to grade level;
RA = Read Aloud; **IR** = Independent Reading

se reparten los diarios

se limpian los calles

se hornea el pan

Cosas que ocurren mientras uno duerme

expansión y contracción de la madera

aire acondicionado o calefacción

refrigerador

de la casa

mapache

lechuzas

de animales

Sonidos nocturnos

catres

hamacas

colchón de agua

colchón de muelles

Camas

La noche

¿Por qué hay día y noche?

mitos y leyendas

explicación científica

los polos: noche perpetua invernal

la luna y las estrellas

estrellas fugaces

constelaciones

Astronomía (Véase la lista de la pagina 92.)

fases de la luna

planetas

Luces

quinqués

luz eléctrica

cocuyos y luciérnagas

faros

fuegos artificiales

DARKIDEA

Shadow Stories   Shadow plays make a good culminating activity for a theme on night. The plays may be original or they may be retellings of stories or plays the children have read.

Younger students can create simple shadow figures with their hands while they improvise stories. Older students can make shadow puppets and write a script prior to the actual performance.

To make a shadow puppet, glue a cardboard shape to a craft stick as shown. Striking profile silhouettes and perforations (at the eyes, for instance) where the light can shine through make for a particularly dramatic effect.

illos

sirenas   aviones

música lejana

de la ciudad

flores que se abren de noche

insectos nocturnos

mapaches y tlacuaches

lechuzas o tecolotes

Animales y plantas nocturnos

El sueño

sueños y pesadillas

estudios científicos sobre el sueño

sonambulismo

conserjes

ente que trabaja de noche

policías   serenos   enfermeras

Whichever method you choose, when the time comes for the performance, pull down the shades, close the doors, turn off the lights, and procure a slide projector and a screen or light-colored wall on which to project the shadows. Then let your "shadow players" give free rein to their imagination.

THEME-RELATED BOOKS

Ada, Alma Flor. *Sale el oso.* Carmel: Hampton-Brown, 1989. Predictable Big Book in which a bear goes out for a walk one night and makes many surprising friends. **K–1:RA/1:IR***

Aguilera, Carmen. *Citlalli en las estrellas.* Mexico City: Novaro, 1982. Set in preconquest Mexico City, this story is about a girl who discovers her grandmother is a goddess that patrols the night sky. **5–6:IR**

Gerson, Sara. *La noche más oscura del mundo.* Mexico City: Trillas, n.d. Fantasy in which the little stars fail to wash their faces and thereby become so dim that they don't brighten the night sky. The world is unhappy, but the next night the little stars wash up and everyone is happy again. **K–1:RA/1:IR**

Lewellen, John. *La Luna, el Sol y las estrellas.* Trans. Lada Josefa Kratky. Chicago: Childrens Press, 1984. Simple introduction to astronomy, with photos and drawings. **3–5:IR**

Robles Boza, Eduardo (Tío Patota). *Chispa de luz.* Mexico City: Trillas, 1984. Modern tale about a spark of light that escapes from a light bulb and tries to find its place in the world. **4:IR**

Sendak, Maurice. *Donde viven los monstruos.* Madrid: Alfaguara, 1988. A brave boy sails to the land of the monsters in his dreams and has a good time there. **K–1:RA/2:IR**

Wylie, Joanne and David. *¿Sabes dónde está tu monstruo esta noche?* Trans. Lada Kratky. Chicago: Childrens Press, 1985. Children must find the monsters that have been hidden in the illustrations of this book. Teaches the hours from one to twelve. **K–1:RA/1:IR**

Zulani, Fausto. *La bolita azul.* Buenos Aires: Plus Ultra, 1981. A boy has a dream in which he goes searching for a blue ball he has lost. **K:RA/1:IR**

See also *Un diente se mueve,* p. 115; *La orquesta,* p. 123; *El Búho en su casa,* p. 125.

*K, 1, 2, etc., refer to grade level;
 RA = Read Aloud; **IR** = Independent Reading

País

días festivos

la familia

las escuelas

la ropa

la gente

los deportes ——— para espectadores
          ——— para participantes

La vida

regionalismos (Véanse las página 35-37.)

la pronunciación

expresiones ——— El idioma

Recursos naturales

industrias principales

turismo

productos de exportación

La economía

temporadas

cantidad de lluvia

temperatura promedio

El clima

Un país de habla española

literatura

pintura/escultura

música

cine

danza

artesanías

teatro

Las artes

Folklore
(Véanse las páginas 47-69.)

mitos
leyendas
cuentos tradicionales
juegos tradicionales
canciones tradicionales
poemas tradicionales

dichos, adivinanzas, trabalenguas, rondas, etc.

BRIGHT IDEA

International Fair An approach to exploring this theme that lends itself well to cooperative/collaborative learning techniques is to ask several small groups to focus each on a different country in preparation for an international fair (feria internacional).

For the fair, which would be held at the end of the time period allotted for the theme, students could create displays and give presentations about the country they have been studying. For example, they might:

- prepare a large topographical map, of the country, showing major mountains, rivers, lakes, etc., or create a travel brochure for it.

- create fact posters or brief almanacs (almanaques) with facts and figures about the country's population, climate, products, geography, holidays, etc.

- prepare a time line or a mural showing important events in the country's history.

- display some of its stamps, money, products, or crafts.

- prepare a dish characteristic of the country.

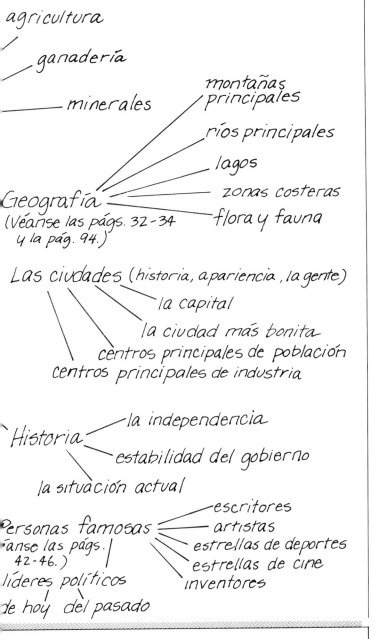

agricultura

ganadería

minerales

Geografía
(Véanse las págs. 32-34
y la pág. 94.)

montañas principales

ríos principales

lagos

zonas costeras

flora y fauna

Las ciudades (historia, apariencia, la gente)

la capital

la ciudad más bonita

centros principales de población

centros principales de industria

Historia

la independencia

estabilidad del gobierno

la situación actual

Personas famosas
(Véanse las págs.
42-46.)

escritores

artistas

estrellas de deportes

estrellas de cine

inventores

líderes políticos

de hoy   del pasado

- record first-person "Get to know me" tapes in which students take the roles of notable people from the country and give a brief explanation of their contributions.

- read aloud a folktale from the country or tell a story written by one of its famous writers.

Note: Part 2 of El Sabelotodo, which deals with the Hispanic cultural heritage and with Hispanic children's literature, contains much useful information for a theme like this. Specific lists have been referenced under topics in the concept map above.

THEME-RELATED BOOKS

Since this theme probably would not be treated in grades K–2, suggestions for theme-related books have been made only for grades 3 and above.

Behrens, June. *¡Fiesta!* Trans. Lada Kratky. Chicago: Childrens Press, 1985. Describes *Cinco de Mayo* celebrations, which commemorate the victory of Mexican troops over French invaders on May 5, 1862. **3–4:IR***

Feliciano Mendoza, Ester. *Sinfonía de Puerto Rico.* San Juan: Instituto de Cultura Puertorriqueña, 1979. Collection of Puerto Rican legends and folktales. **3–4:RA/5–6:IR**

Freire de Matos, Isabel. *ABC de Puerto Rico.* Sharon, Connecticut: Troutman Press, 1979. In the form of an *abecedario,* this collection of poems introduces many words and concepts of Puerto Rican Spanish, as well as others common to the Antilles. Beautifully designed. **3–5:IR**

Grandes biografías hispánicas. Leon, Spain: Everest. Series tells the lives and significance of major figures in Latin American history. Includes *Simón Bolívar, Benito Juárez, José María Morelos, El General San Martín, Pancho Villa,* and *Emiliano Zapata.* **6:IR**

Jacobsen, Karen. *México.* Trans. Lada Kratky. Chicago: Childrens Press, 1985. Discusses the geography and history of Mexico, as well as the ways of life of its people. **3–4:IR**

Rohmer, Harriet. *La tierra de la madre escorpión: Una leyenda de los Indios Miskitos de Nicaragua.* Trans. Rosalma Zubizarreta and Alma Flor Ada. San Francisco: Children's Books Press, 1987. Bilingual book about a courageous Miskito Indian who follows his wife from the land of the living to the spirit world. **5–6:IR**

See also *El cocuyo y la mora: Cuento de la tribu pemón,* p. 109; *Los incas* and *Los mayas,* p. 111; *Citlalli en las estrellas,* p. 117; *Tajín y los Siete Truenos,* p. 125; *La piedra del Zamuro: Un cuento de Tío Nicolás,* p. 127.

*K, 1, 2, etc., refer to grade level;
RA = Read Aloud; **IR** = Independent Reading

Plantas

nomeolvides

girasol dormidera

las flores del desfile "Rose Bow

dibujos hechos con semillas

Plantas con nombres interesantes

plantas decorativas

plantas comestibles

plantas medicinales

lianas

plantas de la selva tropical

Utilidad para los
seres humanos

plantas del desierto

cactos

Habitáculo

Biología de
las plantas

plantas acuáticas

nenúfar

Plantas como símbolos

Plantas

rosa = pasión, amor

laurel = fama

olivo = paz

el frijol que
crece hasta
llegar al cielo

Plantas extraordinarias

de cuentos

Partes

Ciclo anual de las plantas
(cambios asociados con la
distintas estaciones)

el enorme baobab africano

raíz

plantas carnívoras

tallo

pétalos

plantas decíduas

atrapamoscas o dionea

hojas

plantas anuales

ALFABOTÁNICA

Here's an A-to-Z list of plant topics for your students to research or write about.

A aguacate, ajo, alcachofa, alhelí, anón, apio, arroz, avellana

B bambú, banana, baobab, boniato, berenjena, berro, betabel

C cacahuete, calabaza, caña, cebolla, ceiba, centeno, cedro, col, castaño

Ch chicoria, chirimoya, chopo

D dátil, durazno

E ébano, espárrago, estragón

F frambuesa, fresa, frijol

G galán de noche, garbanzo, gardenia, geranio, girasol, gladiolo, guanábana

H haba, habichuela, helecho, heliotropo, henequén, higuera

I izote

J jacinto, jazmín, jícama, judía

L laurel, lechuga, lima, limón, lirio

M maíz, mamey, mango, maní, marañón, melón, melocotón, mostaza

N nabo, naranja, narciso, nenúfar, nomeolvides, nopal

Ñ ñame

O ocote, olivo, olmo, orquídea

plantas que proporcionan fibras
- para hacer papel
- tela
- cuerda o soga

árboles maderables

- plantas deciduas y plantas siempreverdes
- crecimiento
- fotosíntesis
- simbiosis

Microscópicas
- algas microscópicas
- plancton
- hongos microscópicos

Gigantes
- saguaro
- secoya

Lo que necesitan para vivir
aire   tierra   sol   agua

P	palma, papa, papaya, pepino, perejil, pimiento, pino, piña, plátano
Q	quinua
R	rábano, remolacha, roble
S	salsifí, sandía, secoya, sésamo, sorgo
T	tilo, tomate, toronja, trigo, tulipán
U	uva
V	vainilla, verdolaga
Y	yuca
Z	zanahoria, zapote

A good resource of plant photos is the Life Nature Library *(New York: Time-Life Books).*

THEME-RELATED BOOKS

Alonso, Fernando. *La Gallina Paulina y el grano de trigo.* Madrid: Alfaguara, 1975. Story tells about a grain of wheat from germination to becoming a loaf of bread. **3:IR***

Blocksma, Mary. ¡*Manzano, manzano!* Trans. Alma Flor Ada. Chicago: Childrens Press, 1986. Predictable story in which an apple tree offers an apple as a home for a worm. Teaches the seasonal cycle of fruit trees. **K–1:RA/1:IR**

Ionescu, Angela C. *Vivía en el bosque.* Valladolid: Miñón, 1982. Story of a boy who lives in the woods, at harmony with surrounding plants and animals. **5–6:IR**

Kratky, Lada Josefa. *El chivo en la huerta.* Carmel: Hampton-Brown, 1989. Predictable Big Book based on Mexican folktale about a goat who invades a chile patch. **K–1:RA/1:IR**

Levert, Claude and Solé Vendrell, Carme. *Pedro y su roble.* Valladolid: Miñón, 1979. A boy has a special caring for an oak tree and learns about its life cycle. **2:RA/3–4:IR**

Rius, María and Parramón, J.M. *Un día en . . .* Barrons: Woodbury, New York. Illustrated series about the characteristics of various places. Includes *El campo, La ciudad, El mar,* and *La montaña.* **K:RA/I:IR**

Ross, Tony. *El frijol mágico.* Trans. José Emilio Pacheco. Mexico City: Promexa, 1982. Beautiful translation of the classic tale of Jack and the beanstalk. **K–2:RA/3:IR**

Walsh, María Elena. "Sombrera" in *Había una vez.* Buenos Aires: Terra Nova, 1980. Fantasy about a tree on which hats grow. **K–2:RA**

Zendrera, C. *Yaci y su muñeca.* Barcelona: Juventud, 1984. Tale set in the Amazon jungle. A girl buries her doll, made from an ear of corn. After it rains, corn plants grow there. **K–1:RA/1–2:IR**

*****K, 1, 2,** etc., refer to grade level; **RA** = Read Aloud; **IR** = Independent Reading

Sentidos

cocina

sabores

Gusto

ferias y concursos de cocina

¿una melodía _dulce_?

¿A qué huele el verde?

Sinestesia

percepciones extrasensoriales

¿Sexto sentido?

temperatura

Tacto

textura de una superficie

Comunicación

besos   abrazos   darse la mano

alfabeto Braille

Los sentidos

biología/física del sentido de la vista

ojos de distintos animales

Vista

ojos simples y ojos compuestos de los insectos

telescopios/microscopios

ilusiones ópticas

artes visuales

escultura

pintura

colores (véase la página 8)

comunicación

televisión

banderas de señales

SENSUALARIO

Here's a list of words that tell what you feel—or smell, or taste, or hear, or see.

Gusto
ácido, delicioso, dulce, picante, rancio, rico, sabroso, salado

Oído
alto, bajo, chillón, chirriante, escandaloso, estentóreo, estrepitoso, estridente, estruendoso, ruidoso

Olfato
apestoso, aromático, delicioso, fétido, hediondo, oloroso, perfumado

Tacto
áspero, aterciopelado, caliente, duro, frío, liso, pegajoso, pulido, resbaladizo, suave, tibio

Vista
brillante, claro, color (véase la pág. 8), deslumbrante, fluorescente, fosforescente, fulgurante, luminoso, nublado, nubloso, opaco, oscuro, radiante, resplandeciente, sombrío, tamaño (véase la pág. 9), tenebroso

uso del sentido común para evitar
accidentes

reglas de seguridad

Sentido común

cuentos cómicos

Sentido del humor

chistes

comidas

olores agradables

perfumes

Olfato

zorrillos

olores desagradables

biología/física del sentido del oído

onomatopeya: palabras que imitan
un sonido (Véase la página 26.)

Oído

música

comunicación

radio

la palabra hablada

Para todos los sentidos (o varios de ellos)
agradable, delicado, desagradable, intenso,
leve, molesto, penetrante, potente, tenue,
violento

THEME-RELATED BOOKS

Abbado, Claudio. *La casa de los sones.* Madrid:
Destino, 1986. Abbado writes of childhood
experiences that made him decide to become a
conductor. **5–6:IR***

Ballesta, Juan. *Tommy y el elefante.* Barcelona:
Lumen, 1983. A boy whose best friend is an
imaginary elephant outsmarts a wacky psychia-
trist. Good book to tickle anyone's sense of
humor. **2:RA/3:IR**

Broekel, Ray. *Tus cinco sentidos.* Trans. Lada
Kratky. Chicago: Childrens Press, 1984.
Describes in some detail the functioning of the
senses. **3–4:IR**

Chlad, Dorothy. *Pueblo de Seguridad.* Trans.
Lada Kratky. Chicago: Childrens Press. Series
that teaches safety concepts. Includes *Cuando
cruzo la calle; Cuando hay un incendio, sal para
afuera; Es divertido andar en bicicleta; Jugando
en el patio de recreo; Los desconocidos;* and
Viajando en autobús. **1–2:RA/2–3:IR**

Dultzin Dubin, Susana. *Sonidos y ritmos.*
Mexico City: Patria, 1981. Describes sounds
and rhythms, from animal noises to music.
Refers to music of Mexico. **K–1:RA/1–2:IR**

Gerson, Sara. *La orquesta.* Mexico City: Trillas,
1987. Late one night, the instruments in the
orchestra start practicing by themselves, and all
the mice in the theater come to listen. Even the
cat's there. **K:RA/1:IR**

Lionni, Leo. *Frederick.* Trans. Ana María
Matute. Madrid: Lumen, 1986. Beautifully illustrated book about a mouse who collects summer
colors to brighten the winter. **K–1:RA/2:IR**

Rius, María, Parramón, J.M., and Puig, J.J. *Los
cinco sentidos.* Woodbury, New York: Barron's,
1985. Series of books that introduces, in simple
language, the functioning of the senses.
Includes El gusto, *El oído, El olfato, El tacto,*
and *La vista.* **K–1:RA/1:IR**

---

*K, 1, 2, etc., refer to grade level;
 RA = Read Aloud; **IR** = Independent Reading

Tiempo

energía solar —
energía del viento —
energía hidroeléctrica — como fuente de energía

tornados y
ciclones inundaciones tormen

beneficiosos   perjudiciales

el agua y las plantas

sequía

Efectos del tiempo sobre los seres humanos

primavera —
verano —
otoño —
invierno — Estaciones

El tiempo

cirros
estratos
cúmulos — las nubes y su clasificación

frentes fríos, frentes cálidos y
conceptos básicos de meteorología

Meteorología

mapas sinópticos del tiempo

barómetro —
anemómetro —
termómetro — instrumentos meteorológicos

pluviómetro

dichos-

"A mal tiempo, buena cara

BRIGHT IDEA

Weather Report   For active student participation throughout a unit on weather, begin each day with a weather report *(boletín del tiempo* or *boletín meteorológico).* A different individual can report each day or a different group can be responsible for each week, so that everyone has a chance to participate.

For older students, weather reports will be more accurate if you teach them to comment on four elements:

Cielo
   despejado   parcialmente nublado   nublado
Viento
   Dirección: N NE E SE S SO O NO
   Velocidad: calmado ligero fuerte

Temperatura
   fría cómoda calurosa

Precipitación
   neblina lluvia nieve granizo

If you have access to a thermometer, the actual temperature should be noted. If you have access to an anemometer or some way to estimate wind speed (flag on flagpole, surface of a lake or river, etc.), the actual or estimated wind speed should be noted.

lluvia   nieve

neblina

granizo

Mal tiempo

El ciclo del agua

precipitación

drenaje

evaporación

Actividades para días lluviosos/
Actividades para días de sol

En el folklore y la literatura

Canciones   Cuentos

"Que llueva, que llueva"   "La hormiguita"
(Véase la pág. 68.)

Encourage students to record their observations, so that they can see weather patterns at a glance. A good way to do this is to add symbols on a classroom calendar. (See **Bright Idea** on pages 38–39 for some suggestions on classroom calendars.) For example, for sky condition the symbols might be a sun for *despejado,* a sun half hidden by a cloud for *parcialmente nublado,* and a cloud for *nublado.* On Monday of each week, you might have students use the calendar to give a brief recap of the previous week's weather.

THEME-RELATED BOOKS

Climent, Elena. *Triste historia del sol con final feliz.* Mexico City: Trillas, 1986. This humorous story in verse tells how unhappy everyone is when the sun isn't out, and how they cheer up when it finally reappears. Winner of the *Premio Antoniorrobles.* **K–1:RA/1–2:IR***

Garrido, Felipe. *Tajín y los Siete Truenos.* Mexico City: Editoriales Mexicanos, 1962. Totonac legend about thunder and thunderstorms, beautifully retold. **3–4:RA/5–6:IR**

Lobel, Arnold. *El Búho en su casa.* Trans. Pablo Lizcano. Madrid: Alfaguara, 1982. One night, winter invades Owl's house. It's a chilling experience. **K:RA/1:IR**

Rico, Lolo and Blanco, Cruz. *Kalamito tiene miedo.* Madrid: Altea, 1983. Kalamito gets frightened by a rainstorm. Afterward, he's afraid to go out alone, but a friend tells him how to take care of himself in a storm. **1–2:RA/3:IR**

Rius, María and Parramón, J.M. *Los cuatro elementos.* Woodbury, New York: Barron's, 1985. Series of books about the four elements of ancient philosophy. Includes *La tierra, El fuego, El aire,* and *El agua.* **K:RA/1:IR**

Ruillé, Bertrand. *Historia de una nube que era amiga de una niña.* Valladolid: Miñón, n.d. Delightful story tells of the function clouds play for life on the earth. **1:RA/2:IR**

Webster, Vera. *Experimentos atmosféricos.* Trans. Lada Kratky. Chicago: Childrens Press, 1985. Some weather experiments young people can perform. **3–5:IR**

See also *El cocuyo y la mora: Cuento de la tribu pemón, Dinosaurios,* and *Las liebres blancas,* p. 109; *Julie y los lobos,* p. 113; *Pedro y su roble, ¡Manzano, manzano!,* and *Yaci y su muñeca,* p. 121.

***K, 1, 2,** etc., refer to grade level;
 RA = Read Aloud; **IR** = Independent Reading

Yo

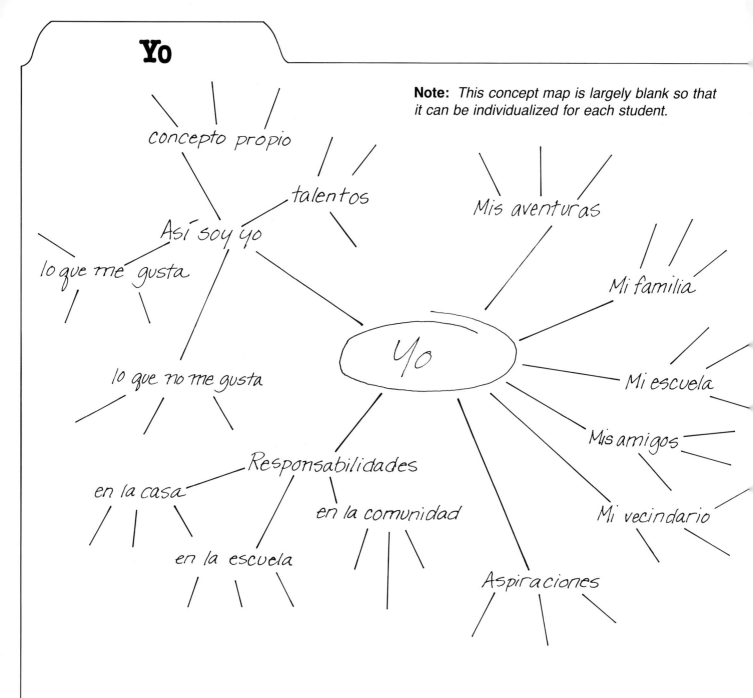

Note: *This concept map is largely blank so that it can be individualized for each student.*

concepto propio

talentos

Así soy yo

lo que me gusta

Mis aventuras

Mi familia

lo que no me gusta

Yo

Mi escuela

Mis amigos

Responsabilidades

en la casa

en la comunidad

Mi vecindario

en la escuela

Aspiraciones

BRIGHT IDEA

Self-Concept Development The following ideas will help foster self-awareness and development of a positive self-concept in your students.

- This activity works well with young children. Set up a large mirror in front of the classroom. Each student comes up to the front of the room and, looking in the mirror, describes himself or herself to the other students, who should close their eyes during the description. After each student has had a turn at the

mirror, distribute drawing paper and have each do a self-portrait.

- For older students, try this activity. Have students list—in one column and skipping two lines between entries—every variation of their names, including nicknames, by which they are known. For example:

  Jorge Luis Martínez Ruiz
  Jorge Martínez
  J. Martínez Ruiz
  Jorgito
  Ogui
  Georgie
  Jorge Luí Comemaní

THEME-RELATED BOOKS

Ada, Alma Flor. *Los seis deseos de la jirafa.* Carmel: Hampton-Brown, 1989. Predictable Big Book about a giraffe who tries on the tails of several other animals, only to find that her own is best. **K–1:RA/1:IR***

Andersen, Hans Christian. *El patito feo.* Mexico City: Promexa, 1982. Trans. Felipe Garrido. Classic tale of the ugly duckling who discovers he's actually a beautiful swan. **K–2:RA/3:IR**

Burmingham, John. *Harquin, el zorro que bajó al valle.* Valladolid: Miñón, 1975. Harquin, a little fox, saves his family from danger that he has inadvertently brought upon them. **K–2:RA/3:IR**

Cantieni, Benita and Gächter, Fred. *Elefantito y Gran Ratón.* Mexico City: Trillas, n.d. A young mouse and an elephant discover they can be good friends despite the difference in their sizes. **K–1:RA/2:IR**

Ende, Michael. *El dragón y la mariposa.* Madrid: Alfaguara, n.d. Humorous tale in lively verse tells of a dragon (named Plácido) and a butterfly (named Bárbara) whose names don't match their personalities. **1–2:RA/3:IR**

Frandsen, Karen G. *Hoy fue mi primer día de escuela.* Trans. Lada Kratky. Chicago: Childrens Press, 1986. Tells about a child's first day in school. **K:RA/1–2:IR**

Next to each variation or nickname, have students note who calls them that and how it makes them feel.

• Another possibility is showing students examples of logos, letterheads, coats of arms, etc., pointing out how symbols are used to tell about the company or person or country. Then have each student design a personal logo, letterhead, or coat of arms for himself or herself. Students may then write a composition explaining the symbolism used.

Lobel, Arnold. *Sapo y Sepo.* Madrid: Alfaguara. Series of books about two friends who look out for one another. Includes *Sapo y Sepo son amigos*; *Sapo y Sepo, inseparables*; *Sapo y Sepo, un año entero*; and *Días con Sapo y Sepo.* **K–1:RA/1–2:IR**

Mis primeros libros. Chicago: Childrens Press. Collection containing many self-concept books. Includes *Escúchame; Igual que yo; A Pedro Pérez le gustan los camiones; Ada, la desordenada; A veces las cosas cambian;* and *Los gatos me gustan más.* **K–1:RA/1:IR**

Ness, Evaline. *¿Tienes tiempo, Lidia?* Trans. Alma Flor Ada. New York: Dutton, 1976. Lidia is so busy with so many projects that she never has time to finish any of them. In this story she finds that she can make time to pay attention to her younger brother. **2:RA/3–4:IR**

Puncel, María. *Abuelita Opalina.* Madrid: Ediciones SM, 1983. Short novel about family life in an imaginary Spanish town. **5–6:IR**

Rico, Lolo and Blanco, Cruz. *Kalamito.* Madrid: Altea. Collection of lively stories about Kalamito, a sensitive boy who changes color as his moods change. Includes *Kalamito va a la escuela, Kalamito tiene miedo, Kalamito tiene una hermanita, Kalamito se aburre, Kalamito quiere otra familia, Kalamito y sus fantasías, Kalamito y sus dos amigos,* and *Kalamito se equivoca.* **1:RA/2–3:IR**

Rivero Oramas, Rafael. *La piedra del Zamuro: Un cuento de Tío Nicolás.* Caracas: Ekaré, 1981. Venezuelan folktale in which a rabbit, who is afraid, finds out through a series of adventures that he is brave and smart. Beautifully retold. **3:RA/4–5:IR**

See also *El cocuyo y la mora: Cuento de la tribu pemón, Nadarín,* and *Las liebres blancas,* p. 109; *El hombrecillo de papel* and *El dolor de muelas de Alberto,* p. 113.

---

*K, 1, 2, etc., refer to grade level;
RA = Read Aloud; **IR** = Independent Reading

PART 5 MANOS A LA OBRA

A catalog of imaginative ideas to promote reading, writing, listening, and speaking

A ESCRIBIR

CUENTOS Y MÁS CUENTOS

*There are more **story-writing options** than you might think. Here, for a start, are 33 ideas. Before students can produce these kinds of stories, they may need to see models of the writing forms. Basal reading programs in Spanish contain many examples; library books in Spanish can also serve as models. Those books appearing in our bibliographies on pages 108–127 that work well as writing models are referenced here, along with some additional titles.*

1 **a day in the life of a . . ./un día típico de un(a) . . .** Students give a chronological account of a typical day in the life of a firefighter (*bombero*) or a frog (*rana*) or a fairy-tale witch (*bruja de cuento de hadas*)—the more unusual the character, the better.

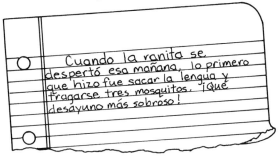

Cuando la ranita se despertó esa mañana, lo primero que hizo fue sacar la lengua y tragarse tres mosquitos. ¡Qué desayuno más sabroso!

2 **all about me/así soy yo** These personal narratives include the author's dreams, fantasies, and wishes.
Model: *El viejo teatro*, see p. 111.

3 **animal adventures/aventuras con animales**
Models: *Nadarín*, see p. 109; *Harquin, el zorro que bajó al valle* and *La piedra del zamuro*, see p. 127.

4 **autobiographical fiction/ficción autobiográfica** Students imagine themselves in a fictional situation. Or, they invent a fictional protagonist who tells about an event in his or her life.

5 **bedtime stories/cuentos para antes de acostarse**

6 cliffhangers/*cuentos de aventuras y de suspenso* These stories are usually written in episodes (*episodios*) at the end of each of which the hero or heroine is placed in a life-threatening situation (*un peligro de vida o muerte*). At the beginning of the next episode, the tension is relieved.

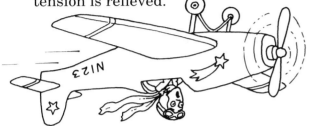

Con un sonido terrible de los motores, el avión del capitán Bruno comenzó a descender vertiginosamente. ¿Se salvará muestro héroe esta vez? ¿O morirá en una pira de metal retorcido y humeante?
Episodio 2
En el último instante posible, el capitán Bruno logra lanzarse del avión en paracaídas.

7 cowboy yarns/*cuentos de vaqueros*

8 fables/*fábulas*
<u>Models</u>: See the collection of fables in *Fábulas* by Arnold Lobel (Madrid: Alfaguara, 1987). For younger children, see *Los seis deseos de la jirafa* on p. 127.

9 fairy tales/*cuentos de hadas*
<u>Models</u>: *Hansel y Gretel*, see p. 113; *El frijol mágico*, see p. 125; *El patito feo*, see p. 127.

10 fantasies/*fantasías*
<u>Models</u>: *Las telarañas de Carlota*, see p. 109; *El hombrecillo de papel*, *El pizarrón encantado*, and *El dolor de muelas de Alberto*, see p 113; *Clara y el caimán*, see p. 115; *Tommy y el elefante*, see p. 123.

11 ghost stories/*cuentos de fantasmas*

12 historical fiction/*ficción histórica*
<u>Model</u>: *Citlalli en las estrellas*, see p. 117.

13 impossible stories/*cuentos imposibles* These are full of irreconcilable differences: *Era de noche y llovía, y el sol rajaba las piedras.*

14 journal/*diario* This story is told through a fictional narrator's journal.

15 jungle adventures/*aventuras en la selva*
<u>Model</u>: See *Cuento de un cocodrilo* by José Aruego (New York: Scholastic Book Services, 1979).

16 legends/*leyendas*
<u>Models</u>: *El cocuyo y la mora*, see p. 109; *La tierra de la madre escorpión*, see p. 119; *Tajín y los siete Truenos*, see p. 125.

17 love stories/*historias de amor* Here are some unusual pining pairs: *dos juguetes abandonados, un ciempiés y un grillo, una nube y una montaña, dos zapatos izquierdos.*

18 manipulations/*manipulaciones* Students can change the setting of a story. For example, they can write a modern version of a fairy tale. They can also expand a scene, change the ending, or write a sequel to a story they know well. Students can also introduce themselves into the story and rewrite it from a personal point of view. Or they can continue the story. Stories that never end (*cuentos de nunca acabar*), such as *Sale el oso* (see p. 117), are an excellent way to encourage students to add episodes to stories.

19 mysteries/*misterios*

Cuando llegué a la casa del conde, estaba lloviendo violentamente. Entre los árboles creí ver unas figuras extrañas que parecían flotar en el aire.

20 patterned stories/*cuentos con frases repetidas*

This highly structured story form is especially good for beginning writers because it has patterned sentences with blanks for students to write their own nouns, verbs, adjectives, or phrases. For example:

> *Al salir el sol, la lechuza dijo: "Uuuu, uuuu".*
> El ___ *dijo*: "___, ___".
> La ___ *dijo,* "___, ___".
> *Y el niño dijo: "Hola, Sol".*

<u>Models</u>: All books in the *Rimas y risas* series, see p. 109; *Chirrinchinchina, ¿qué hay en la tina?* and *El oso más elegante*, see p. 115; *¡Manzano! ¡Manzano!*, see p. 121.

21 pirate adventures/*aventuras de piratas*

—*No sabes con quién te enfrentas. Soy el Corsario Rojo, temido por todo el Caribe.*
—*Conozco tu fama, miserable, pero no te temo ni a ti ni a todos tus hombres. ¡Toma, cobarde!*

22 pourquoi tales/*leyendas explicativas*

<u>Models</u>: *El cocuyo y la mora*, which explains how the firefly got its spark, see p. 109; *Tajín y los siete Truenos*, which explains the origin of hurricanes, see p. 125.

23 repetitive tales/*cuentos con elementos que se repiten*

A repetitive tale is characterized by a plot element that is repeated throughout the story. In "*Los tres cerditos*," for example, the wolf asks the piggies again and again to let him in. Each time they refuse, and he huffs and puffs to blow the house down. Establish the predictable elements and invite students to build a story.

<u>Models</u>: The *Colección "Primeros cuentos"* (Madrid: Altea, n.d.) contains several repetitive tales: *Caperucita roja, Los tres cerditos, Los tres osos, Tres chivos testarudos*.

24 realistic fiction/*ficción realista*

In these stories, contemporary children deal with real-life problems.

<u>Models</u>: *Santiago*, see p. 109; *¿Tienes tiempo, Lidia?*, see p. 127.

25 science fiction/*ciencia-ficción*

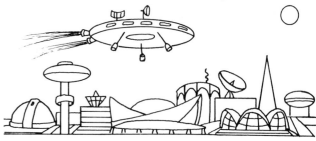

26 sea adventures/*aventuras en altamar*

Desde lo alto de la cofa del palo trinquete, el vigía rugió: "Barco enemigo a la vista, a estribor". En un instante todos los marineros aparecieron sobre cubierta y comenzaron a aprestar los cañones y los garfios de abordaje.

27 sequels/*continuaciones* In the tradition of "*El regreso de . . .*" and "*El hijo de . . .*" stories. Sequels to familiar stories work well for beginning writers because the characters and settings have been already established.

28 sports stories/*cuentos de deportes*

29 spy adventures/*aventuras de espías*

30 tag-on tales/*cuentos acumulativos* See "*En una bella ciudad*" on p. 68 for an example of this technique in a poem.

31 tall tales/*cuentos exagerados* The characters' boasts (*jactancias*) and overstatements (*exageraciones*) make tall tales the ideal story form for experimenting with outlandish language.

32 trickster tales/*cuentos picarescos* Examples include the many Hispanic folktales in which a rabbit or a *tlacuache* outsmarts a coyote. Models: See the many stories in *Cuentos picarescos para niños de América Latina* (Sao Paulo, Brasil: Editorial Ática, 1983). See also *Cuento de un cocodrilo* by José Aruego (New York: Scholastic Book Services, 1979).

33 word-play stories/*cuentos con juegos de palabras* These stories exploit language in a playful way. One technique is to write the same word over and over again, for example: *Mi tío Ángel, que vive en Los Ángeles, compró unos ángeles de cristal . . .*

BRIGHT IDEA

Giving It a New Twist You can inject fresh interest into a familiar writing assignment by challenging students to experiment with:

• **the form of their writing**
For example, a personal narrative might be rewritten as a ballad; a mystery as a radio script; a science report as a propaganda leaflet.

• **the point of view**
Students imagine themselves as giants, elves, animals, persons from the past or from the future, favorite story characters, older or younger persons. Then they write from their imaginary character's point of view. A tantalizing question such as ¿*Qué tipo de carta de amor le enviaría un dragón a una princesa?* can spark students' interest. This approach works for nonfiction topics as well. For example, you might have students interview a mother raccoon about a recent forest fire.

• **the tone**
Students create a mood or feeling—anger, sadness, silliness, fear—and sustain it as they transform their ideas into words. For example, you might ask students to write a silly mail-order catalogue or an angry letter to a restaurant manager from a customer who didn't like the food.

• **the audience**
Students write for an unusual audience, such as an alien from outer space, an animal, or a historical figure.

CIENTO CINCUENTA IDEAS SIN CUENTOS

What else can students write besides stories? Plenty! Here's a list of 150 alternatives to writing a story.

1 adivinanzas/*riddles*
2 advertencias/*warnings*
3 agradecimientos/*thankyous*
4 alabanzas/*praises*
5 alegorías/*allegories*
6 análisis de noticias/*news analyses*
7 anécdotas/*anecdotes*
8 anuncios/*ads*
9 apéndices/*appendixes*
10 aplicaciones para un empleo/*job applications*
11 artículos (de periódico, de diccionario o de enciclopedia)/*articles (newspaper, dictionary, encyclopedia)*
12 autobiografías/*autobiographies*
13 baladas/*ballads*
14 biografías/*biographies*
15 boletines de noticias/*news bulletins*
16 boletines del tiempo/*weather bulletins*
17 calcomanías (de las que se ponen en las defensas de los autos)/*bumperstickers*
18 canciones de cuna/*lullabies*
19 cartas/*letters*
20 cartelones/*posters*
21 catálogos/*catalogues*
22 certificados/*certificates*
23 citas/*quotes*
24 comparaciones/*comparisons*
25 consejos/*advice*
26 consignas/*slogans*
27 constituciones/*constitutions*
28 contratos/*contracts*

29 conversaciones/*conversations*
30 coplas/*couplets*
31 corridos (See **Word Wise** on p. 133.)
32 críticas (de un libro o de una película)/*reviews (book or movie)*
33 cuestionarios/*questionnaires*
34 chismes/*gossip*
35 chistes/*jokes*
36 definiciones/*definitions*
37 descripciones/*descriptions*
38 diálogos/*dialogues*
39 diarios/*diaries*
40 dichos/*sayings*
41 diplomas/*diplomas*
42 directorios/*directories*
43 discursos para otorgar un premio/*speeches presenting awards*
44 discursos políticos/*political speeches*
45 dramas/*dramas*
46 editoriales/*editorials*
47 elogios/*praises*
48 ensayos/*essays*
49 entrevistas/*interviews*
50 epílogos/*epilogues*
51 epitafios/*epitaphs*
52 etiquetas para envases/*product labels*
53 evaluaciones/*evaluations*
54 exageraciones/*exaggerations*
55 exámenes/*exams*
56 exclamaciones/*exclamations*
57 excusas/*excuses*
58 explicaciones/*explanations*
59 fábulas/*fables*

60 fantasías/*fantasies*
61 finales (de cuentos o películas imaginarios)/*endings (for imaginary stories or movies)*
62 forros de libros (con resumen y breve descripción)/*book jackets (with a summary and brief description)*
63 frases/*phrases*
64 guías/*guides*
65 guiones (para películas)/*movie scripts*
66 harengas/*harangues*
67 himnos/*anthems*
68 historiales/*resumes*
69 historietas acumulativas/*cumulative stories*
70 horarios/*schedules*
71 horóscopos/*horoscopes*
72 índices/*indexes*
73 informes/*reports*
74 instrucciones/*directions*
75 insultos/*insults*
76 invitaciones/*invitations*
77 jerigonzas (See **Word Wise** on page 133.)
78 juegos de palabras/*puns*
79 lemas/*mottos*
80 letras de canciones/*song lyrics*
81 listas de mandados/*grocery lists*
82 máximas/*maxims*
83 memorandums/*memorandums*
84 mensajes secretos en clave/*coded messages*

Adapted from IF YOU'RE TRYING TO TEACH KIDS HOW TO WRITE, YOU'VE GOTTA HAVE THIS BOOK! by Marjorie Frank, IP# 62-5, pp. 18–19, ©1979 by Incentive Publications, Inc., Nashville, TN. Used with permission.

WORDWISE

Corridos, Piropos,* and *Jerigonzas These forms are so uniquely Hispanic that a little elaboration is in order.

Corridos are a spontaneous form of folk musical and literary expression. The Mexican *corrido* is a descendant of the *corrido andaluz* and the *jácara*, medieval romance forms that flourished in Spain as early as the sixteenth century. True to their origins, *corridos* remain today popular ballads which narrate and celebrate brave deeds, great loves, and important political events.

Piropos are creative, usually metaphorical compliments said (traditionally) by a man to a woman. The complimenter makes a show of his invention and imagination in coming up with an unusual, well-turned compliment, for example: *Al que te vea sonreír, ¿pa' que le hace falta el sol?* The word *piropo*, by the way, originally meant "garnet," a reddish semiprecious stone, and acquired its new meaning because comparison to a garnet was so often used in conventional compliments.

Jerigonza, from the French *jargon*, meaning "the noises birds make," is a general term to describe any incomprehensible speech, from professional jargon to a system—like pig Latin—that makes language deliberately unintelligible to all but those who know the trick. A common *jerigonza* among children is one that inserts a nonsense syllable—*chi*, for example—in front of every syllable of a word or phrase. For example, *vamos a la escuela* becomes *chi-va-chi-mos-chi-a-chi-la-chi-es-chi-cue-chi-la.*

133

◀█▌INSPIRACIÓN ⟫

*Here is a list of **37 objects and activities that will stimulate students' imaginations** and generate the kinds of thoughts and images from which good writing is born.*

1 antique clothing and jewelry/*ropa y joyas antiguas* Consider inviting an antique dealer (*negociante en antigüedades*) to your classroom to show and describe unusual antiques.

2 cartoons with text deleted/*tiras cómicas con el texto borrado*

3 classified or personal ads/*anuncios clasificados o personales*

4 computer video games/*juegos electrónicos* To construct a plot from the action on the screen is the name of the game.

5 famous paintings/ *pinturas famosas*

6 favorite toys/*juguetes favoritos*

7 field trips/*excursiones* Encourage students to interview, tape record, illustrate, and photograph the people, animals, and things they encounter during an outing. Then have them use what they have gathered as the basis of a writing assignment.

8 foreign or antique coins/*monedas extranjeras o antiguas*

9 grab bags/*bolsas de agarra y mira* Students close their eyes and draw castanets (*castañuelas*), cinnamon sticks (*canela en rama*), conch shells (*conchas de caracol*), and other tantalizing story starters out of a bag.

10 historical artifacts/*artefactos históricos* For example, arrowheads from an archeological dig, or a nineteenth-century pocket knife.

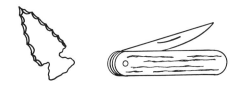

11 holidays/*días de fiesta*

12 horoscopes/*horóscopos* There's no predicting what plot lines these story starters will inspire.

13 in a word/*en una palabra* Students find all the small words in a long word. Then they try to use each small word— as well as the original word—in a story.

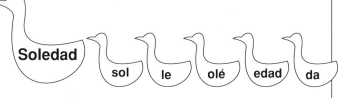

Soledad — sol — le — olé — edad — da

14 invisible or imaginary friends/ *amigos invisibles o imaginarios*

15 jokes/*chistes* Students may pull your leg as they expand their favorite jokes into complete stories.

16 maps/*mapas*

17 mirrors/*espejos* Make them doors into an enchanted world (*un mundo encantado*), make them broken (*roto*) or distorted (*deformado*), make them talk back (*responder*), make them magic (*mágico*)!

18 mood music/*música de fondo*

19 museum catalogs/*catálogos de museo* Museum gift catalogs often provide interesting information about the objects on exhibit. Students can cut out articles and pictures and glue each one on a story-idea card. These can be kept in a file box in the learning center, or shuffled and dealt out during a class writing activity.

20 mysterious-looking natural structures or natural phenomena/*estructuras naturales o fenómenos naturales de apariencia misteriosa*

21 mystery boxes/*cajas misteriosas* Students write a description of what they imagine is in a box wrapped in decorative paper.

22 news headlines/*titulares de primera plana* Consider starting a scrapbook of news headlines and articles that are grade-level appropriate in content and interest.

23 newspaper squares/*recortes de periódicos* Students write a story based on a bit of information found on a scrap of newspaper.

la clase de quim
almuerzo especi
hor del alcalde
cuela. Los estu
gradecerle al o
Avenida de la P

24 night sounds and shapes/*sonidos y siluetas nocturnos*

25 nursery rhyme characters/*personajes de una nana infantil*

26 obituaries/*obituarios* Not as grim as you think, these story starters can provide interesting characters, settings, and plots.

27 photographs/*fotografías* Focus on those that show action, elements of mystery, or conflict.

BRIGHT IDEA

28 pictures of crazy contraptions or inventions/*dibujos de maquinarias o inventos ridículos*

29 pin the tale on the donkey/*pégale el rabo al burro* Students choose a story setting by closing their eyes and pinning a spot on a map (*pegar una tachuela en un mapa*).

30 proverbs and quotations/*proverbios y citas* Especially those that generate self-concept, or realistic fiction. For example:
"Los niños son la esperanza del mundo".
—José Martí.
For examples of proverbs, see page 64.

31 schedules/*horarios* Students may arrive at story-starting points as they study plane, train, and ship schedules.

32 song titles/*títulos de canciones*

33 story-starter strips/*papelitos con principios de cuentos* Often, a catchy beginning is all students need to get them going. Blackine Masters 11–12 on pages 166–167 provide some ideas for younger students, while Blackline Master 13 on page 168 gives prompts for older ones. Store the strips in envelopes on the bulletin board or paste them to the tops of writing paper stored in the writing center. To supply more ideas, take the opening lines of books students haven't read or of papers written by children in other classes. After your students try their hand at continuing the story starter, share the source story.

34 story titles/*títulos de cuentos* Students generate interesting story titles first. Then they write stories to go with the titles.

35 "What if . . .?"/"*¿Qué pasaría si . . .?*" For example:
- *¿Qué pasaría si uno se despertara una mañana y descubriera que se ha puesto del tamaño de una hormiguita?*
- *¿Qué pasaría si pudieras volar como las aves?*
- *¿Qué pasaría si te convirtieras en una estrella de "rock and roll"?*

36 wishes/*deseos* Whether it comes true (*hacerse realidad*) or not, any wish can generate a good story.

37 writer's-block cure/*cura para la falta de inspiración* Help students cure their writer's block by having them toss a cardboard cube (*tirar un dado de cartón*) with a different picture on each side. Students use the pictures that come up as story starters.

◀▮ANTES DE ESCRIBIR ▷

*Exploring a topic, knowing what there is to say about it, limiting the topic, and organizing thoughts are all part of prewriting. Here are **20 prewriting activities** that will help your students nail down their ideas.*

1 a b c/*abecé* Students make an alphabetized list of subtopics, one subtopic for each letter of the alphabet.

2 automatic writing/*composición automática* Students write nonstop (*sin parar*) about whatever comes into their heads, without regard to mechanics or organization.

3 brainstorming/*sesión de ideas* Students let the ideas flow without excluding any possibilities. May be done by partners or by the entire group.

4 concept map/*red de palabras* Students write a topic (*tópico o tema*) on the chalkboard, surround it with as many related concepts (*conceptos relacionados*) as possible, and then draw connecting lines to show the relationships. For examples of concept maps, see Part 4, pages 108–127.

5 cutting out pictures/*recortar dibujos o fotos* This device is good for helping students visualize characters and settings.

6 drawing pictures/*hacer dibujos* This device is especially good for younger students because it helps them plan their plot and sequence events.

7 good news, bad news/*lo bueno, lo malo* Students play this game in pairs to generate a story line (*determinar el argumento general de un cuento*), or opposite points of view (*puntos de vista opuestos*) on a topic. Here's how it works.

- *¡Qué bueno! Me regalaron una bicicleta por mi cumpleaños. Lo malo es que no la sé montar.*
- *¡Qué bueno! Mi papá me prometió que me iba a enseñar. Lo malo es que se fue en un viaje de negocios por tres meses.*

8 guided discussion/*discusión dirigida* Students write or verbalize responses to questions about a drawing or photograph they will write about. Pose questions that are interpretive, such as: *¿Qué les hace sentir esta foto? ¿Qué les hace recordar este dibujo? ¿Qué impresión creen ustedes que quería comunicar el pintor o el fotógrafo?*

9 improvisational drama/*teatro improvisado* Students act out story ideas to find out where the ideas will lead them.

10 interviews/*entrevistas*

11 lists/*listas* Students make lists of names (*nombres*), action verbs (*verbos descriptivos*), descriptive phrases (*frases descriptivas*), rhyming words (*palabras que riman*), etc.

12 outlining/*hacer un esbozo o bosquejo*

13 reading and researching/*lectura e investigación*

14 speculating/*especular* This technique is related to the motivational "What if?" stage of writing, but is more focused because it deals with a topic that has already been chosen. Students think about their topics and ask questions such as: *¿Qué pasaría si [cierto personaje] le tuviera miedo a la oscuridad? ¿Qué pasaría si una manada de dinosaurios irrumpiera de pronto en [un lugar determinado]?*

15 storyboard/*esbozo preliminar en forma de tira cómica* Students draw a series of pictures that illustrate major episodes.

16 story map/*esquema preliminar* Students plan schematically (*por medio de diagramas*) the principal features (*los elementos principales*) of a story they are about to write. For example:

Personajes
un conejito
un lobo

Ambiente
el bosque

Argumento
El lobo quiere comerse al conejo.
El conejo engaña al lobo y se escapa.

17 taking opinion surveys/*hacer encuestas de opinión pública*

18 time lines/*cronologías* Time lines are useful for organizing nonfiction topics.

19 Who? What? When? Where? How?/*¿Quién? ¿Qué? ¿Cuándo? ¿Dónde? ¿Cómo?* Students get to the heart of a story by answering these five basic questions.

20 writing the ending first/*empezar por el final* Sometimes it helps students get started if they know where they're going.

¡QUE SE ENTERE TODO EL MUNDO ➤

*Students should have the opportunity to share their completed drafts not only with their teachers and classmates, but with family, friends, and the world at large. This needn't mean hundreds of copies or mammoth productions. You'll find that a few simple materials, a little imagination, and a great sense of fun add up to a tremendous pride of authorship. Here are **64 publishing ideas** you might consider.*

Act It Out

1 **comedy routines/*actos cómicos***

2 **community-service announcements/*anuncios de servicio a la comunidad***

3 **dances/*bailes***

4 **dialogues/*diálogos***

5 **doll conversations/*conversaciones entre muñecos o muñecas***

6 **finger play/*juegos con los dedos***

7 **home video shows/*videoespectáculos caseros***

8 **impersonation acts/*imitaciones***

9 **mock interviews/*entrevistas simuladas***

10 **monologues/*monólogos***

11 **newscasts/*programas de noticias***

12 **pantomimes/*pantomimas***

13 **puppet shows/*espectáculos de títeres*** See directions for making several kinds of puppets in the Art section of the Activity Ideas in Part 4 (pages 102–103). See suggestions for using puppets in the Language Arts section of the same list (pages 104–105).

14 **radio shows/*programas de radio***

15 **singing telegrams/*telegramas musicales***

16 **skits/"*sketches*"**

17 **tableaux/*cuadros vivos*** Groups of students, perhaps in costume, strike a dramatic pose (*pose dramática*) that portrays a significant moment (*momento importante*) in a story. The trick is to be as still as possible to give the impression of a living painting or sculpture.

18 **three-act plays/*obras en tres actos***

Make It into a Book

19 **ancient scrolls/*rollos de pergamino antiguos*** Students write their compositions on sheets of vellum or parchment (*pergamino*). The pages are then glued together end to end (*a lo largo*) to make a scroll. Each end of the scroll is glued to a dowel (*clavija de madera*). The scroll is then rolled up and tied with a ribbon (*se enrolla y se ata con una cinta*).

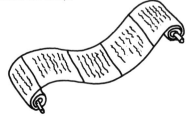

20 flip books/*libros animados* See description of flip books on page 102. Flip books work well as adjuncts to short poems with fast-moving topics, such as a grasshopper (*saltamontes*) or a jack-in-the-box (*muñeco de resorte de una caja sorpresa*).

21 fold-up books/*libros de acordión*

22 great big books/*superlibrotes* Students use an overhead projector to project their writing and illustrations onto large sheets of paper, and trace over the large letters and illustrations with wide-tipped markers or crayons. They then staple the pages together at the top to make an easel book (*libro de caballete*).

23 pop-up books/*libros tridimensionales* To make the basic structural unit, see Blackline Master 1 on page 148. Cut along the dotted lines (*líneas de puntos*) and fold to make a pop-up tab (*lengüeta*). Glue a picture cut-out (*dibujo recortado*) in place as shown. Text goes all around the pop-up tab. To assemble a book, glue two or more units together.

24 shape books/*libros en contorno*

25 single-line books/*libros de un renglón* Students copy their story in a continuous line (*renglón corrido*) on a roll of adding-machine tape (*rollo de papel de máquina sumadora*). Thread story tape through two slits (*ranuras*) in a shoebox lid (*tapa de una caja de zapatos*) as shown. Wind each end (*punta*) of the story roll (*rollo*) around a dowel (*clavija de madera*). You can replay the story over and over again!

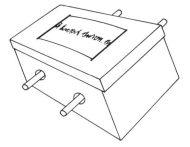

26 teeny-tiny books/*minilibritos* Students use the reduction feature on a copying machine to reduce (*reducir*) each page of their compositions to miniature pages (*páginas en minatura*). Bind miniature story pages into a teeny-tiny book. Miniature poetry could also be laminated (*laminar*) and attached to a keychain (*llavero*).

27 touch-and-feel books/*libros de tacto* Students glue the pages of their stories to pinked swatches (*recortes*) of textured fabric (*tela o material no liso*) and then stitch the pages together (*coser las páginas*).

28 tube books/*libros en tubo* Students decorate a cardboard tube (*tubo de cartón*) in which to store (*guardar*) their compositions.

29 wall books/*libros de pared* Students illustrate each page of their composition, mount (*montar*) the pages on construction paper (*cartulina*) and pin them up in sequence on a bulletin board (*colocarlas en orden en un cuadro de anuncios*) or tape them to a wall (*pegarlas en la pared con cinta adhesiva*).

Do Something Unusual with It

30 banners and bumper stickers/*banderas y calcomanías* Students can print clever sayings (*dichos*) and lovely figures of speech (*tropos o figuras retóricas*) on paper banners or flags. They might also print them on adhesive paper (*papel adhesivo*) and use them as bumper stickers.

Quien sabe dos lenguas vale por dos

31 frame it/*ponerlo en un marco*

32 hang it up, fold it up, wrap it up/*colgarlo, doblarlo, envolverlo* Lines of short poems can be printed on cardboard shapes (*figuras hechas de cartón*) and made into a mobile (*móvil*). Longer poems can be written with black markers on colorful wrapping paper (*papel de regalo de muchos colores*) and used to wrap (*envolver*) a special gift.

33 laminate it/*laminarlo* Use each laminated page as a placemat (*mantelito individual*).

34 mail it/*enviarlo por correo* Students write their final copy on one side of a single sheet of stationery (*papel de cartas*), fold it to make an envelope (*sobre*), stamp it (*ponerle un sello*), and mail it to a friend or relative.

35 puzzles/*rompecabezas* Students illustrate their compositions, glue them onto heavy paper (*papel grueso*), cut them into puzzle pieces (*recortarlas en forma de piezas de rompecabezas*), and take turns putting each other's compositions back together (*armarlas de nuevo*).

Read It Aloud

36 at a meeting/*en una reunión* Could be a parents' meeting, school-board meeting, or a meeting of a civic group.

37 behind a podium/*desde un atril*

38 by candlelight/*a la luz de una vela* A great idea for ghost stories, gothic tales, and poetry.

39 by invitation only/*sólo por invitación* Send cards to individual writers, inviting them to read their work at a special time and place.

40 during a class picnic/*durante un almuerzo al aire libre*

41 for a group of younger children/*a un grupo de niños más chicos*

42 for another class at school/*a otra clase de la escuela*

43 for a Spanish-as-a-second-language adult class/*en una clase de español para personas no hispanoparlantes*

44 for the residents of a retirement or convalescent home/*a los residentes de un asilo de ancianos*

45 in a private home/*en una casa particular*

46 in the school cafeteria during recess/*en el comedor de la escuela durante el recreo* Serve milk and cookies.

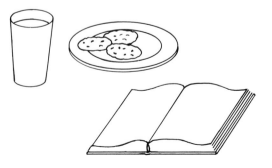

47 in the school library or local library/*en la biblioteca de la escuela o la biblioteca pública*

48 on a "soap box"/*sobre una plataforma improvisada en un lugar público*

49 on a stage/*en un escenario*

50 on cassette tape/*grabado en una "cassette"* Build a class library of talking books.

51 on VCR camera/*captado por una cámara videograbadora* Follow it with an instant replay.

52 to the accompaniment of a slide show/*acompañado por una proyección de transparencias*

53 to the accompaniment of music or sound effects/*acompañado por música o efectos de sonido*

54 while wearing masks or costumes/*con máscaras o disfraces*

Send It Out into the World

55 taped to the side of a school bus or van/*pegado en un autobús escolar*

56 tied to a helium balloon/*atado a un globo de helio*

57 tucked into the seat pocket of a train or tour bus/*puesto en el compartimiento de revistas de un asiento de tren o de autobús de excursión*

Submit It for Publication to

58 children's magazines/*revistas para niños*

59 club newsletters/*boletines de un club*

60 Hispanic organizations /*organizaciones hispanas* See page 46.

61 local newspapers/*periódicos locales*

62 *Reader's Digest* Spanish edition/*edición en español del* Reader's Digest

63 school newspaper/*periódico de la escuela*

64 writing contests/*concursos de composición*

A HABLAR

A VIVA VOZ

*Speaking well builds confidence. Here are **40 powerful ways to involve your students in oral communication**—and that's not just idle talk!*

Demonstrations and Directions

To move beyond "show and tell," students can demonstrate how to:

1 **answer the telephone correctly/ *contestar el teléfono correctamente***

2 **assemble a model or a toy/*armar un modelo o un juguete***

3 **introduce one person to another/ *presentarle una persona a otra***

4 **play a game/*jugar un juego***

5 **perform a science experiment/ *hacer un experimento de ciencias***

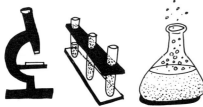

6 **prepare a recipe/*preparar una receta***

Forensics and Public Speaking

Encourage students to give:

7 **debates/*debates***

8 **persuasive talks/*charlas persuasivas***

9 **speeches/*discursos***

Imitations and Impersonations

Have students try their hand at portraying:

10 **a disc jockey/*un locutor de radio***

11 **a historical figure/*un personaje histórico*** Students can improvise (*improvisar*) a TV appearance (*aparición por televisión*) by the historical figure.

12 **a master of ceremonies/*un maestro de ceremonias*** For a classroom variety show (*programa de variedades*) or fashion show (*desfile de modas*).

13 **an auctioneer/*un subastador***

14 **a news announcer or sports announcer/*un locutor de noticias o narrador de un evento deportivo***

15 **a politician/*un político***

16 **a teacher/*un maestro***

17 **a TV comedian/*un cómico de la televisión***

18 **a TV game-show host/*un animador de un programa de concursos de la televisión***

19 **a ventriloquist/*un ventrílocuo***

Oral Games

You could play:

20 **Echo/*Eco***
Spanish Game Directions: *Se forman tres o cuatro grupos. La maestra dice una palabra o frase en voz alta. El primer grupo repite la palabra o frase en voz un poco más baja. El segundo grupo la repite en voz más baja aún, y así sucesivamenta hasta que apenas se oiga la palabra o frase.*

21 **Twenty Questions/*Veinte Preguntas***
Spanish Game Directions: *Un jugador sale del aula y los demás escogen un "objeto secreto". Cuando el jugador regresa, tiene que adivinar el objeto. Puede hacer hasta veinte preguntas que se puedan responder con "sí" o "no".*

22 **"What's My Line?"/"*¿Cuál es mi oficio?*"**
Spanish Game Directions: *Un panel de cuatro estudiantes se turnan en hacerle a otro estudiante (el concursante) preguntas para adivinar la profesión que quiere seguir cuando sea grande. Las preguntas tienen que poderse contestar con "sí" o "no". Cada "no" le gana un punto al concursante.*

Performing

Invite students to put on:

23 **choral readings/*lecturas a coro***

24 **interviews/*entrevistas*** Students can prepare and then perform interviews with a story character (*un personaje de un cuento*), a cartoon character (*un personaje animado*), or an animal.

25 **magic shows/*actos de magia***

26 **mock trials/*juicios simulados***

27 **plays/*obras de teatro***

28 **puppet shows/*espectáculos de títeres*** For some ideas on how to use puppet shows, see page 104.

29 **Readers' Theatre/*teatro leído***

30 **storytelling/*contar un cuento*** This should be a true *performance*. The story should be told from memory (*de memoria*) and be dramatized (*actuada*). Shy students will feel more comfortable telling the story to a younger audience or from behind a mask.

Reading Aloud

Have your students read aloud:

31 **letters from pen pals/*cartas de correspondientes que uno conoce sólo por correo***

32 **newspaper or magazine articles/*artículos de periódicos o revistas***

33 **original or favorite poems and stories/*poemas y cuentos originales o favoritos***

Reciting

Encourage students to practice their elocution with:

34 **famous speeches/*discursos famosos***

35 **finger-play songs/*cancioncitas para juegos con los dedos***

36 **lines from a play/*líneas de una obra de teatro***

37 **lyrics from a song/*la letra de una canción***

38 **nursery rhymes/*nanas infantiles***

39 **poetry/*poesía***

40 **tongue twisters/*trabalenguas***

A ESCUCHAR

TODO OÍDOS

Listening is more than just hearing. It is also processing, reflecting on, and responding to what is heard. Here are **29 ways to promote good listening skills.**

Aural Retention and Recall

To build aural retention, have students try:

1 **asking questions/*hacer preguntas*** Students ask pertinent questions to obtain additional information or clarification of orally presented ideas.

2 **detecting miscues/*detectar errores*** Teacher reads or recites a familiar poem or story, occasionally substituting new words in place of the correct words. Students listen for the substitute words, or "miscues," and say the correct words aloud.

3 **listening for specific information/ *prestar atención para oír datos específicos***

4 **memorizing/*memorizar***

5 **notetaking/*tomar notas***

6 **retelling/*escuchar y contar*** Students listen to and retell jokes, tongue twisters, riddles, stories, oral messages.

7 **summarizing/*resumir*** Students summarize the ideas of a speaker or storyteller.

Collections

Students can collect:

8 **canned sounds/*sonidos en conserva*** Students collect objects such as pebbles, sand, etc., and seal them in cans to make noisemakers. Then they label each can according to the sound it makes, for example: *Sonido de Arena Enlatado.*

9 **familiar sounds/*sonidos familiares*** Students make lists of sounds they hear on the way to school, at home, during different seasons, etc. For example, for *"Sonidos del parque": un subibaja chirriando, una pelota rebotando, etc.*

10 **unusual or unfamiliar sounds/ *sonidos raros*** Students record (*grabar*), for example: radio static (*estática de radio*), the air brakes of a bus (*los frenos de aire de un autobús*), springs in a bed or a sofa (*los muelles de una cama o un sofá*).

Experiments

Have students probe:

11 **sound effects/*efectos de sonido*** Students perform usual classroom activities in different "sound environments": classical music, whale songs, the recorded sounds of ocean waves or of a speaker. Students then fill out a chart telling how each sound affected their work.

12 **the sounds of silence/*los sonidos del silencio*** Students sit in a quiet environment (*un lugar tranquilo*), such as a church or a library reading room, and take note of every sound they hear.

Interpreting

Students will enjoy interpreting:

13 music/*música* Students draw, paint, write, or dance spontaneously (*espontáneamente*) to an unfamiliar piece of music.

14 onomatopoeia/*onomatopeya* Students make up onomatopoetic words (*palabras onomatopéyicas*) for familiar sounds.

15 rhymes and poetry/*rimas y poesías* Students make up finger play and body movements to go with the words.

16 speaker's intent/*intención de la persona que habla* Students listen for words and tones of voice that signal bias (*prejuicio*), facts (*hechos*), and opinions (*opiniones*).

17 voices/*voces* Students listen to a voice on tape or to a concealed individual and try to guess the speaker's mood (*estado de ánimo*), age, sex, and emotion.

Listening Games

Listening skills will be pleasurably enhanced when students engage in:

18 creating cumulative stories/*crear cuentos acumulativos*
<u>Spanish Game Directions</u>: *Para empezar, les voy a dar una oración sencilla, por ejemplo: "Camino del mercado, vi a un hombre con un cerdo". Entonces, cada uno de ustedes repetirá la oración y añadirá una cosa, por ejemplo: "Camino del mercado vi a un hombre con un cerdo y dos sacos de harina". Y así seguiremos hasta que la lista se haga demasiado larga para decir de memoria.*

19 oral games/*juegos orales* See discussion of oral games on pages 142–143.

20 oral spelling bees/*juegos orales de deletreo*

21 playing "Simon Says"/*jugar a "Simón dice"* This familiar game provides good practice for following oral directions. It also teaches students to keep their eyes on a speaker, to listen attentively to what he or she says, and not to interrupt the speaker.

22 playing "telephone"/*jugar "teléfono"*
<u>Spanish Game Directions</u>: *Formen una fila. Le voy a decir un "chisme" en secreto al primer estudiante. Después, el primer estudiante se lo dirá en secreto al segundo, tratando de repetirlo tal como se lo dije. Así seguiremos hasta llegar al último estudiante de la fila. Vamos a ver cómo cambia el chisme.*

Responding on Cue

Students need to listen in order to participate in:

23 choral reading or singing/*leer o cantar a coro*

24 dramatizations/*dramatizaciones*

25 folk dances/*bailes folklóricos o tradicionales*

26 improvisational dances/*bailes improvisados*

27 lip sync'ing/*doblar*

28 rhythm-instrument bands/*bandas de instrumentos de ritmo*

29 role-play situations/*situaciones que requieren representar un papel*

A LEER

ASÍ ME GUSTA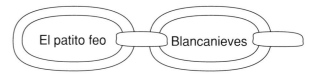

Read, read, read. Silent, sustained, aloud, and in private.
Here are 20 ways to make reading time accessible and attractive *to your students.*

1 Award independent reading time (*tiempo de lectura libre*) for outstanding work and for improved learning performance.

2 Build a class library (*biblioteca privada*) of students' original books, stories, and nonfiction reports.

3 Build a class library of favorite children's books, or start a book exchange (*intercambio de libros*). Include books for every reading level: high, average, and low.

4 Encourage students to write to their favorite writers. Address letters to authors in care of their publishers.

5 Invite a bookstore owner to tell your class why he or she decided to go into the book business and to describe the rewards and pitfalls of running a bookstore.

6 Invite a writer, a book editor, or another person involved in book publishing to tell your class how a book is made.

7 Make space in the classroom for a book display (*exposición de libros*). Students take turns changing the display once every two weeks.

8 Plan a book-awards celebration (*una ceremonia para otorgar premios a libros*). The awards could be set up in the manner of film, TV, or music awards, complete with special categories (*categorías especiales*), secret ballots

(*votación secreta*), and sealed envelopes (*sobres sellados*). Students nominate (*nominar*) favorite books for each category: mystery, fantasy, etc. Students who wish to vote for a book must read all the other books nominated for the same category.

9 Plan a book fair (*feria del libro*). (See **Bright Idea** on page 147.)

10 Plan an art project in which students design and make personalized book marks (*marcapáginas*) and book plates (*etiquetas o placas que dicen a quién pertenece el libro*). (See Blackline Master 5 on page 156 and Blackline Master 14 on page 169.)

11 Provide students with a fun way of keeping track (*llevar un registro*) of the books they read. For example, allow each student to create a book-chain display (*cadena de libros*) like the one below. Students add links (*eslabones*) as they read books.

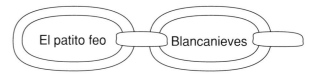
El patito feo   Blancanieves

12 Read aloud to your class. Good read-aloud books have lots of action and suspense. Choose read-alouds that are at least one reading level above your students' average reading level.

13 Read with your class. Schedule blocks of time during which everyone in the class—including yourself—reads silently the book of his or her choice.

14 Schedule a monthly book-lovers' lunch (*almuerzo de aficionados a la lectura*). Students eat their lunch picnic-style as they swap information (*intercambiar impresiones*) about the books they are reading. Older students can hold literary "coffeehouses" (*cafés literarios*).

15 Schedule a weekly visit to the school library and monthly visits to the city or county library.

16 Schedule class time in which students may read aloud passages from books they especially enjoy.

17 Set up a readers-only corner (*un lugar reservado para lectores*) in the classroom. Make it comfortable and inviting. Include a rack of activity books, magazines, and newspapers.

18 Show filmstrips, films, and videos of popular and classic books. Use these to encourage students to read other books by the same author or about the same subject.

19 Stage a book hunt (*caza de libros*). Distribute to individual students clues that lead to books from the school or local library that you feel the students will enjoy. Then send everyone off on a book hunt. Every student may not find the book you had in mind, but chances are they will all find *something* to read.

20 Start book clubs (*asociaciones de aficionados a libros*) for special-interest readers. Each club takes turns planning a display (*planear una exposición*) or giving reports (*presentar informes*) on books about its special interest: mysteries (*misterios*), adventures (*aventuras*), animal tales (*cuentos de animales*), etc.

BRIGHT IDEA

Book Fair Plan a book fair (*feria del libro*) for the end of the semester or school year. Make it an event during which students can share their reading projects and book reports with a wider audience. During the planning stages, students will need to establish all logistics as shown on the following poster:

> ¿Dónde y cuándo tendrá lugar la feria?
> ¿A quién invitaremos?
> ¿Cómo le haremos publicidad?
> ¿Cuál será el tema general de la feria?
> ¿Qué libros se exhibirán?
> Además de libros, ¿qué más habrá en la feria?
> _____comida   _____conferenciantes
> _____refrescos   _____películas
> _____música   _____videograbaciones

Once these decisions are made, form student groups or committees to:

- send invitations (*enviar invitaciones*)
- make posters and announcements (*hacer carteles y anuncios*)
- make theme decorations, costumes and displays (*hacer decoraciones, trajes y exhibiciones basados en el tema general de la feria*)
- collect, keep track of, and return all borrowed books after the fair (*reunir los libros prestados, estar al tanto de ellos y devolverlos*)
- organize refreshments (*organizar la comida y los refrescos*)
- host guest speakers (*atender a los conferenciantes invitados*)
- run the film projector or TV (*operar el proyector o la televisión*)
- explain exhibits to guests (*presentar las exhibiciones a la concurrencia*)
- clean up (*limpiar y recoger*)

During the fair, present special reading awards (*premios de lectura*) to groups and individuals. (See Blackline Masters 14–15 on pages 169–170 for some awards you can make yourself.) Another special event might be a book-awards celebration (see idea number 8 above). Invite someone to make a videotape of the fair.

INNOVACIONES

*Book reports are an integral part of developing a love of reading. But because students do so many book reports, they may run out of interesting ways to present their impressions. Here are some **innovative alternatives to the plain old book report,** broken down into 3 general principles.*

1 Never ask for written book reports. Ask for:

- **book alerts/*boletines bibliográficos*** Students write a brief bulletin announcing that a book is a "must read" (*lectura esencial*). Make it easy by pinning copies of book-alert forms in the corner of a display board. Allow students to tape their completed *boletines* to any wall, window, or door they choose (*en cualquier pared, ventana o puerta que quieran*), and leave it up for a day or two.

- **comic strips/*tiras cómicas*** Students draw a comic strip to retell an important scene (*escena importante*) from the book.

- **critical comments/*críticas*** Not every book is a winner. Offer students an opportunity to write a critical report telling why the book was a bust (*un fracaso o una bomba*).

- **dust jackets/*sobrecubiertas*** Students design the art, write the blurb (*breve resumen*), tell about the author, and fold it around the book.

- **games/*juegos*** Students create a board game (*juego de tablero*), card game (*juego de cartas*), or quiz game (*juego de preguntas y respuestas*) based on the characters and events in the book.

- **letters/*cartas*** Students can offer advice (*consejos*), praise (*elogios*), or encouragement (*ánimo*) to a character in the book.

- **literary letters/*correspondencia literaria*** Students write letters to the teacher telling about the books they are reading. Each letter receives a personal response in which the teacher reacts to the student's remarks.

- **"Most Wanted" posters/*carteles ofreciendo una recompensa por la "captura" de un libro*** Students make a WANTED poster for a favorite book. The poster includes a description (*descripción*) of the book, where it was last seen, and the rewards (*recompensas*) gained for finding and reading it.

- **murals or collages/*murales o "collages"*** Students create a graphic composition (*composición gráfica*) that gives an interpretation (*interpretación*) of the book. They include quotations (*citas*) from the book, and their own reflections (*reflecciones*) about the book's message or theme (*moraleja o idea central*).

- **playbills/*programas de teatro*** Students write a playbill that lists the book's cast of characters (*lista de personajes*), and breaks down the episodes into acts and scenes (*actos y escenas*), giving a brief summary of each.

- **time lines/*cronologías*** Showing the major events (*sucesos principales*) in the book in the order in which they occur (*en el orden en que pasan*).

2 Never ask for oral book reports. Ask for:

- **book auctions/*subastas de libros*** Students auction their book and try to raise bids (*elevar las pujas o posturas*) by describing its merits (*describiendo sus méritos*) to the class. Books to be auctioned should be part of the class or school library. Students who make the winning bids (*pujas o posturas ganadoras*) are allowed to check the book out of the library for a prescribed period.

- **character interviews/*entrevistas con personajes*** Students work with a partner to stage a mock interview (*entrevista simulada*) with a character in the book.

- **dramatizations/*dramatizaciones*** Students act out (*representar*) the story.

- **musical book reports/*informes musicales*** Students deliver (*presentar*) their book report to the accompaniment of music (*con acompañamiento musical*) that matches the mood of the book (*que corresponde al tono del libro*).

- **Readers' Theatre/*teatro leído*** Students do a dramatic reading (*lectura dramatizada*) of an episode in the book.

- **roundtables/*mesas redondas*** Each student in the discussion group assumes the identity (*asumir la identidad*) of a character from the book he or she is reading. Before the discussion, they introduce themselves (*cada personaje se presenta a los demás*). Then they discuss questions asked by the teacher or the class. Quotations (*citas*) from the books the characters come from may also provide springboards for discussion.

- **TV commercials/*anuncios de televisión*** Students promote their book using TV advertising techniques (*métodos utilizados en anuncios de televisión*).

3 Never give up.

Sometimes a small "bribe" might be necessary. Try tokens (*fichas*) made from tagboard or posterboard for each completed book report. Students redeem (*cambiar*) their tokens for sustained-reading (*lectura libre*) time or independent visits to the school library. Tokens may also be used to "bid" for books at book auctions.

SIEMPRE LISTOS

But Where Do We Get the Books? Here is a list of the leading U.S. distributors of imported children's books in Spanish.

Bilingual Publications Company
1966 Broadway
New York, NY 10023
(212) 873-2067 (call collect)

Lectorum Publications, Inc.
137 West 14th St.
New York, NY 10011
(800) 345-5946   (212) 929-2833

Mariuccia Iaconi Book Imports
601 Minnesota St., Loft 106
San Francisco, CA 94107
(415) 285-7393 (call collect)

These publishers carry substantial lines of Spanish-language children's books published in the U.S.

Childrens Press
5440 N. Cumberland Ave.
Chicago, IL 60656
(800) 621-1113
In Illinois, (312) 666-4200 (call collect)

Hampton-Brown Books
P.O. Box 223220
Carmel, CA 93922
(800) 333-3510

Santillana Publishing Co., Inc.
257 Union St.   942 S. Gerhart Ave.
Northvale, NJ   or   Los Angeles, CA
07647   90022
                       (800) 526-0107

149

¡BUEN TRABAJO!

*The following list of **complimentary words and phrases** should help you achieve a little variety as you sing the praises of your students.*

¡Colosal!
¡De primera!
¡Espléndido!
¡Excelente!
¡Fabuloso!
¡Fantástico!
¡Insuperable!
¡Magnífico!
¡Maravilloso!
¡Perfecto!

Note: *For more ways of saying* bueno, *see the list on page 88. For photocopying masters for merit badges and certificates, see Blackline Masters 14–15 on pages 169–170.*

Ahora sí diste en el clavo.
¡Buena observación!
¡Correcto una vez más, como siempre!
El informe te quedó estupendo.
Es evidente que te preparaste muy bien para escribir este informe. Te quedó magnífico.
Es un placer enseñar a estudiantes tan interesados en aprender.
Esa pregunta muestra que estás prestando atención.
Esta anécdota es muy graciosa y está muy bien escrita.
Esta composición te quedó mejor que nunca.
Esta es una composición modelo.
Este es un trabajo de primera categoría.
Felicitaciones. Recibiste muy buena calificación en la prueba.
¡Futuro Premio Nobel de Literatura!
¡Magnífica respuesta!
Me siento orgullosa de ustedes.
¡Qué cuento tan divertido!
¡Qué dibujo más encantador!
Si sigues así, vas a llegar a ser un(a) gran escritor(a).
Siempre haces muy buen trabajo.
Sigues mejorando cada vez más.
Te estás haciendo un experto en esto.
Tu composición ha mejorado muchísimo.
¿Ya ves? Aunque era difícil, lo pudiste hacer.

BRIGHT IDEA

Praiseworthy Pointers The complimentary words and phrases given in this list make good opening lines, but they need development. Research indicates that effective praise is *specific*, so always be sure to make your praise detailed and particular: *¡Qué dibujo más encantador! La expresión en la cara del gallo es comiquísima. ¡Y qué combinación de colores tan brillante!*

Here are a few other praiseworthy ideas:

- You can turn any compliment into a rubber stamp to use on your students' papers. You can have the stampmaker set just the words, or you can create a simple graphic design for the stampmaker. (The blue-ribbon design below could be used.) In any case, try to get a variety of stamps and use them in addition to, not instead of, specific, detailed praise.

- The design below may be photocopied on blue paper and attached to students' papers with tape or staples.

← fold line

¡MUY BUEN TRABAJO!

BLACKLINE MASTERS

NOTE: BI indicates that the Blackline Master is used in a Bright Idea.

Master Number	Contents	Page Number	Pages where Referenced
1	Pop-Up Master	152	13 (BI), 139
2	Collection Master (Single Words)	153	25 (BI)
3	Collection Master (Word Pairs and Trios)	154	25 (BI)
4	Word Wheels	155	17, 89 (BI)
5	Bookmarks	156	46 (BI), 146
6–9	Syllable Cards	157–164	80 (BI)
10	Filmstrip Master	165	93 (BI)
11	Story-Starter Strips (Grade 1)	166	135
12	Story-Starter Strips (Grade 2)	167	135
13	Story-Starter Strips (Grades 3–6)	168	135
14	Bookplates and badges	169	146, 150
15	Award Certificate	170	150

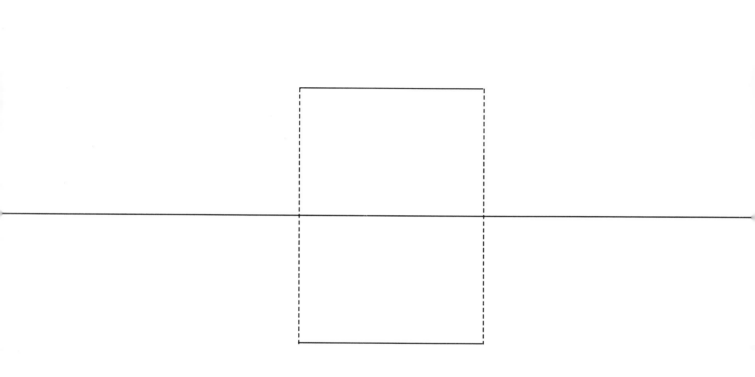

BLACKLINE MASTER 1

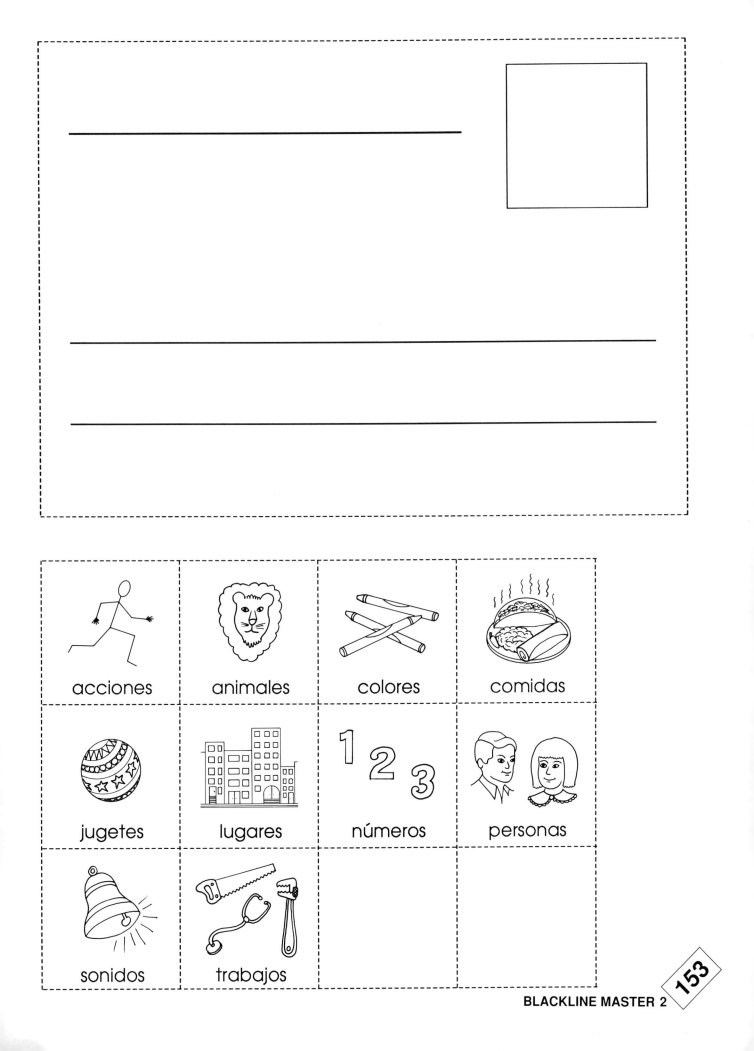

acciones   animales   colores   comidas

jugetes   lugares   números   personas

sonidos   trabajos

153

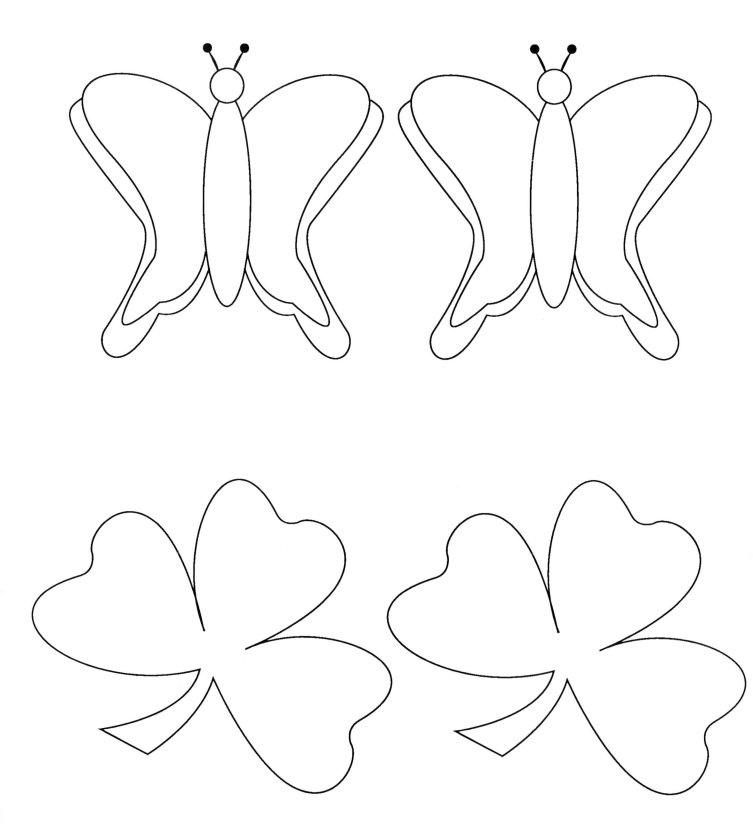

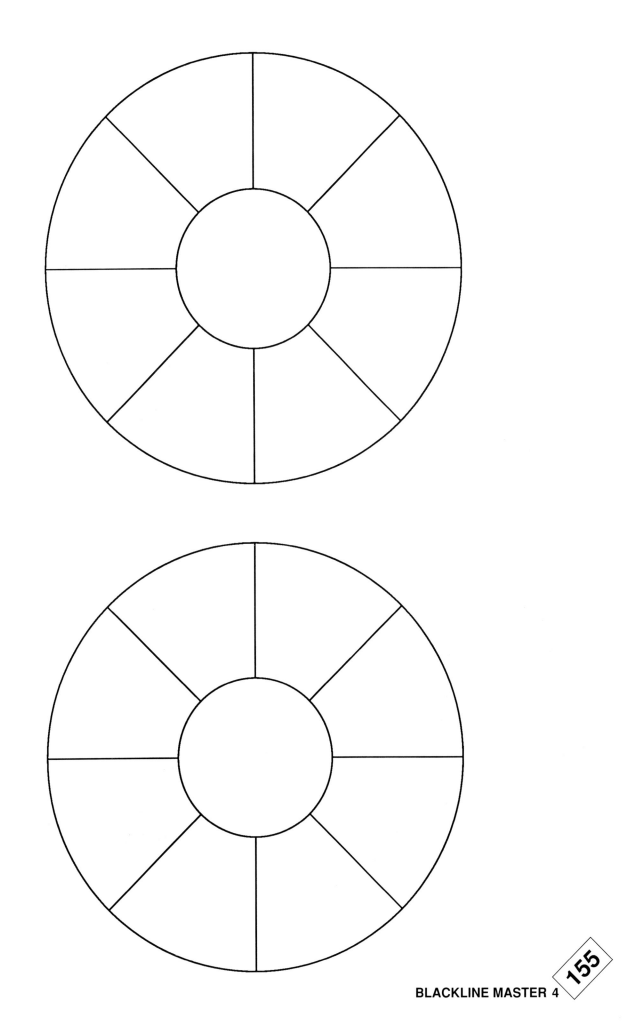

BLACKLINE MASTER 4

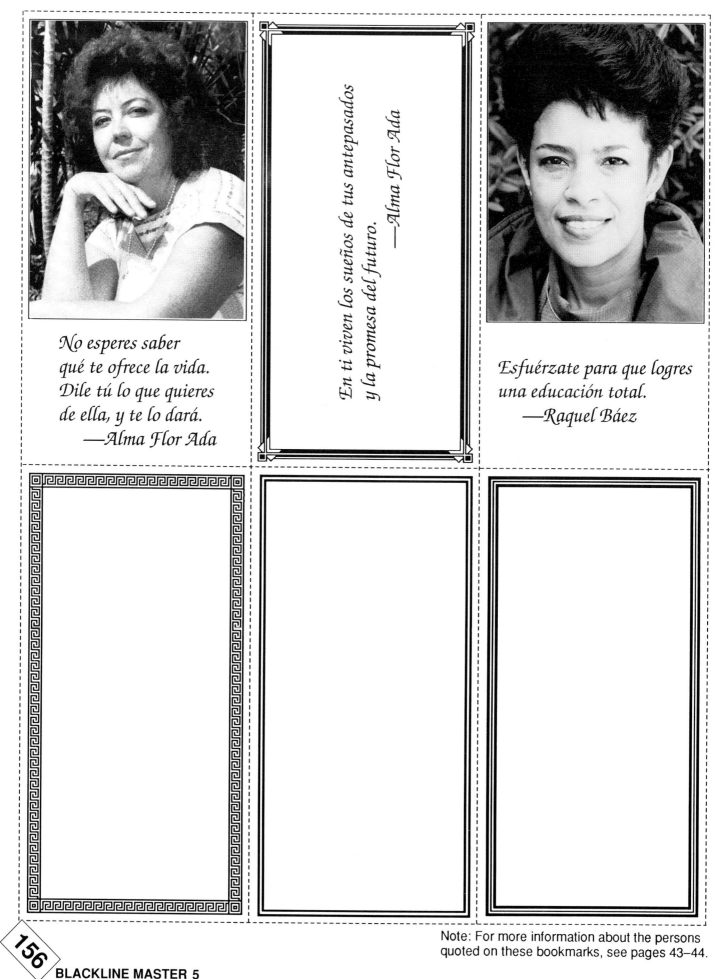

*No esperes saber
qué te ofrece la vida.
Dile tú lo que quieres
de ella, y te lo dará.*
—Alma Flor Ada

*En ti viven los sueños de tus antepasados
y la promesa del futuro.*
—Alma Flor Ada

*Esfuérzate para que logres
una educación total.*
—Raquel Báez

Note: For more information about the persons quoted on these bookmarks, see pages 43–44.

BLACKLINE MASTER 5

BLACKLINE MASTER 6

u	o	i	e	a
mu	mo	mi	me	ma
pu	po	pi	pe	pa
su	so	si	se	sa
tu	to	ti	te	ta

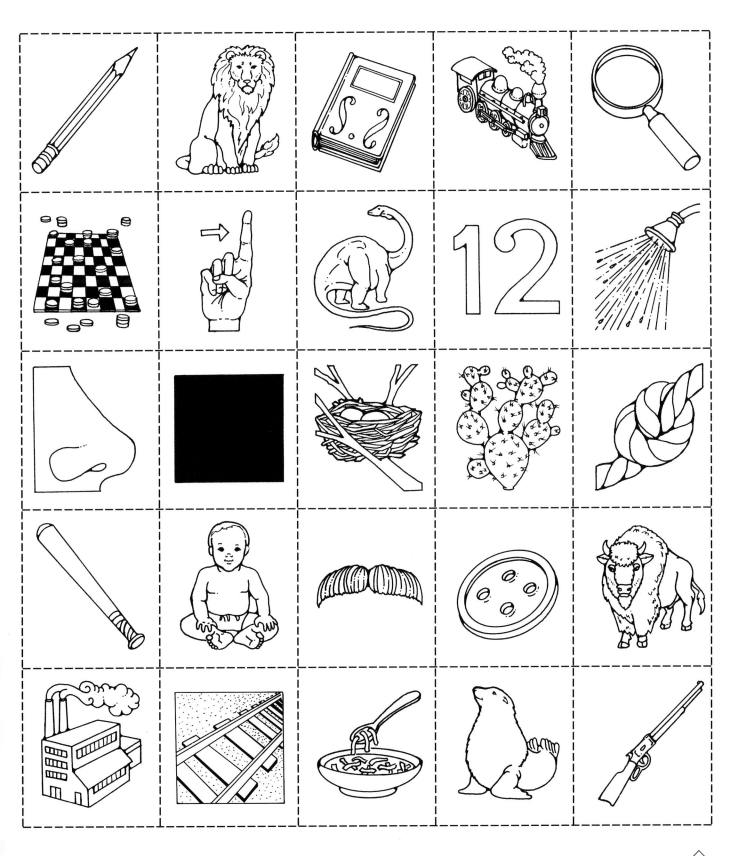

BLACKLINE MASTER 7

lu	lo	li	le	la
du	do	di	de	da
nu	no	ni	ne	na
bu	bo	bi	be	ba
fu	fo	fi	fe	fa

160 BLACKLINE MASTER 7

BLACKLINE MASTER 8

ye	vo	vi	ve	va
ha	gu	go	ga	yo
ca	hu	ho	hi	he
ra	qui	que	cu	co
lla	ru	ro	ri	re

BLACKLINE MASTER 8

cho	chi	che	cha	llu
ji	ja	gi	ge	chu
ci	ce	gui	ju	jo
	zo	zi	ze	za

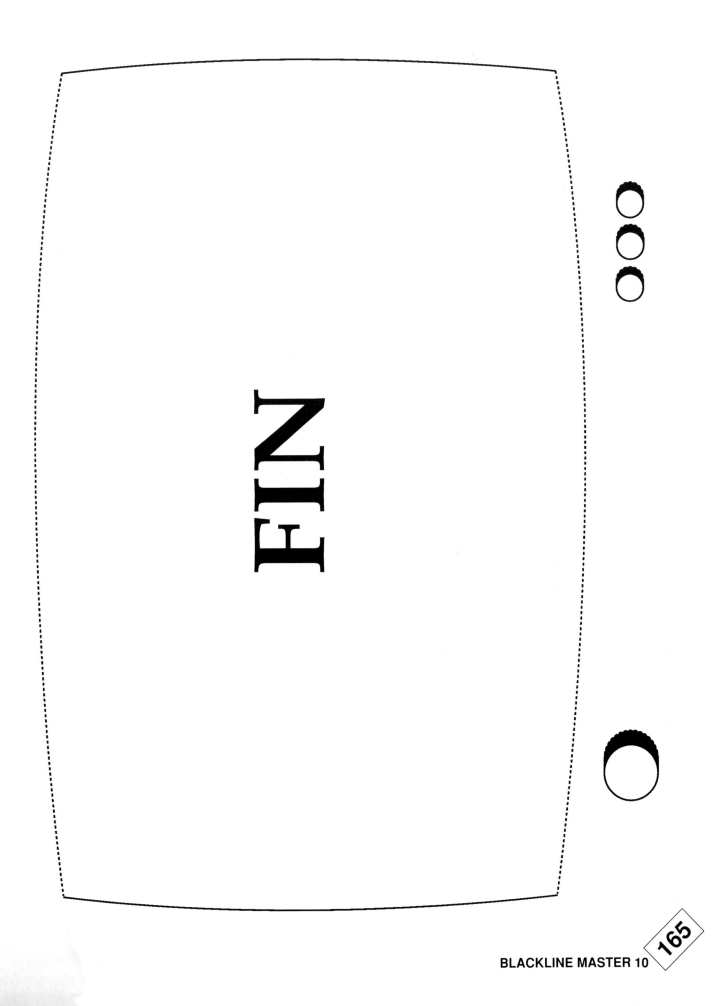

FIN

Debajo de mi cama

Hay algo debajo de mi cama.

Se come todos mis juguetes.

Primero se comió

Lo que quiero ser

Cuando crezca voy a

ser _____ porque

me gusta

El águila y la víbora

Hace mucho tiempo, cuando
el mundo todavía era nuevo, el
águila y la víbora eran amigas.

El niño de la casa de al lado

El niño de la casa de al
lado me pone furioso
cuando

BLACKLINE MASTER 12

Me llamo Bocazo. Soy un perro. Muchos dicen que parezco un coyote, pero soy un perro. Me pasan cosas que ni a un perro le deben pasar. Por ejemplo, un día

—Te doy tres deseos—me dijo la rana—, pero antes de que te los dé tienes que prometer que

Un día cuando papá y yo estábamos limpiando el garaje, un mapa rarísimo se cayó de un libro viejo. Cuando lo vi, sabía que éste sería un verano interesante.

Horacio miraba la extraña nubecita luminosa que flotaba en el aire por encima de los techos. "¡Ahí está otra vez!" pensó. "Pero esta vez sí que la agarro".

Isabel estaba desesperada por que llegara el Cinco de Mayo. Habría una fiesta estupenda. Y también ella tendría algo que contribuir. Se había pasado toda una semana preparando

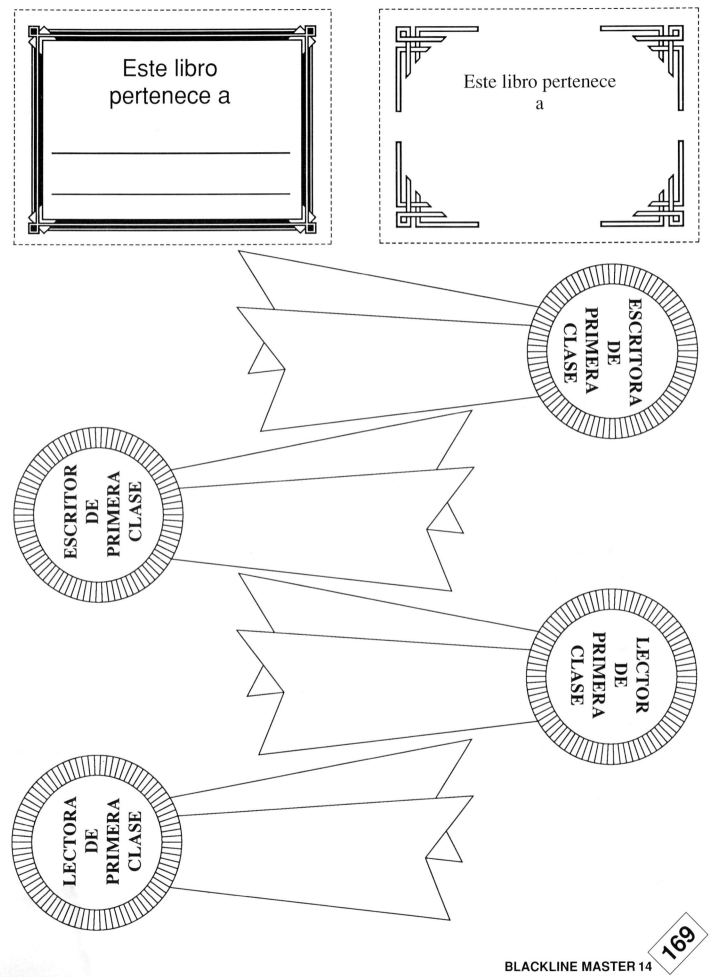

Este libro
pertenece a

_____

_____

Este libro pertenece
a

ESCRITORA
DE
PRIMERA
CLASE

ESCRITOR
DE
PRIMERA
CLASE

LECTOR
DE
PRIMERA
CLASE

LECTORA
DE
PRIMERA
CLASE

CERTIFICADO DE MÉRITO

_____ de 19 _____

Este certificado se le presenta

a

en reconocimiento de la
Alta Calidad de sus Estudios

en

_____
Firma de la maestra

BLACKLINE MASTER 15

ÍNDICE

Nota: las siguientes abreviaturas se usan en este índice:
BI = Bright Idea, SL = Siempre Listos, WW = Word Wise.

INDEX

Note: The following abbreviations are used in this index:
BI = Bright Idea, SL = Siempre Listos, WW = Word Wise.

173

TO ORDER MORE COPIES OF **EL SABELOTODO,**
 • Call Toll Free: 1-800-333-3510
or • Complete this form and mail to **Hampton-Brown Books**
                    P.O. Box 223220
                    Carmel, CA 93922

Date: _____

No. of copies   _____

                  x   *   _____

10% shipping   + _____

CA sales tax   + _____

(shipments to California only)

TOTAL   _____

Charge to:

__VISA or __Mastercard

Account Number _____

Signature _____

expiration date _____

OR

Bill to:

_____
School/Organization
_____
Purchase order number
_____
Name
_____
Position
_____
Street Address
_____
City
_____
State   ZIP
_____
Phone

Ship to:

_____
School/Organization
_____
Name
_____
Position
_____
Street Address
_____
City
_____
State   ZIP
_____
Phone

* Call 1-800-333-3510 for the current selling price.

TO ORDER MORE COPIES OF **EL SABELOTODO,**
 • Call Toll Free: 1-800-333-3510
or • Complete this form and mail to **Hampton-Brown Books**
                    P.O. Box 223220
                    Carmel, CA 93922

Date: _____

No. of copies   _____

                  x   *   _____

10% shipping   + _____

CA sales tax   + _____

(shipments to California only)

TOTAL   _____

Charge to:

__VISA or __Mastercard

Account Number _____

Signature _____

expiration date _____

OR

Bill to:

_____
School/Organization
_____
Purchase order number
_____
Name
_____
Position
_____
Street Address
_____
City
_____
State   ZIP
_____
Phone

Ship to:

_____
School/Organization
_____
Name
_____
Position
_____
Street Address
_____
City
_____
State   ZIP
_____
Phone

* Call 1-800-333-3510 for the current selling price.

From:

_____

_____

_____

To: **Hampton-Brown Books**
P.O. Box 223220
Carmel, CA 93922

fold

Please
provide
first-class
postage

tape here

From:

_____

_____

_____

To: **Hampton-Brown Books**
P.O. Box 223220
Carmel, CA 93922

fold

Please
provide
first-class
postage

tape here